SECOND EDITION

Psychology A2

The Mini Companion
for AQA 'A'

Mike Cardwell • Cara Flanagan

KT-447-224

OXFORD
UNIVERSITY PRESS

EG39283

OXFORD
UNIVERSITY PRESS

Great Clarendon Street, Oxford OX2 6DP

Oxford University Press is a department of the University of Oxford.
It furthers the University's objective of excellence in research, scholarship, and education by
publishing worldwide in

Oxford New York

Auckland Cape Town Dar es Salaam Hong Kong Karachi Kuala Lumpur Madrid
Melbourne Mexico City Nairobi New Delhi Shanghai Taipei Toronto

With offices in

Argentina Austria Brazil Chile Czech Republic France Greece Guatemala Hungary
Italy Japan Poland Portugal Singapore South Korea Switzerland Thailand Turkey
Ukraine Vietnam

Oxford is a registered trade mark of Oxford University Press in the UK and in certain other
countries

British Library Cataloguing in Publication Data

Data available

ISBN 978 0 19 912888 4

10 9 8 7 6 5 4 3 2 1

Printed by Bell & Bain Ltd, Glasgow

Paper used in the production of this book is a natural, recyclable product made from wood
grown in sustainable forests. The manufacturing process conforms to the environmental
regulations of the country of origin.

Acknowledgements
Project development: Rick Jackman (Jackman Publishing Solutions Ltd)
Editorial & project management: GreenGate Publishing Services, Tonbridge
Design & layout: Nigel Harriss
Cover design: Patricia Briggs
Cover photography: Chris Cardwell

Image credits
Shutterstock © Eric Isselée: pages 3, 6, 16, 24, 32, 40, 49, 57, 68, 78, 84, 90, 96, 96, 102, 111,
120, 128, 137

Mixed Sources
Product group from well-managed
forests and other controlled sources
www.fsc.org Cert no. TT-COC-002769
© 1996 Forest Stewardship Council
FSC

Contents

Introduction

This book is a mini version of *Psychology A2: The Complete Companion*. It contains just the basic information needed for the AQA specification 'A' A2 examination. There are no frills and no extras.

When a cook makes a special sauce he or she will boil the liquid for a long time so that it reduces in volume and produces something that is intense and flavoursome. That's what we have done here – producing the nuggets of knowledge necessary to enable you to focus on what you *must* learn in order to do well in the exam as distinct from what you *could* learn. In order to make the most of the material presented in this book you should use it alongside the A2 *Complete Companion* or your own A2 textbook.

The A2 examination

The A2 examination consists of two papers:

Unit 3 (PSYA3) Topics in Psychology

50% of A2 Level marks

Duration: One hour 30 minutes

The exam paper contains eight questions, one question drawn from each of the eight topics in the specification.

You must answer three questions from the following eight topics:

- Biological rhythms and sleep
- Perception
- Relationships
- Aggression
- Eating behaviour
- Gender
- Intelligence and learning
- Cognition and development

Unit 4 (PSYA4) Psychopathology, Psychology in Action and Research Methods

50% of A2 Level marks

Duration: Two hours

The exam paper is divided into three sections:

Section A – Psychopathology

You answer one question chosen from:

- Schizophrenia
- Depression
- Phobic disorders
- Obsessive-compulsive disorder

Section B – Psychology in Action

You answer one question chosen from:

- Media psychology
- The psychology of addictive behaviour
- Anomalistic psychology

Section C – Psychological Research and Scientific Method

One compulsory structured question.

Organisation of this book

This book is organised along the lines of the specification, divided into topics, divisions and subdivisions. At the top of each page in this book you will see:

The chapter title, covering one of the topics above. ➤

Each topic/chapter is divided into three sections.

Each section is further divided into two or more subsections.

Chapter 1		
	Biological rhythms	The nature of sleep and lifespan changes
	Sleep states	Functions of sleep: Restoration theory
Biological rhythms and sleep		Functions of sleep: Evolutionary

Functions of sleep: Restoration theory

Slow wave sleep (SWS)

SWS initiates body repair (Oswald).

Growth hormone

Important in childhood because it stimulates physical growth.

Important throughout lifespan for protein synthesis and cell growth (cells need to be constantly replaced).

If sleep (SWS+REM) is restorative, total sleep deprivation would have negative effects…

Case studies show some support, e.g. DJ Peter Tripp stayed awake for 201 hours and after five days he experienced hallucinations and paranoia; his brain rhythms looked like he was asleep.

Non-human animal studies show that lack of sleep may be fatal. Rechtschaffen *et al.* kept rats on a rotating disc and after 33 days they died, though this may have been due to stress rather than lack of sleep.

There are also some changes to the specification so that some topic areas have been amended, some have been removed and some have been added. Most notably:

- *Perception* – nature–nurture (page 21) removed.
- *Gender* – psychological androgyny (page 54) removed and dysphoria moved to biosocial theory (page 52).
- *Cognition and development* – Bruner (pages 71 and some of 72) removed, Eisenberg (page 74) removed.
- *Addiction* – vulnerability (page 116) now includes stress, peers, age and personality; self-esteem removed.
- *Anomalous* – scientific fraud (page 121), cognitive and biological factors underlying anomalous experience (page 123), functions of paranormal and related beliefs (page 124), deception and self-deception (page 125) all removed – and coincidence and superstition (page 125) expanded.

You can read the changes in detail (and check for any other changes) on the AQA website (**www.aqa.org.uk**).
You can also check our website for updates (**www.oxfordschoolblogs.co.uk/psychcompanion/blog/**).

The exam questions

All A2 exam questions (except 'Psychological Research and Scientific Method') are worth 25 marks. These marks are divided into:

- 9 marks description (AO1) [8 marks after January 2012]
- 16 marks evaluation/how science works (AO2/3)

An exam question might say

*Describe and evaluate **one** theory of perception.*
(9 marks + 16 marks)

This means you should present 9 marks of description of the theory (about 200–250 words) and 16 marks of evaluation (about 400–500 words).

An exam question might say

*(a) Outline **one** evolutionary explanation of group display in humans.*　　*(4 marks)*
*(b) Discuss **one** social psychological explanation of aggression.*　　*(5 marks + 16 marks)*

This means you should present 4 marks describing one evolutionary explanation of group display (about 100–125 words) and a further 5 marks of material describing one social psychological explanation (about 100–125 words), and finally 16 marks of evaluation of the social psychological explanations (about 400–500 words).

The examples on the left show several things:
The division between AO1 and AO2/3 is shown after each exam question – the first mark given indicates the maximum mark available for AO1 and the second mark shows the maximum mark available for AO2/3.

The AO1 and AO2/3 elements are also indicated by exam injunctions, such as

- 'Describe' or 'outline' which indicate AO1,
- 'Evaluate' or 'consider' which indicate AO2/3, or
- 'Discuss' which indicates both.

Note that the wording of the questions is drawn from the specification.

There are three assessment objectives (AOs):
AO1 refers to knowledge and understanding.
AO2 refers to the application of this knowledge, including analysis and evaluation.
AO3 refers to an understanding and evaluation of the research methods used in psychology. Such material can be used as part of effective evaluation but is not required in order to be awarded full marks.

For more information on the exam and how to improve your exam performance, check out our A2 *Exam Companion*.

The topic covered on each page is divided into
- Description (**AO1**) on the left.
- Evaluation (**AO2/3**) on the right.

There is less AO1 than AO2/3 for each topic, reflecting the mark balance in exam questions.

A key feature of the AO2/3 material is the **IDA** points – 'IDA' stands for issues, debates and approaches. The mark scheme for Unit 3 and Section B of Unit 4 rewards the use of issues, debates or approaches as part of your evaluation.

It is important to note that credit is only given to AO2/3 points that are elaborated, including IDA points. If you simply identify evaluative points (including IDA points) you will get only minimal credit.

There is an important thing to notice about the AO2/3 points given in this book – they begin with an emboldened title (such as '*However*' or '*There are individual differences*'). Such 'lead in phrases' are crucial in establishing that you are making an evaluative point (AO2/3) rather than just describing further research (which would be AO1). Use these phrases in your essays.

Biological rhythms and sleep

Division A Biological rhythms

Circadian Rhythms
Infradian and ultradian rhythms
Endogenous pacemakers, exogenous zeitgebers
Consequences of disrupting biological rhythms

Division B Sleep states

The nature of sleep and lifespan changes
Functions of sleep: Restoration theory
Functions of sleep: Evolutionary explanations

Division C Disorders of sleep

Explanations for insomnia
Explanations for other sleep disorders

Specification

Biological rhythms and sleep	
Biological rhythms	• Circadian, infradian, and ultradian rhythms, including the role of endogenous pacemakers and of exogenous zeitgebers.
	• Consequences of disrupting biological rhythms, for example shift work, jet lag.
Sleep states	• The nature of sleep.
	• Functions of sleep, including evolutionary explanations and restoration theory.
	• Lifespan changes in sleep.
Disorders of sleep	• Explanations for insomnia, including primary and secondary insomnia and factors influencing insomnia, for example, apnoea, personality.
	• Explanations for other sleep disorders, including sleepwalking and narcolepsy.

Chapter 1

Biological rhythms >
Sleep states
Biological rhythms and sleep > Disorders of sleep

Circadian Rhythms
Infradian and ultradian rhythms
Endogenous pacemaker, exogenous zeitgebers
Consequences of disrupting biological rhythms

Circadian rhythms

The sleep–wake cycle

Temporal isolation studies provide us with a picture of the free-running circadian rhythm, and demonstrate that the cycle persists despite absence of light, e.g.
- Siffre spent long periods underground with no daylight, radio etc. He found that his sleep–wake cycle generally adjusted to a 24-hour cycle (but sometimes changed dramatically to as much as 48 hours).
- Aschoff and Wever placed participants in an underground WWII bunker with no environmental and social time cues. The participants' cycle was 24–25 hours (sometimes up to 29 hours).

Cycle can be entrained (i.e. brought into phase) to some extent by external cues.

For example, Folkard et al. gradually reduced participants' circadian rhythm using a quickening clock, but at 22 hours the participants' own rhythms took over again, showing a limit for control of internal rhythms by external cues.

However…
In early studies participants were exposed to artificial light, which may have affected their cycle; Czeisler et al. demonstrated that rhythms could be entrained using artificial light.

There are individual differences…
- Cycle length varies from 13 to 65 hours (Czeisler et al.).
- Cycle onset varies, there are innate patterns of sleeping and waking: morning types (rise at 6 am and go to bed at 10 pm) and evening types (rise at 10 am and go to bed at 1 am) (Duffy et al.).

Case studies lack validity…
Siffre's findings were based on one unique individual, so lack generalisability.
However… they have been confirmed by other studies.
On the plus side, he also used an experimental approach, and thus could demonstrate causal relationships.

IDA *Real-world application…*
Chronotherapeutics is the application of biological rhythms to the treatment of disorders, for example, it is advantageous to take medication or engage in activities at certain times of day:
- Taking aspirin to treat heart attacks at 11 pm. Aspirin levels then peak in bloodstream at the time when heart attacks commonly occur (about 3 am).
- People are most alert in the morning and early evening, so those are the best times to work.

Core body temperature

Body temperature is generally lowest at 4:30 am and highest at 6.00 pm.

Post-lunch dip
Tiredness in the afternoon may appear to be due to the effects of having eaten, but it occurs even if you don't eat – due to a circadian temperature rhythm.

Such variation explains…
- Superior recall and comprehension in 12–13-year-old children working in the afternoon rather than the morning (Folkard et al.).
- IQ test results best at 7 pm compared with 9 am or 2 pm (Gupta).

Cause or correlation?…
Giesbrecht et al. deliberately lowered core body temperature and showed that this caused lower cognitive performance.
It is not clear whether the effect is due to the direct effects of core body temperature, or whether the high core body temperature leads to increased physiological arousal and this creates the effect (Wright et al.).

However…
Hord and Thompson found no link between body temperature and cognitive performance.

Hormones

Cortisol levels are lowest at midnight, and peak at about 6 am. When levels are high, this creates alertness – which explains why you can't think clearly when you wake up earlier than normal (your cortisol levels are low and therefore you aren't alert).

Melatonin and growth hormone levels peak at midnight.

IDA *A biological and determinist approach*
All of these explanations suggest our sleep–wake patterns are fixed, caused by either internal mechanisms or by external cues.
- This may be misleading because we do have the power to override such processes, e.g. training ourselves to wake early and be alert in order to function effectively at work.
- On the other hand, it may be helpful to recognise the power of these forces, e.g. when understanding the difficulties experienced by a blind man, who had problems with day-to-day living because he could not adapt his internal rhythm to the demands of society (Miles et al.).

Infradian rhythms

Sleep stages

Descending the sleep staircase:
- *Stages 1 and 2* – relaxed, alpha and theta waves, heart rate slows, temperature drops.
- *Stages 3 and 4* – called deep sleep or slow wave sleep (SWS), delta waves, metabolic rate slows, growth hormone produced.
- *REM sleep* (rapid eye movement) – associated with dreaming, desynchronised EEG activity similar to the awake brain, brain and eyes active but body paralysed (paradoxical state).

One cycle takes about 90 minutes; later in the night there is more REM sleep and less SWS.

There are age differences…
Babies don't have the same stages; they display quiet and active sleep, which are immature versions of SWS and REM sleep. Relatively greater amounts of REM sleep may be related to the considerable learning that is taking place.

Older people experience reduced SWS and an associated reduction in the production of growth hormone. This may explain some of the symptoms associated with old age, e.g. lower bone density (van Cauter *et al.*).

The link between REM sleep and dreams has been questioned…
Dement and Kleitman demonstrated that people awoken during REM sleep were often dreaming, but dreams are not exclusive to REM sleep, often occurring at other times as well.

Neurobiological theories of dreaming make the erroneous assumption that REM sleep equals dreams and explain the function of dreaming in terms of the function of REM sleep.

Basic rest–activity cycle

During the daytime there is also a 90-minute cycle of rest followed by activity. Friedman and Fisher observed psychiatric patients over a 6-hour period, and noted a clear pattern of 90 minutes between eating and drinking 'episodes'.

The value of the 90-minute rhythm…
Ensures that biological processes in the body work in unison. Complex metabolic processes are active in many different parts of the body at any time and some coordination between these is advantageous.

Ultradian rhythms

Monthly cycles

Menstrual cycle determined by fluctuating levels of female hormones that regulate ovulation.

Pituitary gland releases hormones (FSH and LH), egg ripens and triggers production of oestrogen and later progesterone to prepare the lining of the womb for a fertilised egg. If there is no pregnancy, progesterone levels fall and the lining is shed.

Males also have been found to have near-monthly rhythms for temperature and alertness levels (Empson).

Can be controlled exogenously…
Russell *et al.* showed that pheromones can entrain menstrual cycles (by collecting sweat from one group of women and rubbing it on the upper lips of another group of women). This shows that biological rhythms can be entrained by exogenous cues.

May have negative effects…
Premenstrual syndrome (PMS) is associated with certain direct effects: anxiety, depression, mood swings and aggression.

Such behaviours were once considered 'all in the mind' but now there is a recognised biological cause.

Research evidence from Dalton showed that PMS led indirectly to lower academic achievement, suicide and crime.

IDA *A determinist approach…*
Both SAD (seasonal affective disorder) and PMS suggest that certain behaviours are inevitable – and this has been used as a legal defence, e.g. Ms English was placed on probation (rather than a custodial sentence) for the murder of her boyfriend because she was suffering from severe PMS (Johnson).

People can 'will' their biological rhythms to change, e.g. people told to wake up earlier than normal had higher levels of the stress hormone ACTH (Born *et al.*).

Seasonal affective disorder (SAD)

A yearly cycle
People with SAD are depressed in winter and recover in summer.

May be due to the hormones melatonin and serotonin – more darkness means more melatonin, and more melatonin means less serotonin (because melatonin is produced from serotonin). Low levels of serotonin are associated with depression.

Could be explained differently…
SAD might not be an effect of infradian rhythms, but due to a disrupted circadian rhythm, similar to jet lag – happens because we go to bed earlier as it's darker earlier in winter and this puts rhythms out of phase.

IDA *Real-world application…*
Phototherapy developed to treat SAD by exposing sufferers to very strong light (6,000–10,000 Lux).

However, benefits of phototherapy may be due to a placebo effect as, in one study, 32% improved with placebo alone (Eastman *et al.*).

Chapter 1

Biological rhythms	>	Circadian rhythms
		Infradian and ultradian rhythms
Sleep states		**Endogenous pacemaker, exogenous zeitgebers**
Biological rhythms and sleep	> Disorders of sleep	Consequences of disrupting biological rhythms

Endogenous pacemakers

The suprachiasmatic nucleus (SCN)

The SCN is a cluster of nerve cells, in the hypothalamus.
It receives information about light because it is located above the optic chiasma. Even when the eyes are shut, information about light is received by the SCN.

The 'rhythm' is produced by a negative feedback loop:
• One pair of proteins combine (e.g. CLK+BLMAL1).
• This combination then produces a second pair of proteins (e.g. PER+CRY).
• PER+CRY make CLK+BLMAL1 inactive.
• As levels of CLK+BLMAL1 fall, this means PER+CRY are reduced and then levels of CLK+BLMAL1 increase again.

One SCN is in each hemisphere, each divided into:
• *Ventral SCN*, relatively quickly reset by external cues.
• *Dorsal SCN*, less affected by light (Albus *et al.*).

The effect of the SCN has been demonstrated…
In animal studies, e.g. Morgan bred 'mutant' hamsters with 20-hour circadian rhythms. When their SCN was transplanted into the 'normal' hamsters they exhibited the mutant rhythm.

IDA *An issue is the use of non-human animals…*
Animals used in this research are permanently harmed, which can be justified if the research is regarded as important, e.g. it can be argued that it is important for understanding the effects of desynchronised biological clocks in shift workers and providing suggestions for how this might be overcome.

However…
Generalisations made from animal to human behaviour may not be justified as biological systems are different, and also humans have the power of cognitive control over their behaviour, at least in some situations.

This can explain the effects of desynchronisation…
Desynchronisation occurs in jet lag and shift lag, and occurs when the ventral and dorsal portions of the SCN are out of phase.
A study by Folkard observed the effects of isolation in a woman, Kate Aldcroft. While in a cave, her temperature and sleep rhythms became quite different and she experienced symptoms similar to jet lag.

The pineal gland and melatonin

The pineal gland receives signals from SCN, and as a result produces melatonin.
Melatonin induces sleep by inhibiting the brain mechanisms that promote wakefulness.

IDA *The evolutionary approach can help us understand…*
The adaptive nature of biological rhythms, e.g. anticipating daily environmental events. Chipmunks without functioning SCNs were found to be more likely to die, presumably because they were awake at night and making noise, which attracted predators (DeCoursey *et al.*).

Exogenous zeitgebers

Light

Light entrains the free-running biological rhythm.
This affects the SCN and other peripheral oscillators, e.g. Campbell and Murphy shone light on the back of participants' knees and reset circadian rhythms.
Peripheral oscillators contain CRY (cryptochrome), a substance that is sensitive to light.

One issue is whether artificial lighting is enough…
Early studies of biological rhythms exposed participants to artificial lighting and it was assumed this would not be bright enough to entrain rhythms (e.g. Siffre cave study).
But Campbell and Murphy shifted rhythms with light on the back of knees.
Boivin *et al.* found that even normal artificial lighting does have an effect, though bright lighting is better for resetting circadian rhythms.

IDA *Real-world application…*
Living in an artificially lit world may disrupt melatonin production, so leading to increased incidence of cancer (Stevens).

Social cues

Social conventions entrain biological rhythms, e.g. mealtimes reset cells in heart and liver (Davidson).

Temperature

Leaves fall from deciduous trees as the seasonal temperature falls.
Hibernation is triggered by lower temperature.

Problems occur when the biological system fails…
Having a biologically governed system has adaptive advantages but when it goes wrong, it is difficult to override, e.g. *familial advanced sleep-phase syndrome* (FASPS) has been linked to a faulty PER gene, causing sleeping and waking at wrong times, and difficulty leading a normal life (Chicurel).
Physiological changes during adolescence may cause delayed sleep phase syndrome, leading to unusual sleep patterns.

There are advantages with this blended system…
In fact, endogenous and exogenous cues act as one system. Total isolation studies are artificial; in the real world both cues interact to enable internal synchronisation of physiological processes, but also external synchronisation with inevitable environmental changes.

Chapter 1

Biological rhythms >

Sleep states

Biological rhythms and sleep >

Disorders of sleep

Circadian rhythms

Infradian and ultradian rhythms

Endogenous pacemakers/exogenous zeitgebers

Consequences of disrupting biological rhythms

Consequences of disrupting biological rhythms

Shift work and shift lag

Alertness decreases when cortisol levels are lower in the middle of the night, when core body temperature is also lowest (circadian trough) (Boivin et al.).

Sleep deprivation is inevitable because sleeping during the day is disrupted by noises and daylight; sleep length is typically 2 hours less than normal (Tilley and Wilkinson).

Effects on health, e.g. shift workers are three times more likely to develop heart disease (Knutssen et al.).

IDA Real-world application...
Our society relies on shift work and therefore it is essential to understand and reduce the negative effects caused by working shifts.
Many major disasters (e.g. Exxon Valdez) can be blamed on errors arising from the disruption of biological rhythms that are associated with shift work.

An alternative explanation...
Shift work effects are not just due to the direct effects of disruption of rhythms, but indirectly to such things as the associated social deprivation and family disruption, e.g. divorce rates may be as high as 60% in shift workers (Solomon).

IDA Real-world application...
Research has found systems that have fewer negative effects.
• Non-fluctuating shifts are better, i.e. a week of working days, followed by a week of working nights (Gold et al.).
• Forward-rotating shifts (phase delay) are better than backward-rotating shifts (Bambra et al.).

IDA Real-world application...
Artificial lighting can be used to entrain circadian rhythms and promote wakefulness. Boivin et al. showed that very bright lighting can reset the biological clock. They found that, within three days, a group of participants exposed to a very bright light had advanced their biological clock by 5 hours, whereas exposure to an ordinary light advanced participants by 1 hour and dim lighting led to an hour delay.

Laboratory experiments should be verified...
Laboratory experiments demonstrate causal relationships but should be confirmed by more natural studies. Boivin and James studied nurses at work, and found that exposure to bright lights promoted circadian adaptation – supporting their laboratory study.

Jet travel and jet lag

'Jet lag' describes the physiological effects of desynchronised circadian rhythms. Symptoms include nausea, fatigue, disorientation, insomnia and depression.
It is estimated that the dorsal part of the SCN takes several cycles to adjust to large environmental changes.

Phase delay is easier to adjust to – same as staying up later than usual or travelling east to west.

Phase advance is more difficult because you wake up when you're in a circadian trough – same as getting up earlier or travelling west to east.
For example, US baseball results were better for teams travelling east to west – they won 44% of their games over a three-year period compared to 37% wins for teams travelling west to east (Recht et al.).

An alternative explanation...
The effects of jet lag may be due to other factors related to travel, such as long hours of travel, annoyance caused by other passengers and low-oxygen cabin air.

IDA Real-world application...
Melatonin may reduce the effects of jet lag because it naturally induces sleep.
Herxheimer and Petrie reviewed ten studies and found melatonin was very effective if taken just before bedtime, but when taken at other times of day it may delay adaptation to local time.

IDA Real-world application...
Social cues also entrain biological rhythms, so one way to cope with jet lag is to eat and sleep at the right times. This may be because peripheral oscillators, which are found around the body, are reset by eating.
Fuller et al. found that a period of fasting followed by eating at the right time helps to entrain biological rhythms.

It is important to consider individual differences...
Some people are more affected by circadian disruption than others – Reinberg et al. found that people whose circadian rhythms adapt more slowly actually cope best with shift work/jet travel.

Chapter 1

Biological rhythms | The nature of sleep and lifespan changes
Sleep states | > | Functions of sleep: Restoration theory
Biological rhythms and sleep | > | Disorders of sleep | Functions of sleep: Evolutionary explanations

The nature of sleep and lifespan changes

Infancy

Duration

Babies sleep for about 16 hours a day, but not continuously.

They wake every hour or so (cycles less than adult 90-minute cycle).

Patterns of sleep

Active and quiet sleep – version of REM sleep and SWS.

About half of infant sleep is 'active' – more than adult ratio of REM:NREM.

Infants don't go immediately into SWS; they start with very light sleep and are thus easily awoken.

Circadian rhythm

By about six months most children have one main sleep–wake cycle, with a few naps during the day.

IDA *A developmental approach…*

Considering behaviour in terms of how it changes over the lifespan.

For a long time psychology regarded development only up to the beginning of adulthood. We now realise there are significant psychological and physical changes throughout the lifespan.

IDA *An evolutionary approach…*

Suggests that infant sleep patterns evolved so that parents can get on with daytime chores.

Infant sleep patterns evolved because infants have small stomachs and must wake and eat regularly.

There is a reason why infants have large amounts of active sleep…

Active (REM) sleep is associated with the production of neurotransmitters and consolidation of memory – both apply to infant development.

This is supported by…

Research that shows that premature babies (whose brains are even less mature) spend 90% of sleep time in active sleep.

Childhood

Children typically sleep about 12 hours a day, and EEG patterns resemble adult patterns.

Amount of sleep gradually decreases.

Parasomonias common in childhood, such as sleep walking and night terrors.

There are cultural differences…

Tynjälä *et al.* found considerable differences in sleep patterns across European countries in children 11–12 years, e.g. Israeli children sleep an average 9 hours and Swiss children sleep an average 10 hours.

This suggests that… sleep is influenced by cultural values and lifestyles.

Adolescence

Sleep duration increases in adolescence.

Boys often have orgasm and ejaculation during sleep.

Phase delay

Circadian rhythms shift so teenagers stay awake later, and wake up later.

Adolescent sleep can be explained by hormone changes…

Adolescence is a time when there are major changes in sex hormones.

These changes disrupt sleep because hormones are predominantly released at night. Many 'symptoms' of adolescence (e.g. moodiness, lack of motivation) may be due to sleep problems.

A consequence of phase delay…

Schools should adjust their school day to fit delayed sleep phase syndrome, which is typical of adolescents and means they have poor attention spans in the morning (Wolfson and Carskadon).

Adulthood

Typically 8 hours per night, 25% of which is REM sleep.

Increasing frequency of sleep disorders such as insomnia and apnoea.

Too much sleep is not necessarily a good thing…

Kripke *et al.* surveyed 1 million adults and found that sleeping for 6–7 hours was associated with reduced mortality, whereas an average of 8 hours had a 15% increased risk of mortality and sleeping more than 10 hours was linked to a 30% increased risk.

Correlational data does mean a cause has been demonstrated…

It is likely that underlying illness is an intervening variable.

Old age

Sleep patterns change

More difficulty going to sleep, and wake more frequently.

REM sleep decreases to 20% of total sleep time.

SWS decreases to 5% of total sleep time.

Phase advance: go to sleep earlier and wake earlier.

May nap during day to satisfy sleep needs.

Reduced sleep is a consequence of…

Physiological changes, but also problems staying asleep, e.g. insomnia and reduced SWS means people are awoken more easily.

A consequence of sleep changes is…

Less growth hormone is produced (because less SWS), which may explain some of the symptoms of old age, e.g. lack of energy and lower bone density (van Cauter *et al.*).

Lack of sleep may also explain impaired cognitive functions.

IDA *Real-world application…*

Sleep quality can be improved through the use of melatonin.

Chapter 1

Biological rhythms

The nature of sleep and lifespan changes

Sleep states

> Functions of sleep: Restoration theory

Biological rhythms and sleep > Disorders of sleep

Functions of sleep: Evolutionary explanations

Functions of sleep: Restoration theory

Slow wave sleep (SWS)

SWS initiates body repair (Oswald).

Growth hormone

Important in childhood because it stimulates physical growth.

Important throughout lifespan for protein synthesis and cell growth (cells need to be constantly replaced).

Secreted to some extent during the day but mainly in SWS. This is demonstrated by reversing the sleep–wake cycle and then GH is produced during the day when SWS takes place (Sassin et al.). Also the amount of GH correlates with the amount of SWS (van Cauter and Plat).

Immune system

Body's defence against viruses and bacteria. Lack of SWS is associated with reduced immune functioning (Krueger et al.).

REM sleep

REM sleep initiates brain repair (Oswald).

Brain growth

Infants have a greater proportion of REM (i.e. active) sleep than adults, which suggests that REM sleep may be important to brain growth.

Siegel suggests that the amount of REM sleep in any animal is proportional to the immaturity of offspring at birth, e.g. platypus young are very immature and have about 8 hours REM, whereas dolphin young are very mature and have almost no REM sleep.

Neurotransmitter function

Siegel and Rogaski suggest that during REM sleep neurotransmitters are not produced, allowing neurons to regain their sensitivity.

Antidepressant drugs such as MAOIs abolish REM activity – and also replenish monomaine neurotransmitters, supporting the link between REM and neurotransmitter recovery (antidepressant drugs increase neurotransmitter levels).

Memory

REM sleep may permit memories to be sorted and discarded if unwanted (Crick and Mitchison).

REM may be important in the consolidation of procedural memory (memory for *doing* things), whereas SWS is important for semantic and episodic memory (memory for events and meanings) (Stickgold).

If sleep (SWS+REM) is restorative, total sleep deprivation should have negative effects…

Case studies show some support, e.g. DJ Peter Tripp stayed awake for 201 hours and after five days he experienced hallucinations and paranoia; his brain rhythms looked like he was asleep.

Non-human animal studies show that lack of sleep may be fatal. Rechtschaffen et al. kept rats on a rotating disc and after 33 days they died, though this may have been due to stress rather than lack of sleep.

However…

Sleep-deprived individuals may actually be getting some sleep, e.g. laboratory observations have found that sleep deprivation for more than 72 hours results in periods of microsleep while participants are apparently awake (Williams et al.), i.e. sleep deprived participants are only apparently awake but experiencing some of the benefits of sleep.

Another case study (Randy Gardner) found no psychotic symptoms after 11 days without sleep and there are reports of individuals (e.g. Hai Ngoc) who haven't slept for years with no ill effects. However, such individuals may be experiencing microsleep.

There are methodological issues…

Case studies relate to unique individuals, and other sleep studies often use volunteers who also might have unique characteristics (e.g. have less need for sleep than the norm) – so results might lack generalisability.

Non-human animal studies might lack generalisability because animals have different sleep requirements to humans.

If SWS is important, SWS deprivation should have negative effects…

Demonstrated in 'rebound effects' – when people are deprived of SWS they show need for more SWS on subsequent nights.

Acoustic stimulation is used to wake sleepers as soon as brain waves show SWS (Ferrara et al.).

If REM sleep is important, REM sleep deprivation should have negative effects…

REM deprivation results in as much as 50% more REM sleep on subsequent nights (Empson).

If sleep (SWS+REM) is restorative, exercise should increase the need for sleep…

Exercise should use up proteins etc so necessitating the need for more sleep for restoration.

Shapiro et al. found that marathon runners slept 2 hours longer after a race.

However…

Horne and Minard found that a series of exhausting tasks led people to go to sleep faster but not for longer.

IDA The evolutionary approach…

The main alternative to restoration theory is the evolutionary approach, which claims that sleep has no specific benefit except protection (to conserve energy or keep an animal safe from predators), rather than performing some specific biological function as claimed by the restoration approach.

The restoration approach doesn't explain, for example, why some species sleep one hemisphere at a time (e.g. dolphins).

Nor does it explain why lack of consciousness is necessary.

It looks like environmental pressures are important in shaping sleep processes, which can be explained by the evolutionary approach.

Chapter 1

Biological rhythms	The nature of sleep and lifespan changes
Sleep states >	Functions of sleep: Restoration theory
Biological rhythms and sleep >	Disorders of sleep	**Functions of sleep: Evolutionary explanations**

Functions of sleep: Evolutionary explanations

Energy conservation

High expenditure of energy
Warm-blooded animals use energy to maintain temperature.

This is especially true for small animals with a high metabolic rate.

Predicts a negative correlation between body size and sleep…
Supported by… Zepelin and Rechtschaffen, who found smaller animals sleep more than larger animals, although there are exceptions, e.g. sloths, who are large and sleep lots.

However, not supported by… Capellini *et al.* who found a positive correlation. This study used carefully selected, standardised data and therefore may be more reliable than older evidence.

Energy only conserved in NREM sleep…
In REM sleep the brain is relatively active so energy may only be conserved in NREM sleep.

Benefit of sleep
Sleep provides period of enforced inactivity to conserve energy, such as hibernation (Webb called it the *hibernation theory of sleep*).

Therefore small animals should sleep lots to conserve energy.

Suggests that… Only NREM (not REM) sleep evolved for energy conservation. More primitive animals (e.g. reptiles) only have NREM sleep, supporting the view that NREM sleep evolved first (for energy conservation) and REM sleep evolved later (to maintain brain activity).

If this is correct we would expect… A negative correlation only between body size and NREM sleep. Supported by Allison and Cicchetti but not by Capellini *et al.*

Foraging requirements

Time spent asleep (conserving energy)
is constrained by time needed for eating.
- Herbivores (e.g. cows) have to spend a lot of time eating because their food is poor in nutrients.
- Carnivores (e.g. lions) can afford to sleep a great deal.

Predicts a trade-off between foraging needs and sleep…
Capellini *et al.* found that animals with a greater need for foraging (because of high metabolism or diet low in energy) had lower sleep rates, supporting foraging needs as an explanation for sleep patterns.

Predator avoidance

Time spent asleep (conserving energy)
is constrained by risk of predation (being eaten).
- Predators can sleep for longer.
- Prey species are in danger while sleeping, therefore if sleep is vital, it should be done when least vulnerable, e.g. in the dark.

Predicts a trade-off between predation risk and sleep…
Alison and Cicchetti found that species with a high risk of predation did sleep less. Though there are exceptions, e.g. rabbits (high risk of predation) slept as much as moles (low risk of predation).

However…
Capellini *et al.* found the relationship is complex, e.g. animals that sleep socially sleep fewer hours – but ought to sleep more because there is safety in numbers.

Waste of time

Sleep is wasting time
Meddis proposed that sleep is what animals do when they have nothing else to do with their time (e.g. when not eating, mating, hiding from predators, etc.).

For most animals this means sleeping at night and sleeping out of sight (e.g. in a burrow).

Being awake is dangerous
Siegel also pointed out that being awake is dangerous not just because of predation, but also because an animal is more likely to be injured.

The best adaptive strategy is to sleep as long as you can.
For example, the little brown bat (small mammal, high metabolism) should sleep little. However, it has a very specific diet of insects that are around for a short time and the little brown bat is awake only then.

IDA ***The evolutionary approach…***
Suggests that sleep must be adaptive in some way, otherwise why do all animals do it, but their patterns of sleeping differ? This suggests that these patterns are in some way adaptive to the species' environment.

The 'phylogenetic signal' provides key support…
The fact that animals that are close together on the phylogenetic scale share close similarities in their sleep patterns supports the view that such patterns have evolved through adaption to environmental pressure.

Capellini *et al.* concluded that foraging and predation risks act as selective pressures (i.e. a demand resulting in one set of genes being favoured over another).

IDA ***The restoration approach…***
Restoration theory suggests that sleep evolved not just to occupy wasted hours, but because vital functions are performed.

Horne proposed a way to combine both approaches:
- Core sleep (= SWS), essential for bodily restoration.
- Optional sleep (= REM and some NREM sleep), dispensable but useful for occupying unproductive hours.

Explanations for insomnia

Insomnia may relate to going to sleep and/or staying asleep and may occur transiently, intermittently or chronically (more than once a month).

Causes of insomnia

Secondary insomnia

A single underlying cause:
- Medical (e.g. heart disease).
- Psychiatric (e.g. depression).
- Environmental (e.g. too much coffee).

It is a symptom of the main cause.

Primary insomnia

Defined by DSM as a problem with no known cause, which has occurred for more than a month. May be due to:
- Bad sleep habits (e.g. drinking coffee in the evening, having naps during the day).
- Expectations of sleeping problems because of previous cause (e.g. depression). The original problem has disappeared but there is still an expectation of sleep problems, which is a self-fulfilling prophecy.

IDA *Real-world application...*

The distinction between primary and secondary insomnia is important when deciding on treatment, because either you should treat the insomnia (if it is primary insomnia) or you should treat the underlying cause (in the case of secondary insomnia).

For example, in the case of insomnia arising from depression it might be unhelpful just to treat the insomnia.

However...

It is not always clear whether insomnia is simply a symptom of the main cause (i.e. secondary) or in fact primary. A survey of 15,000 Europeans found that insomnia often preceded depression i.e. was primary. This suggests that insomnia *should* be treated (Ohayon and Roth).

IDA *Real-world application... the cognitive approach...*

Attribution theory is an example of the cognitive approach in psychology. It concerns the way we think about the causes of our own (and other people's) behaviour. In the case of insomnia, if a person believes they cannot sleep because of insomnia this produces self-fulfilling expectations, i.e. they don't sleep as a result.

Attribution therapy suggests that an individual needs to think differently about the causes of their behaviour, i.e. learn to make a different attribution about why they are not sleeping.

Storms and Nisbett tried this with insomniacs. They gave the insomniacs a pill and told them it would either stimulate them or make them sleepy. Those insomniacs who expected the pill to stimulate them went to sleep faster because they attributed their usual bedtime arousal to the pill and therefore relaxed.

Risk factors influencing insomnia

Age

Teenagers also experience insomnia due to delayed sleep phase syndrome, a condition that is common in adolescence.

Older people have increasing physical problems (e.g. arthritis), which disrupt sleep.

Gender

Increased incidence in women may be due to hormonal fluctuations (e.g. the menopause).

Sleep apnoea

Individual stops breathing while asleep, for a few seconds or as much as a minute. May occur up to 30 times an hour and disrupts sleep.

Other parasomnias

Sleep walking, snoring, teeth grinding all disrupt sleep.

Personality

Insomniacs may tend to internalise psychological disturbance rather than acting out emotional problems (Kales *et al.*). Such internalisation would mean higher levels of emotional arousal and feelings of anxiety.

There is supporting evidence for adolescent insomnia...

A survey of 4,000 11–17-year-olds showed that 25% experienced insomnia and 5% said it interfered with their ability to function (Roberts *et al.*). A year later 41% reported continuing problems.

IDA *A genetic approach...*

It is possible that some people are predisposed to develop insomnia because of inherited factors.
- Twin studies show a 50% variance in the risk for insomnia is related to genes (Watson *et al.*).
- Such genetic factors might lead to physiological differences, such as hyperarousal (a state of increased psychological and physiological tension). Insomniacs have been found to experience hyperarousal during the day and night time (Bonnet and Arand).

IDA *Nature and nurture – genetics and environment...*

Spielman and Glovinsky distinguished between risk factors that predispose, precipitate or perpetuate insomnia. Genetic factors (nature) *predispose* an individual to insomnia.

Environmental stressors (nurture) trigger or *precipitate* primary insomnia (the diathesis-stress model of vulnerability + stress).

Perpetuating factors include expectations of having difficulty sleeping, leading to a self-fulfilling prophecy.

IDA *Real-world application...*

Treatments focus on factors that perpetuate insomnia, e.g. relaxation techniques and improving sleep hygiene (reduce caffeine, cut down daytime naps, sleep in darker room).

Phototherapy can be used for circadian disruption to entrain rhythms.

Chapter 1

Biological rhythms		
Sleep states		Explanations for insomnia
Biological rhythms and sleep >	Disorders of sleep >	Explanations for other sleep disorders

Explanations for narcolepsy

Main characteristics
- Feeling sleepy.
- Episodes of cataplexy (loss of muscular control).
- Triggered by emotional arousal.

IDA *Biological versus psychological approach…*
Most explanations are biological (see left) but there have been some psychological explanations.
For example, sudden attacks of sleepiness might occur to disguise sexual fantasies (Lehrman and Weiss).

Malfunction of REM sleep
Popular explanation in the 1950s, makes sense because classic symptoms of narcolepsy match REM sleep, for example:
- Paralysis (lack of muscle tone).
- Intrusion of REM-type sleep (hallucinations) into daytime.

There is some research support…
Vogel observed the sleep patterns during narcoleptic episodes in one patient, and found (as predicted) that REM patterns were present at the beginning of each episode.
Siegel recorded activity in brainstem of narcoleptic dog, and found the same activity during cataplexy as found in REM sleep.
However…
Generally there is little research support for the REM malfunction explanation.

Mutation in HLA
HLA (human leukocyte antigen) is part of the immune response.
A mutation (HLA-DQB1*0602) has been found in narcoleptics (Honda et al.).

HLA unlikely to be the sole explanation…
Mignot et al. found that the HLA mutation was present in many, but not all, narcoleptics and was also reasonably common in the general population.

Mutation in hypocretin (orexin)
The neurotransmitter hypocretin plays a role in maintaining wakefulness.
Narcoleptic dogs found to have abnormal gene for processing hypocretin (Lin et al.).

There is research support…
Findings from dogs are confirmed in humans, e.g. narcoleptics have lower levels of hypocretin in their cerebrospinal fluid (Nishino et al.).
Low levels of hypocretin are likely to be due to brain injury, diet, stress or auto-immune attack (body's immune system turns on itself).
Low levels of hypocretin are not linked to inherited factors because narcolepsy doesn't run in families and not concurrent in twins (Mignot).

Explanations for sleep walking (somnambulism)

Main characteristics
- Sleep walking is a term that covers any activity that takes place during sleep but is more common while waking.
- More common in childhood, affecting 20% of children.
- Only occurs during NREM sleep/SWS.
- Sleep walker not conscious of activity.

IDA *Nature and nurture – genetics and environment*
The evidence for a genetic basis for sleep walking:
- Prevalence of sleep walking in first-degree relatives is ten times greater than in the general population (Broughton).
- There is 50% concordance in MZ twins compared with only 15% in DZ twins (Lecendreux et al.).
- Gene identified (DQB1*05) (Lecendreux et al.).

The environmental component acts as a 'stressor' as in the diathesis-stress model, for example:
- Maturity of relevant brain circuits (immaturity leads to sleep walking).
- Amount of SWS sleep, e.g. factors such as sleep deprivation increase SWS, which explains why sleep walking becomes more likely.
- Being a child is related to both of the above (i.e. immature and high levels of SWS).

Due to incomplete arousal
EEG recordings during sleep walking show delta waves (typical of SWS) plus beta waves (typical of awake state).
Person in SWS is awakened but arousal is incomplete.
This incomplete arousal may be genetic.

IDA *Real-world application…*
Research has suggested a way to diagnose vulnerability to sleep walking. For example, 40 patients referred to a clinic for suspected sleep walking were observed during two nights' sleep – before and after a period of 25 hours' sleep derivation. Before sleep deprivation 50% of the patients showed episodes of sleep walking; afterwards this rose to 90% (Zadra et al.).
This supports the view that some people have a vulnerability for sleep walking, which is triggered by factors such as sleep deprivation.

Other factors
Sleep walking is increased by sleep deprivation, fever, stress, alcohol and psychiatric conditions.
Hormonal changes in puberty and menstruation may also be triggers.

Why children?
Might be because the system that usually inhibits motor activity in SWS isn't fully developed in children and may be under-developed in some adults (Oliviero).
One study did find that adult sleep walkers showed immaturity in the target neural circuits.

IDA *Real-world application…*
More research is needed in order to understand the extent to which a person does or doesn't have personal control during sleep walking, as it is used as a defence in criminal trials (Pressman et al.).
For example, Jules Lowe killed his father while sleep walking, found not guilty due to *insane automatism*. Brian Thomas killed his wife while sleeping, thinking she was an intruder, found not guilty and not insane.

Perception

Division A Theories of perceptual organisation
Gregory's top-down/indirect theory of perception
Gibson's bottom-up/direct theory of perception

Division B Development of perception
Perceptual development: Infant studies
Perceptual development: Cross-cultural studies
Perception and the nature–nurture debate

Division C Face recognition
Bruce and Young's theory of face recognition
Visual agnosias

Specification

Perception	
Theories of perceptual organisation	• Gregory's top-down/indirect theory of perception. • Gibson's bottom-up/direct theory of perception.
Development of perception	• The development of perceptual abilities, for example depth/distance, visual constancies. • Infant and cross-cultural studies of the development of perceptual abilities. • The nature-nurture debate in relation to explanations of perceptual development.
Face recognition and visual agnosias	• Bruce and Young's theory of face recognition, including case studies and explanations of prosopagnosia.

Chapter 2

Theories of perceptual organisation >

Development of perception

Gregory's indirect theory of perception

Perception > Face recognition

Gibson's direct theory of perception

Gregory's top-down/indirect theory of perception

Perception as hypothesis formation

A top-down process

According to this view, perception relies on stored knowledge to make sense of the physical information received by the senses.

This is necessary because the physical information is often inadequate.

Perception is based on an interaction between

- Knowledge stored in the brain.
- Sensory data.

A hypothesis or inference is developed based on previous knowledge and then tested against reality.

There is research support for this...

Hypotheses, once formed, are tested against reality. For example, Khorasani et al. found that the Müller-Lyer illusion had less effect once participants were told about the illusion.

However...

This is not true for all visual illusions, e.g. Necker cube reversals continue even after reality-testing (Shopland and Gregory).

This suggests that hypothesis testing may sometimes, but not always, contribute to the final perception.

Role of previous knowledge and expectation

Internal expectations are based on past experience

For example, people who are shown false playing cards (black hearts or red spades) 'see' brown or purple because expectations distort perception (Bruner et al.).

Generally expectations produce accurate perception

For example, a table viewed from any angle still looks rectangular (because of our expectations) even though the retinal image is rarely that shape.

There is research support for this...

Participants were shown a contextual scene, e.g. a kitchen. In this context participants often mistakenly identified a potentially ambiguous object such as a mailbox as a loaf of bread (Palmer). The kitchen context led to an erroneous hypothesis, which affected what was seen.

The digits 1 and 3 are perceived as the letter B when viewed in the context of a set of letters but as the number 13 in a set of numbers (Bruner and Minturn).

IDA Real-world application...

The effect of expectations can explain real-world events such as the error made by the US Navy in mistaking an Iranian passenger jet for an enemy aircraft about to attack and shooting it down with a missile, resulting in the death of 260 people.

Visual illusions

'Misapplied' hypotheses lead to errors of perception, e.g. visual illusions.

These are not accidental mistakes of perception but, rather, are 'lawful' and illustrate normal perceptual processes.

Examples

- *Converging lines* are used in two-dimensional (2D) paintings to suggest perspective.
- *Necker cube* – the red dot appears at front or back depending on which hypothesis about the shape is accepted.
- *Müller-Lyer illusion* – arrow with outward fins looks longer because equivalent to corner of a room, and thus looks farther away. The arrow with inward fins is equivalent to nearer corner of a building.

There is research support for Gregory's explanation of the Müller-Lyer illusion...

People who don't live in carpentered environments (e.g. live in round huts) are less likely to perceive the illusion, which might be because they are not used to seeing corners of rooms or edges of buildings.

Strengths of the top-down approach...

Can explain how the perceptual system copes with ambiguous situations and/or incomplete data.

Can help in the design of computer systems to 'see' the world, such systems are programmed to draw on experience.

Limitations of the top-down approach...

May not explain much of real-world perception because it is based on situations with ambiguous/incomplete data.

Can't explain why visual illusions persist even when you know the reality; reality testing should lead to the formation of new hypotheses.

Some concepts of the theory are imprecise, e.g. hypothesis testing doesn't explain what information is selected from the retinal image (Marr).

IDA The bottom-up approach

Gregory's top-down approach can be contrasted with Gibson's bottom-up/direct theory, which suggests that physical data are sufficient to explain perception.

See also 'Reconciling Gibson and Gregory' on the next page.

Chapter 2

Theories of perceptual organisation >

Development of perception

Gregory's indirect theory of perception

Perception > Face recognition

Gibson's direct theory of perception

Gibson's bottom-up/direct theory of perception

The optic array

A bottom-up process

According to this view, the pattern of light received at the senses (the optic array) provides sufficient information for perception.

Perception is simply the detection of information.

Optic flow

As we move forward, objects straight in front remain stationary, whereas objects to the side flow past; the further away, the faster the flow.

The importance of movement

Perceptual information is received as the observer moves around the environment.

Ecological aspects of perception

Perception can only be understood by observing how it operates in the environment (i.e. ecological).

For example, depth/distance is indicated by texture gradient (objects further away have a finer texture).

Such information can be picked up directly.

The role of invariants in perception

Some aspects of the environment don't change as we move about (i.e. are invariant).

Examples of such invariants:

• Texture gradient
• Horizon-ratio relation – the proportion of an object above and below the horizon line is constant for objects of the same size standing on the same ground.

Using the optic array

Resonance

Animals 'pick up' perceptual information from the environment in the same way that a radio picks up radio waves.

Picking up information = resonance.

Affordance

The meaning of an object is directly perceived and tells you how the object can be used, i.e. its action potential.

For example, a handle looks like something to be grasped, i.e. it 'affords grasping'.

The concept of affordance links perception and movement, as objects afford potential for action.

The usefulness of perception

Perception is not simply the detection of information, but the detection of useful information. It enables an animal to respond to its environment in an adaptive way.

Biological motion demonstrates direct perception...

(Perception of movement directly from a changing array of dots.)

Johansson placed small lights on a moving body, and found that observers 'saw' movement from changing array of lights.

Even young babies (Fox and McDaniel) and animals (Blake) respond appropriately when shown changing dots, which suggests this is an innate ability.

Time-to-contact demonstrates direct perception...

(Judging the responses to be made when approaching an object.)

Long jumpers change stride length as they approach take-off (Lee et al.).

Gannets close their wings at a constant time when they are making a vertical dive into water (Lee).

Both examples support the view that perception is directly perceived from the environment.

Movement can be shown to be important in perception...

Wraga et al. showed that the Müller-Lyer illusion disappeared when participants walked around a three-dimensional (3D) version.

Visual illusions can demonstrate direct perception...

Gregory's indirect approach explains visual illusions as an example of a misapplied hypothesis, but the direct theory can also explain them.

For example, the Ames room illusion has been explained in terms of top-down processing (expectations about rectangular rooms), but could also be explained in terms of horizon-ratio relation because the illusion persists even without walls and floor.

IDA Nature and nurture...

The question about whether perceptual abilities are largely due to nature or nurture is discussed on page 21. Explanations related to 'nature' support the direct theory of perception.

For example, Gibson and Walk (using the visual cliff) found that infants and animals perceive depth innately, which supports direct perception.

IDA Real-world application...

Principles of direct perception have been successfully applied in designing autonomous robots that learn about the meaning of objects in their environment (Şahin).

Strengths of the bottom-up approach...

This approach highlights the richness of data in the optic array.

Examples described show that direct theory can explain some aspects of perception.

Limitations of the bottom-up approach...

Cannot explain research related to the effects of experience (see previous page).

Best for explaining the evolution of perceptual abilities in a species but not the development of perceptual abilities in an individual, e.g. an African bushman can only learn the affordance of a red pillar box through personal experience.

IDA The top-down approach...

Gibson's direct theory can be contrasted with Gregory's top-down approach, which suggests that physical data are not sufficient to explain perception.

Reconciling Gibson and Gregory...

Bottom-up processes function in good visual conditions (e.g. daylight) whereas top-down processes function in ambiguous visual conditions.

Ventral stream of visual processing deals with object recognition (top-down) whereas dorsal stream deals with spatial/movement perception (bottom-up).

Chapter 2

Theories of perceptual organisation

Development of perception >

Perceptual development: Infant studies

Perceptual development: Cross-cultural studies

Perception > Face recognition

Perception and the nature–nurture debate

Perceptual development: Infant studies

Depth perception

Monocular cues (using one eye)

Dynamic cues (e.g. motion parallax) appear before static cues (e.g. occlusion) i.e. cues from movement versus cues from a static position. For example

- Gibson and Walk found motion parallax was the most likely cue in the visual cliff studies. Infants (with a patch over one eye) refused to crawl over the side of the display, which looked deeper (in reality covered with glass).
- Hofsten et al. showed that three-month-old infants used motion parallax. They assessed perception using the habituation method – infants habituated to (got used to) three rods while being moved about and later showed more interest in three equidistant rods (matching the effect of motion parallax).
- Granrud and Yonas found a response to occlusion around the age of six months.

Binocular cues (using both eyes)

Bower et al. tested retinal disparity by presenting different information to each eye so a 3D image appeared. Infants of one week responded by trying to grasp the object, showing depth perception.

Age-related changes in the use of perceptual cues.

For example, the use of shadows for depth perception tested by displaying two toys, one apparently closer because of shadows (one eye covered to remove binocular cues). Older infants (30 weeks old) responded, whereas younger infants (21 weeks old) didn't (Yonas et al.).

Visual constancy

Shape constancy (shape of object 'looks' the same despite differing retinal images).

Infants aged two months conditioned (being rewarded) to prefer a rectangle slanted at 45 degrees, later showed preference for this shape even when the retinal image was different, showing shape constancy (Bower).

Size constancy (an object, such as an apple, looks the same size despite different retinal images due to distance).

Infants habituated to certain cubes. When shown two cubes that had the same retinal size but one was more distant, they still responded to the new one, thus showing size constancy (Slater et al.).

Pattern perception

Newborn infants showed a preference for face-like patterns (Fantz).

They also showed a preference for complex patterns once their visual acuity (focus) has matured (Brennan et al.).

Criticisms have been made of the visual cliff studies...

The infants tested were six months old and had plenty of sensorimotor experience and therefore depth perception may be learned, not innate.

However...

Campos et al. tested two-month-old infants by measuring their heart rates; the infants showed fear (raised heart rate) when wheeled over the (apparent) deep side of the visual cliff.

Further support...

The young animals tested who were mobile from birth (e.g. day-old chicks and young goats) avoided the deep side, suggesting depth perception is innate (Gibson and Walk).

IDA Conclusions from infant studies support the innate approach...

The fact that many perceptual abilities are apparent at birth or once the visual system has matured sufficiently supports perception as an innate, bottom-up process.

However, this is not true for all perceptual processes...

Perceptual completion (bridging gaps in retinal image, e.g. Kanizsa triangle) is not displayed in two-month-old infants (Ghim).

Occlusion (part of object hidden by something in foreground) is an example of perceptual completion. At about two months infants treat the objects as if they were separate (Slater et al.).

This shows that...

Some aspects of perception require knowledge about object properties (e.g. perceptual completion), as top-down theorists would argue.

Bottom-up theorists counter-argue that seeing the 'hidden' parts in such illusions is part of cognitive development (learning to differentiate between items – Gibson and Gibson's differentiation theory) rather than part of the perceptual process.

IDA Cross-cultural research supports the nurture approach...

Studies of perceptual abilities in different cultural groups suggest that perception is more affected by experience i.e. nurture more than nature.

For example, McGurk and Jahoda found that all children they tested displayed some ability to interpret depth cues in pictures, however, children got better at this as they got older and Scottish children did better than Ghanaian children (suggesting experience does matter).

IDA Problems with studying nature and nurture in infants...

It is not always easy to decide what counts as an innate process (nature). Just because a process is present at birth does not mean it is innate – an infant has experiences in the womb and may learn to coordinate some sensorimotor processes.

Equally, just because an ability appears later in development it doesn't necessarily mean it is due to learning (nurture), because some innate abilities only appear when the nervous system is sufficiently mature.

There are methodological problems studying infants...

The conclusions from infant studies presume that we are actually testing infant abilities, whereas all of the techniques used rely on assumptions, e.g. assuming that an infant will express surprise at a novel object (the basis of the habituation method).

Infants might simply respond to subtle cues from the researcher (investigator bias), or might be sleepy and that's why they fail to show interest rather than because they were habituated.

Infants also have very poor visual acuity (the ability to focus). This means they may not be really seeing very much, or might mean they are actually more capable than they appear to be.

Chapter 2

Theories of perceptual organisation	Perceptual development: Infant studies
Development of perception >	Perceptual development: Cross-cultural studies
Perception > Face recognition	Perception and the nature–nurture debate

Perceptual development: Cross-cultural studies

Depth perception

Forest dwellers

Kenge, a Bambuti pygmy (forest dweller), interpreted distant buffalo as being insects. This shows lack of experience with depth cues (Turnbull).

The use of pictorial cues

Hudson tested children in South Africa using pictures that looked three-dimensional because of the use of depth cues such as occlusion, linear perspective and object size.

European children, by the end of primary school, could use depth cues (e.g. could correctly identify which animal was nearer) but the Bantu children couldn't interpret the pictorial depth cues.

Jahoda and McGurk tested depth perception using cues such as texture gradient, linear perspective and size. Participants had to arrange a 3D model to represent the position of two girls in the picture. They found (1) the more depth cues available, the better participants performed, (2) the older the children the better they did, (3) Scottish children did better than Ghanaian children but all children showed some ability to interpret depth cues.

Visual constancies

Shape constancy

Zulus who live in rural areas without windows could not 'see' the *trapezoid window illusion* (window appears to swing back and forth instead of around because it is shaped like a trapezium). Urban Zulus could see the illusion, indicating that experience leads to shape constancy (Allport and Pettigrew).

Size constancy

Zulus were found to be less susceptible to the Müller-Lyer illusion (Segall *et al.*). This may be because they lived in circular huts (not a carpentered environment). Gregory suggested that the illusion may be due to experience with edges of rooms and buildings, and Zulus would lack this.

IDA *Conclusions from classic cross-cultural studies support the nurture approach…*

The studies described on the left are from the 1960s (with the exception of Jahoda and McGurk). These studies suggest that many perceptual abilities are due to experience because people from different cultural groups, who each have different experiences, appear to have different perceptual capabilities. In this research the IV is cultural/perceptual experience and the DV is perceptual capabilities. This supports the view that perception is a top-down, learned process.

However…

More recent research (post-1970) has found contrary evidence. For example, Page repeated Hudson's research, using a different style of questioning (asking 'which is nearer to you, the antelope or the elephant?' instead of 'which is nearer to the man, the antelope or the elephant?'). Zulus could cope better than in Hudson's study.

The studies on pictorial depth cues appear to be contradictory…

Hudson found experience did matter, whereas Jahoda and McGurk concluded experience mattered less.

One possible explanation for this is…

Some 2D pictures are more difficult to interpret. Deregowski proposed an important distinction between images:

- Epitomic illustrations provide poor or no information about depth, as in Hudson's pictures (and also e.g. a silhouette).
- Eidolic illustrations look 3D because they use more easily interpreted cues (e.g. texture gradient), as in Jahoda and McGurk's pictures (and also impossible figures, e.g. three-pronged trident).

This explains why there were more 3D responders on Jahoda and McGurk's task.

Another explanation is…

The difference between cultural groups may be because of using culturally relative depth cues rather than innate depth cues.

For example, Europeans use converging parallel lines to represent distance. This is a cultural convention (developed in 15th century paintings) as opposed to a true reflection of reality – it is true that parallel lines converge but only at infinity and the horizon of our visual field is rarely at infinity (Berry *et al.*).

There are methodological problems with cross-cultural studies…

- Imposed etics – Using tests or procedures developed in one country/culture which may not be valid in the other culture, such as using the trapezoid illusion to test people unaccustomed to 3D pictures which therefore might not make sense to them.
- Representativeness – The group of participants tested may not be representative of that culture.
- Language – Participants and investigators, who rely on translators, may not understand each other.
- Natural experiments – The IV (cultural) is not specifically manipulated and therefore we cannot claim that it causes changes in the DV, we can only conclude that there is an association between experience and ability.

IDA *Cultural bias…*

These studies are all conducted assuming that the physical process of perception is the same in all people. However, the pigmentation of the retina has been found to vary with skin colour and is linked to difficulties in perceiving edges of objects (*retinal pigmentation hypothesis*). High pigmentation, found in African people, could explain why they are less likely to 'see' certain visual illusions.

IDA *Cross-cultural studies can be contrasted with…*

Infant studies (see previous page), which provide support for the influence of bottom-up innate factors.

Chapter 2

Theories of perceptual organisation	Perceptual development: Infant studies
Development of perception >	Perceptual development: Cross-cultural studies
Perception >	Face recognition	Perception and the nature–nurture debate

Perception and the nature–nurture debate

The nature position

Differentiation theory (Gibson and Gibson)

Perceptual development involves learning to see the *differences* between objects, i.e. differentiation. Continued experience with an object allows us to identify the properties that make two or more objects different and results in differentiation.

The implication of differentiation theory is that…

Sensory (direct) information provides all we need to interpret the environment, as proposed by Gibson's direct theory. See page 18 for evidence related to this theory.

IDA *This evidence shows that…*

Perception occurs without cognitive input, i.e. nature and not nurture; bottom-up processing.

Infant and cross-cultural research

Infant studies show infants have some highly developed and presumably innate perceptual abilities.

People from different cultures display the same perceptual abilities, as long as questions are phrased to make sense.

There are methodological problems with such research…

Infants may simply respond to subtle cues from the researcher (investigator bias) or might be sleepy and that's why they fail to show interest rather than because they were habituated.

In cross-cultural studies participants may not interpret the questions they are asked appropriately and/or researchers may misunderstand their answers. Methods for testing perceptual abilities be an imposed etic.

Pattern perception (Hubel and Wiesel)

The biological basis of perception (bottom-up) lies in cells in the visual cortex, each of which responds to one type of information (e.g. lines of unique orientation, a moving dot, etc). Complex and hypercomplex cells respond to groups of simple cells and are organised into functional columns which predispose the brain to make certain comparisons, e.g. for depth perception.

This research has been used to demonstrate the effects of visual deprivation…

Hubel and Wiesel tested the kittens in Blakemore's research (see left column) and found that the cells that usually respond to horizontal lines were absent in the vertically reared kittens, providing support for the conclusions on a neurophysiological level.

This effect only occurs if kittens are visually deprived before the age of eight weeks, a critical period – a time window during which development can take place and therefore time can be affected.

The nurture position

Enrichment theory (Piaget)

Piaget's theory of cognitive development proposes that we draw on cognitive schemas (expectations) to *enrich* the sensory data surrounding us (see page 69).

The implication of enrichment theory is that…

What we perceive is based on expectations derived from previous experience, as proposed by Gregory's indirect theory. See page 17 for evidence related to this theory.

IDA *This evidence shows that…*

Perception relies on cognitive input, i.e. nurture and not nurture; top-down processing.

IDA *Nature and nurture…*

The two different approaches may be reconciled in various ways:

- Each explains different aspects of perception, e.g. in good and poor conditions (see 'Reconciling Gregory and Gibson', page 18).
- 'Theory' theory – infants do have substantial innate knowledge, but cognitive development also requires the construction of theories (hypotheses about how the world works), which are tested against reality (Gopnik and Meltzoff).
- The development of the innate, physical system depends on interactions with experience for fine tuning, experience causes brain development. For example, rats raised in an enriched environment have larger brains because the nerve cells in their brains form more connections when compared with rats raised in a more deprived environment (Diamond).

Infant and cross-cultural research

Infant studies show that perceptual abilities change as babies get older, so support nurture.

Cross-cultural studies show an association between living in urban, carpentered environments and abilities to interpret depth cues.

Deprivation studies with animals

Blakemore and Cooper's kittens lost innate visual abilities when reared in a restricted environment (e.g. exposure to stripes only).

Held and Hein showed that perceptual development depends on sensory plus motor input; the passive kitten in a basket didn't develop normal vision, whereas the active kitten did.

The animal studies have been supported by human case studies…

For example, SB's vision was restored after a lifetime of being blind from cataracts. However, he never was able to really 'see' – his innate visual system was no longer capable of learning to make sense of the physical data.

IDA *There are ethical issues with animal studies…*

Animals in perceptual deprivation experiments are left permanently perceptually impaired.

Chapter 2

Theories of perceptual organisation
Development of perception   **Bruce and Young's theory of face recognition**
Perception   > Face recognition   > Visual agnosias

Bruce and Young's theory of face recognition

A serial model

Each stage or node is accessed one after the other (serially). At any time only some of the units (or 'nodes') are activated.

Step 1: Structural encoding

The details of a person's face are encoded as specific information about the features and expressions on the person's face.

Step 2: Route A – Familiar faces

- *FRUs (face recognition units)* – information about familiar faces, activated if there is a match.
- *PIN (person identity node)* – information about a person's identity, e.g. occupation, their interests etc.
- *NRU (name recognition unit)* – person's name retrieved.

Names can only be accessed once the person has been identified; there is no direct link from face to name. Consistent with the fact that people rarely remember a name without knowing any personal identity information, whereas the opposite is common.

Activation of any of these three nodes may draw on the *cognitive system* to decide whether the match is close enough to constitute recognition or merely a 'resemblance'.

Step 2: Route B – Facial expressions

- *Expression analysis* – work out the meaning of facial expressions.
- *Facial speech analysis*, e.g. use lip movements to understand what someone is saying.
- *Directed visual processing* – processing other facial information.

This route is used when dealing with unfamiliar faces, which accounts for the finding that some people with brain damage can match familiar faces but not unfamiliar faces (Malone *et al.*).

Step 3: The cognitive system

All of the units/nodes are linked to the cognitive system, which provides information as required.

This might be information about stereotypes (e.g. actresses tend to be attractive) or information about the people we know (e.g. who you are likely to see in your local shopping centre).

There is research evidence to support the model…

Participants kept a diary for eight weeks of their mistakes when recognising people. They could often recall information about a person but not their name, but not vice versa, supporting the serial nature of the model (Young *et al.*).

In another study Young *et al.* found participants were faster at identifying whether a particular face was that of a politician than identifying the politician's name.

Research on prosopagnosiacs shows they can decode emotional expressions, despite being unable to recognise faces. Deficits of emotional understanding are located in a different region of the brain (the amygdala) than object recognition (Groome).

However, not all research has not confirmed the model's predictions…

For example, Stanhope and Cohen found that participants could retrieve names for faces, despite having no information about personal identity (PIN).

Strengths of the theory…

The theory generates precise predictions that can be tested, which can further our knowledge of face recognition.

The theory makes clear distinction between the way familiar and unfamiliar faces are processed.

Limitations of the theory…

The details of unfamiliar face processing are vague.

Other components of the model, such as the cognitive system, are also not clearly specified.

An updated model…

Burton and Bruce produced a connectionist model (*IAC model*). This model proposes that face recognition involves a large number of nodes (FRUs, PINs, etc) with complex connections rather than serial links.

This matches the behaviour of the nervous system – lots of interconnected neurons, which fire when activated by sufficient incoming links.

IDA Real-world applications…

- Assisting police in recognising unfamiliar faces (Identikit pictures).
- Designing machines that will recognise faces for security, e.g. facial *cognitive biometric systems* (measure biological characteristics and match them against a database).

Are faces special?…

If face recognition is nothing more than object recognition, there is no need for a special model.

Face recognition is special…

- Studies have shown that infants have an innate preference for face-like stimuli, not just complex patterns (Fantz, Goren *et al.*).
- It makes adaptive sense to have a dedicated face processor because faces are important, e.g. recognising an enemy or decoding emotional expressions.
- The *fusiform face area* (FFA) is active when processing faces and not as active when identifying other objects (Kanwisher and Yovel).

Face recognition isn't special…

- Research on prosopagnosia suggests that face recognition isn't unique, i.e. is not different to object recognition generally.
- Some research has shown that the FFA is also active when recognising other objects, e.g. bird experts identifying birds or when trained to recognise *Greebles* (computer-generated novel objects) (Gauthier *et al.*).
- Face processing may simply be a form of expert object recognition.

Chapter 2

Theories of perceptual organisation
Development of perception
Bruce and Young's theory of face recognition

| Perception | > | Face recognition | > | Visual agnosias |

Visual agnosias

Apperceptive agnosia

Inability to perceive the form of the object.

Patients can't draw objects, match objects or describe component parts.

For example, Benson and Greenberg studied a young man who could not name or match letters, objects or familiar faces, yet he could identify numbers and colours and could respond to spoken language.

Associative agnosia

A failure, which occurs at a later stage in the object recognition process.

Patients can draw objects, match similar objects and describe the component parts. However, they cannot associate these details with stored knowledge about the objects in order to recognise them.

For example, HJA suffered brain damage, he was able to copy and match objects but couldn't name them; found it hard to search for an upside down letter T in rows containing the letter right way up (couldn't group similar items together), and couldn't recognise faces (but could recognise individual features) (Riddoch et al.).

JBR had difficulties identifying certain classes of object – more successful identifying non-living things (e.g. toasters) than living things (e.g. lions) – 90% versus 6% (Warrington and Shallice).

Prosopagnosia

Individuals can describe a person's face and its expression, but cannot recognise whose face it is unless they use other non-facial information such as hair, gait, clothing or voice.

Special characteristics
- **Prosopagnosiacs can recognise objects** (If face recognition was a special case of object recognition, this shouldn't be true). For example, VA could recognise objects but was poor at naming famous faces from pictures (may have 'cheated' by imagining the faces and then matching faces to pictures) (De Renzi and di Pellegrino).
- **Prosopagnosiacs can recognise their individual farm animals**, for example, Mr W. (Bruyer et al.).
- **Prosopagnosiacs have unconscious recognition of faces**. Patients shown familiar and unfamiliar faces and unable to identify which faces were familiar but showed a positive GSR to them (Bauer).
- **Some cases of prosopagnosia may be inherited**. Duchaine et al. studied ten family members who showed face and object recognition deficits, but not facial emotion recognition task deficits.

There are problems with the use of case studies…
Inevitably the study of abnormal behaviour relies on case studies (because such behaviours are rare).
- It is difficult to reach firm conclusions because many cases produce contradictions. For example, it appears that some prosopagnosic farmers can recognise their individual cows (Assal et al.) or individual sheep (McNeil and Warrington).
- Difficult to fully and reliably test any individual to be certain what they can and cannot do. This is due to many things – different methods used by different researchers, the motivation of patients to do their best when tested (some may be quite depressed because of their condition, which may mask their true abilities) and so on.

There are problems with studying brain-damaged individuals…
One of the reasons for studying abnormal behaviour (e.g. visual agnosia) is to understand 'normal' visual perception.
However…
- We often don't know what their abilities were before the damage, so can't conclude that current abilities are due to damage.
- Just because an area of the brain (such as the FFA) is associated with an inability to recognise faces doesn't mean that part of the brain is responsible.

IDA Ethical issues…
The privacy of individuals in case studies is protected by using their initials (e.g. HJA), although it is relatively easy to discover a person's true identity.
There are concerns about psychological harm because patients may be subjected to intensive testing to fully establish what they can or can't do, and this continues for many years.

IDA Real-world application…
Insights from research can offer help to people with agnosias, if only to help them realise that their problems are not imaginary.

Are there different modules in the brain?…
The fact that some people perform better on certain object recognition tasks than others suggests there are different mental modules, e.g. JBR (on left) was better at recognising non-living than living things, prosopagnosiacs are less able to recognise faces than other objects.
- It could be that one category is more familiar, and thus more easily recognised, than the other. When familiarity was controlled patients with agnosia performed equally well with living and non-living animals.
- The difficulty with classifying living things and classifying faces may be due to the specificity of the task. There are more specific categories for non-living things and face recognition requires recognition of specific features.
Both of these explanations suggest that there are not separate modules for different kinds of tasks.

Is face recognition special?…
Prosopagnosia may simply be one end of the object recognition continuum and not an independent disorder.
Farah proposed that apperceptive and associative agnosias are not separate, but that they all result from the disruption of two separate processes which lie on a continuum:
- Decoding structure (feature analysis, a kind of configural process).
- Computing relationships among the parts (a holistic process).
Not all of the evidence fits, e.g. HJA showed some evidence of holistic processing (Groome), and face inversion did not affect his performance, i.e. lack of holistic processing (Boutsen and Humphreys).
Another suggestion is that prosopagnosia might result from a disconnection between perception and memory for faces, because it affects the recognition of familiar faces in particular (Takahashi et al.).

Relationships

Division A Romantic relationships

The formation of romantic relationships
The maintenance of romantic relationships
The breakdown of relationships

Division B Human reproductive behaviour

Sexual selection
Parental investment

Division C Effects of early experience and culture

Influence of childhood and adolescent experiences on adult relationships
Relationships in other cultures

Specification

Relationships	
Romantic relationships	• Theories of the formation, maintenance and breakdown of romantic relationships: for example, reward/need satisfaction, social exchange theory.
Human reproductive behaviour	• The relationship between sexual selection and human reproductive behaviour. • Evolutionary explanations of parental investment: for example, sex differences, parent–offspring conflict.
Effects of early experience and culture on adult relationships	• The influence of childhood and adolescent experiences on adult relationships, including parent–child relationships and interaction with peers. • The nature of relationships in different cultures.

Chapter 3

	Romantic relationships	>	The formation of romantic relationships
	Human reproductive behaviour		The maintenance of romantic relationships
Relationships >	Effects of early experience and culture		The breakdown of relationships

The formation of romantic relationships

Reward/need satisfaction theory

We are attracted to people who provide us with direct reinforcement

Rewarding stimuli lead to positive feelings and punishing stimuli lead to negative feelings (operant conditioning).

Therefore:

- We enter into some relationships because that person creates positive feelings in us, which makes us feel happy, secure etc.
- We do not enter into relationships with some individuals because they create negative feelings in us, making us feel unhappy, threatened etc.

There is research support for this…

An experiment by Griffitt and Guay found that participant rating (for liking) of an experimenter was highest when the experimenter had positively evaluated them, producing positive feelings in them.

IDA *There are individual differences…*

This theory does not account for cultural and gender differences in the formation of relationships, suggesting that this is not a universal explanation of the formation of relationships.

- Lott suggests that in many cultures, women are more focused on the needs of others than receiving reinforcement.

There is a lack of mundane realism…

Most of the studies in this area have been laboratory studies, which don't necessarily show the principles of need satisfaction in real life.

However…

Some studies (e.g. Caspi and Herbener) have been conducted on real-life couples and have tended to support the claims of this theory.

We are also attracted to people who are associated with pleasant events

They *acquire* positive value because of their association with something else that makes us happy (classical conditioning).

A relationship is likely to succeed when the positive feelings outweigh the negative feelings, and is likely to fail when the negative feelings outweigh the positive feelings.

There is research support for this…

In the Griffitt and Guay study, onlookers who witnessed the experimenter's evaluation were also more likely to be liked by the participant when the onlooker had witnessed a positive evaluation of the participant than a negative one.

In these conditions, participants gave the same ratings of 'likeability' to both the experimenter and onlooker, supporting the claim that attraction may be influenced through association with a pleasant event, and this makes the formation of a relationship with that person more likely.

Similarity

Similarity (of personality and attitudes) promotes liking

- We first sort potential partners for dissimilarity, avoiding those who are too different.
- From those remaining, we can then choose those who are most similar to ourselves.
- We are therefore more likely to form relationships with people similar to ourselves.

There is research support for this…

Lehr and Geher carried out an experiment to test whether attitude similarity would be important in determining whether someone would be liked more. Descriptions of an imaginary stranger had varying degrees of similarity with the participant's own attitudes.

- The imaginary stranger was liked more (and seen as more suitable as a potential date) if he or she was similar to the person doing the rating.
- The stranger was more likely to be liked if the description had already indicated that they liked the participant.

This indicates importance of similarity *and* reciprocal liking in attraction.

Personality

We are more likely to be attracted to those with similar rather than dissimilar or complementary personality traits.

Married couples with similar personalities are more likely to be happy than those with dissimilar personalities (Caspi and Herbener).

Similarity is important in the formation of relationships because…

- By ruling out dissimilar people, we lessen the chance of being rejected as a partner.
- When people share our attitudes and beliefs, it tends to validate them, which is also rewarding.

But…

Rosenbaum suggests that *dissimilarity* rather than similarity is the more important factor in determining whether relationships will form.

Attitudes

If partners' attitudes toward important issues differ, the process of attitude alignment may occur, as one or both partners modify their attitudes to produce similarity.

IDA *There are cultural similarities…*

This 'dissimilarity-repulsion' hypothesis has been tested and supported across a number of different cultures including Singapore and the USA. By demonstrating cultural similarities, this suggests that sorting prospective partners initially according to *dissimilarity* is a universal phenomenon.

Chapter 3

Romantic relationships	>	The formation of romantic relationships
Human reproductive behaviour		The maintenance of romantic relationships
Relationships >	Effects of early experience and culture	The breakdown of relationships

The maintenance of romantic relationships

Social exchange theory

People exchange resources (e.g. form relationships with others) with the expectation that they will earn a 'profit' – i.e. rewards exceed costs incurred.
- Rewards include: being cared for, companionship and sex.
- Costs include: effort expended developing a relationship, financial investment and time wasted.
- Commitment to a relationship is dependent on its profitability, with less profitable relationships being more vulnerable to termination.

There are limitations…
The main criticism concerns the selfish nature of the theory, i.e. the claim that people are only motivated to maintain relationships out of selfish concerns. It is possible that the principles of social exchange theory apply only in individualist cultures, which are characterised more by individual concerns.

IDA *There is a cultural bias in this theory…*
Moghaddam suggests that social exchange theory would only apply to relationships in Western cultures, and only to short-term relationships among individuals with high mobility (e.g. students).

Long-term relationships within less mobile population groups (e.g. in non-Western cultures) are more likely to value security rather than personal profit.

This suggests that social exchange theory does not represent a universal explanation of the maintenance of relationships, i.e. it is culturally biased.

We develop a comparison level (CL) against which new relationships are judged. It is the product of experiences in previous relationships plus expectations of the current relationship.
- If potential profit from new relationship exceeds CL, it will be judged worthwhile.
- Comparison level for alternatives (CLA) – potential increase in rewards from new partner minus costs of ending current relationship.

There are limitations…
The theory does not explain why people leave relationships despite having no alternative, nor does it suggest how great the disparity in CL has to be for it to become unacceptable.

IDA *Real-world application…*
The concept of CLA can be used to explain why some women stay in an abusive relationship. Rusbult and Martz argue that when investments are high (e.g. children, financial security) and alternatives are low (nowhere else to live, no money), this might be considered a profit situation, and so the woman might choose to stay in the relationship.

Equity theory

People strive to achieve fairness in relationships and feel distressed if they perceive unfairness.

Inequitable relationships exist when a person perceives that they:
- Give a great deal in a relationship and get little in return.
- Receive a great deal and give little in return.

Both are inequitable relationships and would leave them feeling dissatisfied. The greater the inequity the greater the dissatisfaction.

There is research support for this…
Stafford and Canary surveyed 200 married couples concerning equity and relationship satisfaction. They found that:
- Relationship satisfaction was highest for spouses who perceived their relationships to be inequitable.
- Satisfaction was lowest for spouses who perceived themselves to be most under-benefitted in their relationships.

Limitations of this theory…
Clark and Mills argue that a concern for equity may only characterise relationships between colleagues or business associates rather than relationships between friends or lovers (romantic relationships).

They claim that romantic relationships are governed by a desire to respond to the needs of the partner rather than any concerns about equity.

Ratio of inputs and outputs
An equitable relationship is one where one partner's benefits minus their costs equals the other partner's benefits minus their costs.

Perception of inequality in a relationship motivates a person to try to restore it (e.g. by changing perceptions of relative inputs and outputs) or end the relationship.

IDA *Gender bias…*
Steil and Weltman studied married working couples. They found that the women generally rated their husbands' careers as more important than their own.

They concluded that because women tend to seek less for themselves in a relationship, this makes equity a less relevant explanation of relationship satisfaction in real-life relationships.

Because of this, it challenges the universality of equity as a determinant of relationship satisfaction.

Chapter 3

Romantic relationships	>	The formation of romantic relationships
Human reproductive behaviour		The maintenance of romantic relationships
Relationships > Effects of early experience and culture		The breakdown of relationships

The breakdown of relationships

Reasons for relationship breakdown (Duck)

Lack of skills

Some people lack the interpersonal skills to make relationships mutually satisfying. These include being poor conversationalists and poor at indicating interest in others. Others then find them unrewarding and the relationship breaks down.

There is research support for this explanation…

Boekhout *et al.* found that extramarital affairs were typically a direct reaction to a perceived lack of skills and/or stimulation in the existing relationship.

Undergraduates judged sexual boredom and the need for excitement as the main reasons for infidelity among males, and lack of attention and emotional dissatisfaction as the main reasons for infidelity among females.

Lack of stimulation, e.g. boredom

Often quoted when breaking off a relationship. People expect relationships to change and develop; if they do not this is seen as sufficient justification to end the relationship.

Despite this…

Long-distance relationships are increasingly common in our mobile society, and yet Holt and Stone found there was little decrease in relationship satisfaction provided that lovers are able to reunite regularly.

This suggests that people use different management strategies to successfully maintain long-distance relationships.

Maintenance difficulties

Some circumstances (e.g. going away to university or a military tour of duty) make maintenance of relationships difficult to manage because partners do not see each other often enough. This places a strain on relationships, which may be responsible for their breakdown.

IDA *Real-world application…*

The importance of social skills deficits in relationship breakdown has led to the development of training programmes to enhance relationship skills.

For example, Cina *et al.* compared couples who had received relationship skill training with those who did not. The 'trained' couples later reported much higher marital quality compared to couples in the control group.

A model of breakdown (Duck and Rollie)

Relationships that are inequitable or where there are reasons for breakdowns as outlined above, are likely to create dissatisfaction in one of the partners. This may lead to:

Breakdown
One partner becomes dissatisfied with the relationship.
Threshold: I can't stand this anymore.

▼

Intrapsychic processes
Person broods on their partner's faults and on relational 'costs'.
Threshold: I'd be justified in withdrawing.

▼

Dyadic processes
Person confronts their partner and begins to discuss their feelings and the future.
Threshold: I mean it.

▼

Social processes
Dissatisfaction spills over to friends and family and so speeds partners toward dissolution.
Threshold: It's now inevitable.

▼

Grave-dressing processes
Partners construct a representation of the failed relationship that avoids putting them in an unfavourable light.
Threshold: Time to get a new life.

▼

Resurrection processes
Each partner prepares themselves for new relationships by redefining themselves and building on past experience.
What I've learned and how things will be different.

There is research support for this explanation…

Tashiro and Frazier surveyed undergraduates who had recently broken up with a romantic partner. They typically reported that they had not only experienced emotional distress, but also personal growth. Breaking up with their partner had given them new insights into themselves and a clearer idea about future partners (i.e. resurrection processes).

This model is important because…

It emphasises the value of communication in relationship breakdown. Paying attention to what people say and the ways in which they talk about their relationship gives a clue as to the stage they are at and therefore appropriate repair strategies that might be employed.

IDA *Ethical issues in breakdown research…*

Carrying out research in such a sensitive area raises significant ethical issues because participants may experience distress when revisiting the issues that led to the breakdown.

This means the researcher faces the dilemma of pursuing valuable information or terminating a study to prevent the participant experiencing further distress.

IDA *A heterosexual bias…*

A limitation of models of relationships is that they tend to be developed from the experiences of white, middle-class, heterosexual participants, which may not represent the experience of other groups.

Gender differences

Women are more likely to stress unhappiness and incompatibility as reasons for dissolution (Brehm and Kassin).

Men are more likely to cite 'sexual witholding'.

Sexual selection

Inter- and intrasexual selection

Intrasexual selection

Members of one sex (usually males) compete with other members of their own sex for access to members of the opposite sex (mate *competition*).

Whatever traits lead to success in this competition will be passed on to the next generation.

Intersexual selection

Members of one sex (usually females) show preferences for members of the opposite sex who possess certain characteristics (mate *choice*).

These indicate the chances of the mate being able to give protection and support to offspring which makes them more attractive as a potential mate.

IDA *A non-evolutionary explanation*…

Some critics reject sexual selection as an explanation for male preferences for younger women. An alternative explanation is based on social power; younger women are easier to control and are therefore preferred as mates.

Kenrick *et al.* rejected the claim that males consistently prefer younger women (a fundamental claim of sexual selection theory), finding that teenage males are most attracted to woman that were actually five years older than them, even though the older women show no interest in them!

IDA *Real-world application*…

Many of the studies carried out in this area have been restricted to expressed mate preferences rather than real-life mate choice.

However…

A study of actual marriages (Buss) confirmed that men do choose younger women.

Statistics also show that men who divorce and remarry tend to choose women who are increasingly younger than they are.

Short-term mating preferences

Parental investment theory claims

that men evolved a greater desire for casual sex and would ideally seek sex earlier in a relationship.

Female behaviour would not be subjected to the same evolutionary pressures.

In contrast to women, men appear to lower their standards in the context of short-term mating opportunities and show a marked decrease in attraction following sex (Buss).

There is research support for this…

Clarke and Hatfield's study with students on a college campus provides compelling evidence that men have evolved psychological mechanisms to ensure success in short-term mating, including a desire for sexual variety, the tendency to seek sex early in a relationship and a willingness to consent to sex with strangers.

IDA *Gender bias in short-term mating preferences*…

Although parental investment theory predicts that men more than women would have a preference for casual sex, Greiling and Buss suggest that women may also profit from short-term mating as a way of leaving a poor-quality relationship or to produce more genetically diverse offspring.

Long-term mate preferences

Sexual selection should favour high levels of choosiness in *both* sexes.

Poor mate choice is disadvantageous for both sexes who will have wasted valuable resources, but is particularly disastrous for women.

Women have an obligatory biological

investment in their children, therefore are predicted to be very particular in their choice of mate. Therefore women are attracted to men who:

- Are able to invest resources in her and any offspring.
- Are able to protect her and any offspring.
- Show promise as a good parent.
- Are sufficiently compatible to ensure minimal costs to her and offspring.

Men are attracted to women who

display signals of fertility, an indication of their reproductive value (e.g. youth and physical attractiveness).

There is research support for this…

Buss explored mate preferences among men and women in 37 cultures. The main results were:

- Women more than men desired mates who were good financial prospects (i.e. had resources or ambition).
- Men placed more importance on physical attractiveness in a mate, cues to a woman's fertility and reproductive value.
- Men wanted mates who were younger than them, an indication that men value increased fertility in potential mates.
- Both sexes valued intelligence in potential mates (linked to parenting skill), kindness and dependability.

IDA *Hormonal factors in attraction*…

Mate preferences are also subject to factors other than those predicted by sexual selection. Some research suggests that women near the most fertile point of their menstrual cycle are more attractive to men.

There is research support for this…

This was confirmed by a study of lap dancers. Miller *et al.* calculated the tips earned by lap dancers at various stages of their menstrual cycle. Those in the most fertile stage of their cycle (i.e. in oestrus) earned twice the value of tips compared to girls who were not in oestrus.

Chapter 3

Romantic relationships
Human reproductive behaviour > Sexual selection
Relationships > Effects of early experience and culture | **Parental investment**

Parental investment (PI)

Sex differences in parental investment

What sex differences?

Males can opt out of parental investment in a way that females cannot.

The implication is that…

Males should be unwilling to invest resources that are not their own. However, a study by Anderson *et al.* challenges this. They found that men did not discriminate financially between children born to a current partner in a previous relationship and their own child from a previous relationship.

Why do females invest more?

Mothers make the greater *prenatal* contribution (pregnancy) and greater *postnatal* contribution (extended period of childcare), because of the relative immaturity of their offspring.

One explanation for this…

It is possible that these men would invest in their stepchildren to convince their current partner that they are a 'good provider' in order to promote future mating possibilities.

Costs of maternal investment

Maternal investment (e.g. internal fertilisation, nine months pregnancy, breast feeding) is considerably higher than paternal investment, making random mating more costly for females.

Consequences of high maternal investment include…

Infant dependency means females want good male providers, and the expense of childrearing means females want good quality males (to provide good quality offspring).

Baker and Bellis suggest one option is to marry a man who is kind and has resources but seek extramarital affairs with good quality males.

Bellis suggests that as many as 14% of children are the product of such extramarital matings.

Paternal investment and cuckoldry

When males do invest parentally (provision of time or resources), they must protect themselves from cuckoldry, so have greater concern over the fidelity of their mates.

IDA There is physiological research support for this…

Sex differences in jealousy have been explored physiologically. Buss *et al.* found that when asked to imagine scenes of sexual or emotional infidelity involving their partner, males showed much higher physiological responses (e.g. increases in heart rate and EMG response) for sexual rather than emotional infidelities.

Sexual and emotional jealousy

Men are likely to be jealous of sexual infidelity (to avoid the possibility of cuckoldry) while women are more likely to be jealous of emotional infidelity (to avoid loss of resources).

IDA This can be better explained in terms of social learning…

Harris questions whether such sex differences are an adaptive response as predicted by parental investment theory. She found that males respond with greater arousal to any sexual imagery regardless of its context, suggesting that sex differences in jealousy are more likely to be a product of social learning than evolutionary history.

Parent–offspring conflict

Parental and offspring fitness

Resource allocations that maximise parental fitness are not identical to those that would maximise offspring fitness.
- Parents and children will be in conflict about *when* the child should be weaned.
- Parents would encourage children to value their siblings more than they are naturally inclined to.

IDA An evolutionary perspective…

According to PI theory, first-born (closer to reproductive age) and last-born (more vulnerable and so more needy) would receive more PI than middle-born children.

This is supported by…

Andrews studied 1,600 US adolescents, and found that suicide attempts were more common among middle-born children than first or third-born children; their suicide attempts were a risky effort to extort increased parental investment (love, resources etc.).

Conflict before birth

Pre-eclampsia – dangerous rise in maternal blood pressure caused by foetus secreting hormones when it perceives need for more nutrition.

There is research support for conflict before birth…

Research has found that mothers who experience high blood pressure during pregnancy have fewer spontaneous abortions and larger babies at birth, supporting the adaptive value of pre-eclampsia for the foetus.

Conflict after birth

When children become older, parents attempt to maximise their own reproductive interest by directing resources away from older children and toward vulnerable younger children.

IDA Cooperation as an alternative evolutionary strategy…

Salmon and Daly suggest many younger children opt out of competition for parental attention and develop traits such as cooperativeness to help them form alliances instead. This suggests that children may develop cooperativeness as an equally adaptive alternative to competing with siblings for parental investment.

Sibling rivalry

Individual offspring try to maximise their fitness (in terms of parental resources) at expense of other offspring.

Coping with sibling rivalry

Lalumière *et al.* suggest that sibling rivalry and conflict for resources can be reduced by steering siblings along different developmental paths, so that there is reduced sibling competition, and each is able to maximise their strengths without taking resources from the other(s).

Influence of childhood and adolescent experiences on adult relationships

Childhood experiences

Parent–child relationships

Bowlby claimed that later relationships are a continuation of early attachment styles (secure or insecure) because the behaviour of the primary attachment figure promotes an internal working model of relationships, which leads the infant to expect the same in later relationships.

Children also learn about caregiving by modelling the behaviour of the primary attachment figure. This is then reflected in their own behaviour as adults.

Interactions with peers

Qualter and Munn found that children also learn from their experiences with other children. This determines how the child thinks about him/herself.

Through these interactions, children develop a sense of their own value, which determines how they approach adult relationships.

The experience of having a friend to confide in promotes feelings of trust and acceptance, both important in adult relationships.

There is research support for this…

The relationship between attachment style and later relationships is supported by a meta-analysis (Fraley) which found correlations ranging from +.10 to +.50 between early attachment type and success in adult relationships.

However…

It is also possible that an individual's attachment type is caused by the current relationship, which is why happily married individuals tend to be securely attached.

There is research support for this…

An ongoing longitudinal study (Simpson *et al.*) supports the claim that expression of emotions in adult romantic relationships can be traced back to attachment experiences during earlier social development. The study found that securely attached infants were more socially competent as children, closer to their friends as adolescents and more emotionally attached to their romantic partners as adults.

IDA *Determinism in the development of adult relationships…*

Research appears to suggest that early experiences have a fixed effect on later adult relationships. However, researchers have found many examples where participants were experiencing happy adult relationships, despite not having been securely attached as infants.

This suggests that an individual's past experiences do not *determine* the future course of their adult relationships.

IDA *Links to psychopathological disorders…*

Some children find any close relationships difficult. They may suffer from an attachment disorder, caused by early abuse or neglect. The resulting behaviour and emotions create a disturbed way of relating to others, which can interfere with subsequent adult relationships.

Adolescent experiences

Parent–child relationships

Allen and Land claim that adolescent relationships are shaped by an internal model of relationships based on early parent–child experiences plus experiences from current relationships.

Adolescents thus develop relationship experience with each relationship affecting the next.

Autonomy is not the only important thing…

Breaking free from parental control (i.e. developing autonomy) is important in adolescent development but Coleman and Hendry suggest that autonomy is most healthy when accompanied by continuing warm and close relationships with parents as well (connectedness).

Research by Larson *et al.* found that time spent with each parent individually remained consistent throughout adolescence.

This suggests that…

Adolescent relationships *supplement* rather than replace relationships with parents.

Interactions with peers

In adolescence, attachment shifts from parents to peers. Romantic relationships in adolescence serve a number of purposes including:

• They achieve the goal of separation from parents.
• They allow the adolescent a type of emotional and physical intimacy different to that with parents.

Madsen's study of dating behaviour among adolescents found that some dating in adolescence is advantageous for adult relationships, but too much can be maladaptive.

There are sampling limitations in research studies…

In many studies on adolescent romantic relationships, there has been a reliance on a highly selective sample of adolescents from one school or city.

A major disadvantage of such samples is that they do not adequately represent the experiences of adolescents in other areas or other cultures. If social factors determine adolescent experiences, then it is difficult to generalise findings from one highly specific culture to *all* cultures.

Adolescent relationships can also have adverse effects…

• Haynie found adolescent romantic relationships increased some forms of deviance in adolescence by 35%.
• Neemann *et al.* found that romantic involvement in middle adolescence was associated with decreases in academic achievement and increases in conduct problems.

In late adolescence, romantic relationships were no longer associated with these negative effects, suggesting it is the *timing* of romantic relationships in adolescence that determines what influence they have.

Chapter 3

Relationships	>	Effects of early experience and culture	>
		Romantic relationships	Influence of childhood and adolescent experiences on adult relationships
		Human reproductive behaviour	
			Relationships in other cultures

Relationships in other cultures

Western and non-Western relationships

Voluntary or non-voluntary relationships

Western cultures are predominantly urban, ensuring relatively easy social and geographical mobility, and therefore interaction with a large number of people. This leads to a high degree of choice over who people interact with on a voluntary basis.

Non-Western cultures lack these urban settings, therefore people have less social and geographical mobility, interaction with fewer others on a daily basis, and therefore less choice over who they form relationships with.

There is research support for this…

Epstein found that in societies with reduced mobility, non-voluntary (arranged) marriages seem to work well, with low divorce rates and surprisingly high levels of love between the partners.

Myers *et al.* also found no difference in marital satisfaction between Indian couples in arranged marriages and non-arranged marriages in the USA.

However…

A Chinese study (Xiaohe and Whyte) found that women who had married for love were happier than women who were in arranged marriages.

IDA *Evolutionary explanation for universal love…*

Pinker claims romantic love is a 'human universal' that evolved to promote survival and reproduction among humans.

Jankowiak and Fischer support this claim with their finding that romantic love existed in 90% of the 166 non-Western cultures they studied.

Individual or group-based relationships

Attitudes in individualist cultures, where individual interests are more highly regarded than group goals or interests, are consistent with the formation of relationships based on freedom of choice, whereas collectivism leads to relationships that may have more to do with the concerns of family or group.

Voluntary relationships are not necessarily the most successful…

Although we might expect relationships based on love to produce more compatible partners than relationships based on family or financial reasons, this may not necessarily be the case.

For example, parents may be in a better position to judge long-term compatibility than young people who are 'blinded by romantic love' and who ignore areas where they may be incompatible.

Despite this, however, Xiaohe and Whyte's Chinese study found that freedom of choice in relationships appeared to promote marital stability rather than instability, suggesting greater long-term compatibility in non-arranged marriages.

Continuity and discontinuity

Cultures differ in the degree to which they value heritage and ancestry (many non-Western cultures) or progress (most Western cultures).

This is consistent with relationships in these cultures, with non-Western cultures emphasising continuity and therefore permanent relationships. Western cultures emphasise change and discontinuity, so favour more temporary relationships.

IDA *Real-world application…*

The increase in divorce rate in India is considered to be due to increasing urbanisation and changing lifestyle. This has led to the development of an industry of 'divorce tourism', where tourism companies have put together packages to help couples rescue their marriages.

IDA *There may be an historical bias…*

The increase in discontinuous and non-permanent relationships in Western cultures is relatively recent, with divorce in the UK being rare 50 years ago.

This suggests that the drift to discontinuous and more temporary relationships may be more a product of the greater urbanisation that has characterised Western cultures in the last 50 years, rather than any inherent difference based on the cultural norms and values of Western cultures.

Norms

Act as guidelines for behaviour within a culture. The norm of reciprocity stresses that for a benefit received an equal benefit should be returned.

In individualist cultures, reciprocity in personal relationships tends to be voluntary, whereas in collectivist cultures it is more obligatory (e.g. Japan has a norm of reciprocal gift-giving) (Ting-Toomey).

Culture is an important factor in the study of relationships because…

Social psychologists have traditionally ignored culture in their study of human relationships because of an emphasis on the experimental method as the preferred method of study.

However, although cultural background may be seen as a problematic extraneous variable in such research, it is clear that culture itself is an important variable that influences the relationship processes being studied.

Moore and Leung, in a study of romantic love among Australian students, found differences between Anglo-Australian and Chinese-Australian students in their attitude to romantic relationships, love and loneliness.

Rules

Argyle *et al.* found different relationship rules applied to different cultures (e.g. UK, Italy, Hong Kong and Japan), although there are also similarities.

All four cultures acknowledged the importance of courtesy and respect in relationships and the avoidance of social intimacy.

IDA *Cultural bias in cross-cultural research…*

Knowledge of the norms and rules underlying relationships in a particular culture is important in understanding that culture. However, a problem with research such as Argyle's where the list of rules and ways of measuring these was formulated in the culture of the researcher, is that this may have resulted in a failure to include rules specific to one particular culture.

This represents an imposed etic, where a culture-specific idea or measure is wrongly imposed on another culture where it is less relevant and may lead to misleading conclusions.

Chapter 4

Aggression

Division A Social psychological approaches to explaining aggression
Social learning theory
Deindividuation
Institutional aggression

Division B Biological explanations of aggression
Neural and hormonal mechanisms
Genetic factors

Division C Aggression as an adaptive response
Evolutionary explanations of human aggression
Explanations of group display

Specification

Aggression	
Social psychological approaches to explaining aggression	• Social psychological theories of aggression, for example, social learning theory, deindividuation. • Explanations of institutional aggression.
Biological explanations of aggression	• The role of neural and hormonal mechanisms in aggression. • The role of genetic factors in aggression.
Aggression as an adaptive response	• Evolutionary explanations of human aggression, including infidelity and aggression. • Explanations of group display in humans, for example, sports events and lynch mobs.

Chapter 4

Social psychological approaches to aggression	>	Social learning theory
Biological explanations of aggression		Deindividuation
Aggression	> Aggression as an adaptive response	Institutional aggression

Social learning theory (SLT)

Observation

We learn aggressive behaviour through observation and imitation

People learn the specifics of aggressive behaviour and also its consequences by seeing others being rewarded or punished for their aggressive behaviour (vicarious reinforcement).

By observing the consequences of aggression, they learn when it is and isn't appropriate.

IDA Real-world application…

Studies of the effects of social learning are not restricted to laboratory studies of children. Philips found that murder and assault rates in the USA almost always increased in the week following a major televised boxing match, suggesting that viewers were imitating some of the aggressive behaviour they had observed in the boxing.

IDA Explains cultural differences…

Aggression is rare among the !Kung San people because parents do not reward physical aggression in children (lack of direct reinforcement), nor do they model aggression, therefore there is no motivation for children to act aggressively.

The Bobo doll studies

Bandura et al. found that children who observed an adult behaving aggressively toward a Bobo doll were likely to reproduce those specific modelled behaviours.

This was particularly so if they observed the adult being rewarded for their aggression toward the doll.

The Bobo doll studies lack validity because…

Children in these studies may well have been aware of what was expected of them and responded accordingly (i.e. they responded to demand characteristics). Noble supports this claim with a report that at least one child reported that 'that's the doll we have to hit'.

The studies have also focused on aggression toward a doll rather than a real person; however, Bandura carried out a study using an adult beating up a live clown. Children who observed this behaviour later did imitate it.

Mental representation

For social learning to take place mental representations are required

The child must also represent possible rewards or punishments for their aggressive behaviour in terms of expectancies of future outcomes.

If opportunities for aggressive behaviour arise in the future, children display the learned behaviour, provided the expectation of reward is greater than the expectation of punishment.

There is research support for this…

Evidence for the role of expectancy and self-efficacy in aggressive behaviour was provided by Perry et al. They found that children who were described as highly aggressive by their peers reported greater confidence in their ability to use aggression to successfully resolve interpersonal conflicts than did children rated as less aggressive by their peers.

Context-dependent aggression can be explained by SLT…

People behave differently in different situations because they have observed that aggression is rewarded in some situations and not in others, i.e. they learn behaviours that are appropriate to different contexts. This is a strength of this theory in that it can predict whether aggressive behaviour is likely in any specific situation dependent on previous experiences.

Production of behaviour

Maintenance through direct experience

An individual who is rewarded for their behaviour (e.g. is praised by others) is likely to repeat that action in similar situations in the future.

For example, a child who has a history of successfully bullying other children learns that aggression towards other children is likely to produce rewards.

A strength of social learning theory is…

Unlike operant conditioning theory, SLT can explain aggressive behaviour in the absence of direct reinforcement.

For example, in the Bobo doll studies, although participants behaved more aggressively after observing an aggressive model, at no point were these participants directly reinforced for their aggressive behaviour. The concept of vicarious reinforcement is necessary to explain these findings i.e. that children have learnt by observing the actions of others, particularly where they see these actions rewarded.

Self-efficacy expectancies

Children must also develop confidence in their ability to successfully carry out the learned aggressive behaviours. Children who have been unsuccessful in their use of aggression in previous situations may develop less self-efficacy concerning their ability to use aggression and turn to other means of resolving conflict.

IDA Ethical issues make it difficult to test SLT experimentally…

Exposing children to aggressive behaviour (either in real life or on film) with the knowledge that they may reproduce it in their own behaviour raises ethical issues concerning protecting participants from psychological harm.

As a result, experimental studies such as the Bobo doll studies would no longer be allowed. This means that it is difficult to test experimental hypotheses about the social learning of aggressive behaviour in children.

Chapter 4

Social psychological approaches to aggression	>	Social learning theory
Biological explanations of aggression		Deindividuation
Aggression > Aggression as an adaptive response		Institutional aggression

Deindividuation

The nature and process of deindividuation

Nature of deindividuation

It is a psychological state characterised by lowered self-evaluation and decreased concerns about evaluation by others.

This leads to an increase in behaviours that would normally be inhibited by personal or social norms.

The psychological state of deindividuation is aroused when individuals are in:
• Crowds or large groups.
• Situations that increase anonymity.
• A state of altered consciousness (e.g. through drugs or alcohol).

Process of deindividuation

People move from an individuated to a deindividuated state when inhibitions concerning aggressive behaviour are removed.

In a large group, the individual loses awareness of their individuality and feels faceless and anonymous.

As a result, inner restraints are reduced and inhibited behaviours (such as aggression) are increased.

Deindividuation does not necessarily lead to aggression…

Johnson and Downing showed that, rather than aggression being an automatic consequence of deindividuation, behaviour was more likely to be the product of local group norms.

They found that participants dressed in an anonymous mask and overalls (looking like Ku Klux Klansmen) delivered more shocks than a control group dressed normally.

Participants dressed anonymously in nurses' uniforms delivered fewer shocks than the control group.

This suggests that participants felt that aggression was more appropriate when dressed like Ku Klux Klansmen than as nurses.

There is a lack of research support…

Evidence for deindividuation theory is mixed. For example, a meta-analysis of 60 studies of deindividuation (Postmes and Spears) concluded that there was insufficient support for the major claims of deindividuation theory, particularly the claim that aggressive behaviour is more common in large groups and anonymous settings.

There are prosocial consequences of deindividuation…

Rather than engaging in behaviour based on primitive urges, people may be conforming to a local group norm. This need not necessarily be antisocial, and would account for the fact that some studies have found increased *prosocial* behaviour in large crowds.

Spivey and Prentice-Dunn found that deindividuation could lead to either prosocial or antisocial behaviour depending on situational factors. When prosocial cues were present (e.g. a prosocial model), deindividuated participants performed significantly more prosocial acts and significantly fewer antisocial acts compared to a control group.

Research on deindividuation

Delivering shocks

Zimbardo divided undergraduates into two groups:
• One group was in a deindividuated condition (in lab coats and hoods).
• The other group was in an individuated state (wearing normal clothing and wearing a name tag).

Those in the deindividuated state shocked a 'learner' for twice as long as did those in an individuated state.

Group sports

Rehm *et al.* investigated whether wearing a uniform while playing sports (deindividuation through greater anonymity) increased aggression in group sports.

Children playing handball while wearing the same colour shirts were consistently more aggressive than children wearing their normal street clothes.

IDA *There is a gender bias…*

Aggression as a result of deindividuation may be more of a male characteristic than a female one.

Cannavale *et al.* found that male and female groups responded differently under deindividuation conditions. An increase in aggression was obtained only in the all-male groups.

There are cultural differences…

Research by Watson found that tribes that significantly changed their appearance through war paint or body decoration (i.e. became deindividuated) when going to war were far more aggressive (e.g. torturing and mutilating their victims) than those who did not.

IDA *Real-world application…*

Mann used the concept of deindividuation to explain the behaviour of 'baiting crowds'. Suicide jumpers were encouraged to jump (verbal aggression) when crowds were under conditions of deindividuation (e.g. large crowd, nighttime, some distance from the potential jumper etc.).

The concept of deindividuation can also be used to explain the behaviour of lynch mobs. Mullen found that the more people there were in the mob (a contributing factor in deindividuation), the greater the savagery with which they killed their victims.

Chapter 4

Social psychological approaches to aggression	>	Social learning theory
Biological explanations of aggression		Deindividuation
Aggression	>	Aggression as an adaptive response	Institutional aggression

Institutional aggression

Institutional aggression within groups

The importation model

Irwin and Cressey claim that in prisons, inmates bring with them (i.e. *import*) their own social histories and violent characteristics and this influences their behaviour in prison.

There is research support for the importation model...

Harer and Steffensmeier, in a study of 58 US prisons, found that patterns of misconduct for particular groups *within* prisons tended to parallel differences observed *outside* prison.

They found that black inmates showed significantly higher rates of violent behaviour within prison and white inmates showed higher rates of drug- and alcohol-related misconduct, reflecting behaviour outside prison.

These differences reflect the statistical differences found in US society generally, thus suggesting that they were *imported* into the prison environment.

The deprivation model

Prisoner aggression or patient aggression (in mental institutions) is a consequence of stressful and oppressive conditions, including overcrowding, physical conditions of heat and noise, and a lack of any meaningful activity. Crowding, for example, is assumed to increase fear and frustration levels, which then leads to aggression.

There is research support for the deprivation model...

McCorkle *et al.* found that overcrowding, lack of privacy and a lack of meaningful activity all significantly increased interpersonal violence in prisons, supporting the view that aggression was a direct consequence of situational factors that deprived prisoners of normal living standards.

IDA *Real-world application of the deprivation model*...

Most violence occurs in environments that are hot, noise polluted (e.g. shouting, banging cell doors) and overcrowded. Wilson showed that changes to such deprived environments (e.g. reducing levels of noise, heat and crowding) resulted in a dramatic decrease in violent conduct among inmates at HMP Woodhill.

However...

This application of the deprivation model does not work in all types of institution. Nijman *et al.* found that, in psychiatric institutions, increasing personal space failed to decrease violent behaviour among patients.

Hazing

A type of behaviour whereby members of a group cause another group member to suffer any activity that is cruel, abusive or humiliating.

These 'initiation rituals' can spiral out of control and cause lasting physical or psychological damage.

Reasons why it happens include
- *Situational* influences (e.g. deindividuation within institution).
- *Cultural* notions of male toughness and need for obedience to superiors.
- *Conformity* pressures and 'bonding' beliefs within the group.

There is research support for this explanation...

McCorkle found that, in prisons, domination of the weak was seen as essential to maintaining status among inmates. Passive behaviour was seen as a sign of weakness and likely to invite exploitation.

The claim that hazing may be a product of cultural notions of male toughness is supported by research that reports that of the 60 or so reported deaths that have been a consequence of hazing, only three have been women.

Problems of definition...

Problems arise in determining what is and what is not 'aggressive behaviour' (rather than 'harmless fun'). Many victims do not report hazing because they don't recognise it in these terms.

In a survey of US students, 1 in 5 had experienced behaviours that would be classified as hazing, although only 1 in 20 regarded themselves as having experienced this.

Institutional aggression between groups

Genocide

Acts committed with intent to destroy in whole or in part, a national, ethnical, racial or religious group.

Staub claims genocide is more likely if a less powerful group within society is scapegoated for the social problems experienced by others.

This can lead to dehumanisation of the target group. In this process, minority group members (e.g. Jews in Nazi Germany) are seen as worthless animals and so not worthy of moral consideration due to fellow humans. This then leads to intergroup violence and mass killings.

There is support for this explanation...

There is historical evidence for the power of dehumanisation to influence mass violence against specific groups in society. For example, the actions of Nazis against Jews during the Holocaust, where Nazi propaganda referred to Jews as the 'Jewish disease'.

In the Rwandan genocide in 1994, the minority Tutsi were referred to as 'inyenzi' (cockroaches) by the majority Hutu, and their murder referred to as 'the work'.

Both of these examples of genocide show how killings were made easier by the dehumanising of victims.

IDA *Ethical issues in dehumanisation research*...

There are additional problems for researchers in that there are significant ethical issues in studying people who have been subjected to dehumanising violence. For example, recalling such incidents may cause significant distress for the participant and may also be traumatic for the researcher.

Neural mechanisms

Serotonin

Low levels of serotonin are associated with aggressive behaviour

Serotonin usually reduces aggression by inhibiting responses to stimuli that might otherwise lead to aggressive behaviour.

Low levels of serotonin have been associated with an increased susceptibility to impulsive and aggressive behaviour.

Drugs that deplete serotonin (e.g. *dexfenfluramine*) have been shown to increase aggression levels in participants (Mann *et al.*).

IDA *Evidence from studies using non-human animals* …

Evidence for the importance of serotonin comes from studies of animals that have been specially bred for domestication and for increasingly docile temperaments. These animals have shown a corresponding increase, over generations, of levels of serotonin in the brain.

Evidence from the use of antidepressants …

If drugs that deplete serotonin activity lead to raised aggression levels, then drugs that raise serotonin levels should lead to lower levels of aggression. This is exactly what was found in clinical studies of antidepressant drugs, further supporting the link between serotonin and aggression.

IDA *Gender bias* …

In Mann *et al.*'s study, an increase in aggression was found only in male participants, not female participants, suggesting that the role of serotonin in aggression may possibly be different for males compared to females.

Dopamine

Increases in dopamine levels have been shown to produce increases in aggressive behaviour.

Demonstrated in studies that used amphetamines (to increase dopamine activity in the brain) and found an associated increase in levels of aggressive behaviour (e.g. Lavine).

Studies that have reduced dopamine levels through the use of antipsychotics have reported a reduction in aggressive behaviour (Buitelaar).

Evidence is inconclusive …

Evidence for the causal role played by dopamine in aggression is inconclusive, but a study by Couppis and Kennedy suggests that it may be a consequence rather than a cause. Some individuals may seek out aggressive encounters because dopamine is released as a positive reinforcer in the brain when they engage in aggressive behaviours.

There is research that challenges this …

A meta-analysis (Scerbo and Raine) examined neurotransmitter levels in antisocial children and adults. They found lower levels of serotonin in individuals described as aggressive, but found no significant rise or fall in dopamine levels for this group compared to 'normal' individuals.

Hormonal mechanisms

Testosterone

Testosterone is thought to increase aggression in adults due to its action on brain areas involved in controlling aggression.

Studies (e.g. Dabbs) have found that criminals with the highest levels of testosterone tended to have a history of mainly violent crimes, whereas those with the lowest levels had committed mainly non-violent crimes.

The *challenge hypothesis* proposes that testosterone would only rise above baseline level in response to social challenges (e.g. to status), with a resultant rise in aggressive behaviour.

Evidence is inconsistent for this link …

Albert *et al.* point out that although many studies show a link between testosterone and aggressive behaviour, many others do not, particularly those that compare testosterone levels for aggressive and non-aggressive individuals. Most of the studies that do find a positive correlation between testosterone levels and aggression have used small samples of men within prisons relying on self-reports of aggressive behaviour. This means that research has both a gender bias and a possible social desirability bias, as some inmates may report higher than their actual participation in violence.

IDA *Gender bias* …

Most studies of the links between testosterone and aggression have involved male participants, yet research suggests that the link between testosterone and aggression may be even stronger for females (Archer *et al.*). Studies suggest that successful women have higher testosterone levels, possibly as a result of being more assertive than other women when faced with challenging situations.

Cortisol

High levels of cortisol inhibit testosterone levels and so inhibit aggression.

Low levels of cortisol have been reported in habitual violent offenders (Virkkunen) and violent schoolchildren (Tennes and Kreye).

This suggests that, although testosterone may be the main biochemical influence on aggressive behaviour, low cortisol levels increase the likelihood of aggressive behaviour.

There is support for this explanation …

The moderating effect of cortisol on aggressive behaviour is supported by research with boys with aggressive conduct disorder (McBurnett *et al.*). Boys with consistently low cortisol levels had three times the level of aggressive symptoms compared to boys with high or fluctuating levels of cortisol. This demonstrates that cortisol levels are strongly and inversely related to levels of aggression.

Why does this relationship exist? …

One possible reason is that boys who have low cortisol levels may be less afraid of punishment. As a result, such children may not experience anxiety at the threat of punishment and so do not avoid aggressive situations in the same way as do other children.

Genetic factors

Twin and adoption studies

Twin studies

MZ twins share all of their genes, while DZ twins share a maximum of 50%. If MZ twins are more alike than DZ twins in terms of their aggressive behaviour, then this suggests a strong genetic influence.

Studies of adult twins suggest that at least 50% of the variance in aggression can be explained in terms of genetic factors.

Adoption studies

If a positive correlation is found between an adopted child's aggressive behaviour and that of a biological parent, this implies a genetic effect.

If the correlation is stronger between the adopted child and their rearing (i.e. adoptive) family, then this suggests environmental influences are stronger.

A study (Miles and Carey) of adopted boys with criminal convictions found that a significant number had biological parents who also had criminal convictions, suggesting a strong genetic influence was at work.

There is research support for this…

A meta-analysis of 24 twin and adoption studies (Miles and Carey) found evidence of a strong genetic influence in the development of aggressive behaviour. In younger individuals, both genetic and environmental influences contributed to aggression, but in older individuals, environmental influences were less important and genetic influences more important in determining aggressive behaviour.

This finding was supported in a later meta-analysis (Rhee and Waldman) of 51 twin and adoption studies. They concluded that aggressive and antisocial behaviour was largely the product of genetic contributions.

However…

In both these studies, several variables moderated (i.e. contributed to the strength of) the genetic influence on aggression. These included the age of the participant and the method used to assess aggression.

This suggests that genetic factors are important in the development of aggression, but other factors determine the expression of aggressive behaviour.

There are problems in assessing aggression…

Most studies have relied on either parental or self-reports of aggressive behaviour. In the Miles and Carey study, those that found a stronger genetic influence on aggressive behaviour had used parental or self-reports, whereas those that had used observational techniques found significantly less genetic influence. This suggests that the method used to assess aggression is a significant influence on the findings of a study.

A gene for aggression?

The role of MAOA

One of the genes responsible for producing MAOA is associated with aggression. MAOA regulates the metabolism of serotonin in the brain, and low levels of serotonin are associated with aggression.

A study of a violent Dutch family found that many of the men had abnormally low levels of MAOA and also had a defective gene for the production of MAOA.

Gene–environment interactions

Caspi *et al.* discovered two variants of the gene for MAOA, one associated with high levels of MAOA and one with low levels. Those with low levels were significantly more likely to display aggressive behaviour, but only if maltreated as children. This suggests that it is the interaction between genes and environment that determines aggression, not genes alone.

There are problems of sampling…

Most studies have focused on individuals convicted of violent crime. There are two problems with this. First, these individuals represent a very small minority of those who regularly engage in aggressive behaviour. Second, a person who is imprisoned for a single violent offence (e.g. murder) is not necessarily a consistently violent individual. This means that the validity of conclusions drawn from these studies may be suspect.

There are difficulties in determining the role of genetic factors…

It is difficult to establish genetic contributions to aggression because:
• More than one gene contributes to a given behaviour.
• As well as genetic factors, there are many other influences on the manifestation of aggressive behaviour (e.g. social learning, environmental factors).
• These factors interact with each other.

IDA *The value of animal research…*

Studies of rodents (e.g. Young) have the advantage of allowing researchers to eliminate a single gene from an experimental group to see its effect.

Thus researchers can identify a genetic mutation that causes aggressive behaviour in mice. Although a counterpart to this gene exists in humans, its exact function is not yet known.

Genetics and violent crime

Research suggests that inherited temperament or personality characteristics make some people more likely to commit violent crimes. Adoption studies have shown that the highest rates of criminal violence occur when both biological and adoptive parents have a history of violent crime, clear evidence of a genetics/environment interaction.

IDA *Real-life applications…*

The possibility of a genetic influence in violent crime has led some to suggest using genetic engineering to prevent crime, or even using chemical castration to 'treat' potential violent offenders.

However…

This raises significant ethical concerns about the consequences of labelling someone as a threat to society on the basis of their genetic inheritance, particularly when the evidence for genetic influences in aggressive behaviour is far from conclusive.

Chapter 4

Social psychological approaches to aggression
Biological explanations of aggression
Evolutionary explanations of human aggression

Aggression > **Aggression as an adaptive response** > Explanations of group display

Evolutionary explanations of human aggression

Infidelity and jealousy

Cuckoldry and sexual jealousy

Unlike women, men may experience parental uncertainty, therefore they are at risk of cuckoldry. The consequence of this would be that a male might unwittingly invest his resources in offspring that are not his own.

The adaptive value of sexual jealousy, therefore, would have been to deter a mate from sexual infidelity, thereby minimising the risk of cuckoldry.

IDA *Gender bias...*

Most studies of infidelity have focused solely on men's mate retention strategies and male violence against women. However, this view is gender biased because women also practise mate retention strategies and engage in violence against their partner.

This behaviour is not always adaptive...

If the social environment is dynamic rather than static (which evidence suggests is the case), then the only kind of mind that makes humans adaptive is one that is flexible and responsive. In some environments it might be adaptive for males and females to act in this way, but not in all. This challenges the claim of these being universal human behaviours.

Mate retention and violence

Buss claims that males have evolved strategies that deter mates from infidelity. These include:

- *Direct guarding* (e.g. vigilance against male attention). Women who claim their partners dislike them talking to other men are twice as likely to experience violence from partners (Wilson *et al.*).
- *Threats.* Women perceived to be prone to infidelity are more at risk of violence. A study of battered women (Dobash and Dobash), found most cited sexual jealousy as a key cause.

There is research support for this...

Shackelford *et al.* used a survey to investigate the use of mate retention strategies and the use of intersexual violence. In keeping with the claims detailed left, men's use of mate retention strategies (such as direct guarding) was positively correlated with violence scores. Women's responses confirmed this, with reports of direct guarding and the use of threats from their partner being positively correlated with their experience of violent behaviour towards them.

IDA *Real-world applications...*

The use of mate retention tactics by males can be an early indicator of violence against the female partner. The findings from these studies suggest that awareness of the use of mate retention strategies by the male partner can be used to alert friends and family members to the danger signs that violence may follow. At this point, help can be sought (or offered) before inter-mate violence ever happens.

Uxorocide (wife-killing)

Men guard against their partner's infidelity by conferring benefits (e.g. resources, kindness) or inflicting costs (e.g. violence or threat of violence).

If men cannot offer benefits, they may resort to inflicting costs. Daly and Wilson argue that wife-killing may be the unintended consequence of behaviours that were designed to control a partner, rather than kill her.

An alternative explanation is...

Shackelford studied more than 13,000 cases where a man had killed his wife and discovered that younger women had a much greater risk of uxoricide, regardless of the age of their partner. This is puzzling because the younger they are, the more they are 'prized property'.

A theory that can explain this is the *evolved homicide module theory* (Duntley and Buss). A partner's infidelity carries a double loss for the male if the female is still of reproductive age. He loses a partner (decreasing his reproductive fitness) and in addition, a competing male gains a partner and increases the competing male's fitness. By killing his wife, he at least prevents another man gaining at his expense.

The evolution of homicide

Lack of resources

A study of homicides in Detroit (Wilson and Daly) found that more than 40% of the perpetrators and victims were unemployed, despite unemployment figures at the time of just 11%. This suggests that a lack of resources and an inability to attract long-term mates may lead to increased male–male competition and homicide (murder).

A consequence of the evolution of homicide is...

Humans have also evolved anti-homicide defences (e.g. being able to read homicidal intent). Homicide then becomes far more costly as a strategy, its success rate becomes lower and increasingly dangerous for the person doing the killing.

As a result, evolution has favoured adaptations that conceal homicidal intent to avoid activating homicidal defences.

Loss of status

A key motive of male–male homicide is protection of status within the social group. Loss of status would have been catastrophic for our ancestors. Although this is no longer adaptive, the same conditions still trigger this response.

There are limitations of the evolutionary perspective on homicide...

An evolutionary perspective cannot explain why people react in such different ways when faced with the same adaptive problem. Two major problems:

- Buss and Shackelford suggest that an evolutionary perspective cannot account for why different men confronted with a wife's infidelity will choose totally different responses (e.g. homicide, getting drunk etc.).
- An evolutionary perspective cannot explain why some cultures (e.g. the *Yanomamo*) appear to require male violence to attain status, whereas in others (e.g. the *!Kung San*) aggression leads to irreparable reputational damage.

Sexual jealousy

A study of same-sex killings (Daly and Wilson) involving 'love triangles' (two males were love rivals for the same woman), found that 92% were male–male homicides and only 8% female–female homicides.

Chapter 4

Social psychological approaches to aggression
Biological explanations of aggression   Evolutionary explanations of human aggression

Aggression   > Aggression as an adaptive response   > Explanations of group display

Explanations of group display

Lynch mobs

Social transitions and the need for conformity

When groups feel at risk, survival of the group becomes vital, so cooperative group defence and antagonism to outsiders (aggression) are more likely.

Patterson claims lynch mobs were more active during social transition after the abolition of slavery because of a fear of negroes, with 'lynch law' used as a form of social control.

There is research support for this…

Boyd and Richerson support the power of social conformity in group displays. Groups in which cooperation thrived were also those that flourished. This explains why, when a group is threatened as a result of social change, individual self-interest gives way to 'groupishness'.

Lynch mobs and deindividuation…

Mullen carried out an archival analysis of 60 newspaper reports of lynchings, and found an alternative explanation of these events, based on deindividuation theory. As the lynch mob grew in size, this led to a breakdown in self-regulation processes and an increase in aggression directed towards the victim.

Power-threat hypothesis

Groups that pose a threat to the majority are likely to be discriminated against and subject to violent action.

The 'threat' of homicides and assaults by blacks against the white majority were frequently cited 'threats' and used to justify the lynching practice.

There is research that challenges this…

From a comparative study of lynchings in Brazil, Clark concluded that the evidence contradicted the claim that the threat of 'dangerous classes' in society was a major causal factor in lynchings.

For example, in Sao Paulo, the percentage of Afro-Brazilians (i.e. a 'dangerous class') in the community was negatively correlated with incidents of lynch-mob violence.

Religious rituals

Costly signalling theory

Explains why some religious groups indulge in self-inflicted painful acts (e.g. self-flagellation). Sosis argues that by engaging in painful group rituals, individuals are signalling their commitment to a group.

The significant costs of such acts act serve as a deterrent for outsiders, who might otherwise try to take advantage of the benefits offered by group membership.

The adaptive value of such group displays is ultimately to promote and maintain cooperation within a group without leaving the group open to others, who may take the benefits and provide nothing in return.

There is research support for this…

Sosis and Bressler found that religious groups imposed twice as many costly commitments on members as did non-religious groups.

This shows that groups that require the greatest displays of commitment from their members produce the most commitment and so last the longest. Painful rituals, therefore, have an adaptive value for the group.

There is research support for this…

The costs of religious group displays should be related to the incentives of group membership. Chen found during the Indonesian financial crisis of the 1990s, Muslim families devoted a greater proportion of their resources to religious institutions.

Chen claimed that in times of need, religious groups provide collective social insurance, supporting the most needy of the group members.

IDA *An evolutionary approach…*

If intra-group solidarity is the adaptive advantage of religious membership promoted by costly group displays, then the adaptive disadvantage is the potential for inter-group hostility. Roes and Raymond found societies with stricter religious practices tend to have higher levels of inter-group conflict.

Sports events and xenophobia

Xenophobia

Natural selection favours genes that cause human beings to be altruistic toward members of their own group, yet intolerant towards outsiders (to prevent 'free-riders').

From an evolutionary perspective, it would be adaptive to exaggerate negative stereotypes of outsiders, as the overperception of threat would be less costly than its underperception.

There is research support for this…

Foldesi found support for this view in a study of Hungarian football crowds, with violent incidents based on racist or xenophobic attitudes being observed at all stadia. Gypsies, Jews or Russians were the usual targets.

In recent years, these group displays have been attributed to the rise of the extreme right-wing Jobbik party, which has been accused of anti-Semitism and xenophobia and has led to an increase in violent attacks on minorities.

IDA *Real-world application…*

The power of xenophobic group displays to invoke violence has motivated football clubs to take steps to minimise its influence.

For example, in December 1992, all the teams in the German Bundes-league played in shirts displaying the slogan, 'My friend is a foreigner'.

In Scotland, the Glasgow teams Celtic and Rangers have both introduced initiatives to end xenophobic sectarian displays by their supporters, and so end violence on the terraces.

Xenophobia in sports displays

Podaliri and Balestri analysed the behaviour of Italian football crowds. Group displays in the form of chants and banners were not only openly xenophobic, but also stressed the differences between the different cultural groups.

Eating behaviour

Division A Eating behaviour
Attitudes to food and eating behaviour
Explanations for the success or failure of dieting

Division B Biological explanations of eating behaviour
Neural mechanisms in eating and satiation
Evolutionary explanations for food preference

Division C Eating disorders
Psychological explanations of anorexia nervosa
Biological explanations of anorexia nervosa
Psychological explanations of bulimia nervosa
Biological explanations of bulimia nervosa

Specification

Eating behaviour	
Eating behaviour	• Factors influencing attitudes to food and eating behaviour, for example, cultural influences, mood, health concerns. • Explanations for the success or failure of dieting.
Biological explanations of eating behaviour	• The role of neural mechanisms involved in controlling eating and satiation. • Evolutionary explanations of food preference.
Eating disorders	• Psychological explanations of one eating disorder, for example, anorexia nervosa, bulimia nervosa, obesity. • Biological explanations, including neural and evolutionary explanations of one eating disorder, for example, anorexia nervosa, bulimia nervosa, obesity.

Attitudes to food and eating behaviour

Social learning

Impact of observing others

Parental modelling of attitudes to food affects children's own attitudes. Brown and Ogden found correlations between parents and their children in terms of snack food intake, eating motivation and body dissatisfaction.

There is research support for this...

Meyer and Gast surveyed 12-year-olds and found a positive correlation between peer influence and disordered eating. 'Likeability' of peers was the most influential factor.

Birch and Fisher found that the best predictors of daughters' eating behaviours were their mothers' dietary restraint and their perception of the risk of their daughters becoming overweight.

Media effects

MacIntyre et al. found the media has a major impact on what people eat and their attitudes to certain foods. However, many attitudes (e.g. healthy eating) are limited by personal circumstances (e.g. income and age). Therefore, people learn attitudes from the media, but then place these within the broader context of their lives.

Attitudes are about much more than just learning...

Social learning explanations focus exclusively on how children acquire attitudes towards eating from exposure to models (e.g. in the media).

However... Evolutionary explanations suggest that our preference for fat and sweet foods is the direct result of an evolved adaptation.

IDA *There is a gender bias...*

Most studies have focused solely on women's attitudes to eating behaviour, yet research has shown that homosexual men are also at risk of developing disordered eating attitudes and behaviour, including body dissatisfaction and higher levels of dieting than heterosexual men.

Cultural influences

Ethnicity

Research suggests that body dissatisfaction and related eating concerns and disorders are more characteristic of white than black or Asian women (Powell and Khan).

Ball and Kenardy studied 14,000 Australian women of various ethnic origins. The longer they had spent in Australia, the more they reported eating attitudes similar to Australian-born women (the acculturation effect).

There is research that challenges this...

Mumford et al. found more evidence of body dissatisfaction and eating disorders among Asian schoolchildren than among white counterparts.

Striegel-Moore et al. found more evidence of a 'drive for thinness' among black girls than among white girls.

IDA *There is a cultural bias...*

Rozin et al. explored the way food functions in the minds of people in four different cultures. Americans tended to associate food with health, whereas the French associated it with pleasure. Females of all four cultures had attitudes more similar to those of the Americans. Cultural background influences attitude to eating and therefore means the measurement of attitudes in one culture tells us little about attitudes in a different culture.

Social class

Body dissatisfaction and eating concerns are more common among middle and higher class individuals.

Dornbusch et al. surveyed 7,000 American adolescents and found that higher class individuals had a greater desire to be thin and were more likely to be dieting to achieve this, than were lower class individuals.

There is research that challenges this...

The relationship between social class and attitudes to eating is not as straightforward as suggested by the Dornbusch et al. study. In a sample of American students, Story et al. found that higher social class was related to greater satisfaction with weight and *lower* rates of weight control behaviour.

There are problems of generalisability...

Some studies in this area are from clinical populations (e.g. people with bulimia nervosa), some sub-clinical (with certain disordered behaviours), and some non-clinical. This makes it difficult to generalise from one group to another and draw valid conclusions about the causal factors in attitudes toward eating.

Mood and eating behaviour

Binge-eating

Individuals with bulimia experience anxiety prior to bingeing. The same relationship between anxiety and binge-eating appears to hold for sub-clinical populations as well.

Wegner et al. found that people who binged had low mood before and after binge-eating. Although low mood may make binge-eating more likely, it does not alleviate the low-mood state.

The reinforcing qualities of binge-eating are not clear...

Although a number of studies have shown that low mood tends to precede a binge-eating episode, any reinforcement is fleeting and many studies report a drop in mood immediately after the binge. As a result, it is difficult to see what the reinforcing qualities of a binge-eating episode might be.

However, a recent article by Wedig and Nock identified four types of reinforcement that might explain why individuals engage in binge-eating behaviour. These include social negative reinforcement (to avoid interactions with others or escape their demands) and intrapersonal positive reinforcement (to increase the strength of a desired positive emotion).

Comfort-eating

Garg et al. observed food choices of participants as they either watched an upbeat movie or a depressing one. 'Happy' participants chose healthy food, but 'sad' participants went for the short-term pleasure of junk food.

Comfort-eating may not work...

Our attitude toward comfort foods such as chocolate is based largely on the belief that it can lift our mood. However, a study by Parker et al. found that chocolate, if used repeatedly, is more likely to prolong a negative mood than to alleviate it. This challenges the view that low mood causes comfort-eating, because comfort-eating may not be that effective in overcoming low mood.

Chapter 5

Eating behaviour >
Biological explanations of eating behaviour | Attitudes to food and eating behaviour
Eating behaviour > Eating disorders | Explanations for the success or failure of dieting

Explanations for the success or failure of dieting

Restraint theory

Disinhibition

Restrained eating has become synonymous with dieting, but Herman and Mack's restraint theory suggests that attempting not to eat may actually increase the probability of overeating. It is the disinhibition (loss of control) of restraint that is the cause of overeating in restrained eaters.

Wardle and Beales randomly assigned obese women to one of three groups for seven weeks; restrained eating, exercise or non-treatment. Women in the restrained eating group ate more than women in the other two groups.

The boundary model

This model explains the failure of dieting in terms of the greater distance between hunger and satiety in dieters. It takes dieters longer to feel hungry and therefore more food to reach a state of satiety.

In addition dieters have a self-imposed desired intake. Unlike non-dieters, when they go over this threshold of desired intake, they experience a 'what the hell' effect, and continue to eat until they reach satiety, i.e. beyond the maximum level imposed as part of their diet.

Restraint theory has limited relevance…

Ogden argues that restraint theory may explain the overeating of some groups with disordered eating patterns (e.g. dieters, bulimics and some anorexics).

However…

The behaviour of restricting anorexics (where weight loss is achieved by restricting calories) cannot be explained in this way. If trying not to eat results in overeating, claims Ogden, then how do restricting anorexics manage to starve themselves?

IDA *Real-world application*…

Restraint theory suggests that restraint leads to overeating, yet the treatment of obesity typically recommends restraint as a way of losing weight. As a result, overeating may be a consequence of obesity treatment, leaving many obese individuals depressed, feeling a failure and unable to control their weight.

Cultural differences in obesity…

Some cultural groups appear to find it harder to diet successfully because of a natural inclination to obesity. Asian adults are more prone to obesity than Europeans (Park *et al.*). Asian children and adolescents have a greater central fat mass compared to other ethnic groups (Misra *et al.*)

IDA *Psychology as science – the limitations of anecdotal evidence*…

Many studies of dieting success or failure rely on personal accounts, and this evidence is then used to justify claims about particular dieting strategies. However, such anecdotal evidence has two problems that properly controlled scientific studies do not have:

• The main limitation is that memory is not 100% accurate.
• Assessment of the success or failure of dieting tends not to be objective.

Both these create problems for the reliability of anecdotal accounts.

The role of denial

The theory of ironic processes of mental control

Attempting to suppress a thought frequently has the opposite effect, making it even more prominent.

Central to any dieting strategy is the decision not to eat certain foods. This results in a state of denial as dieters attempt to suppress thoughts about foods 'forbidden' as part of their diet.

Wegner suggests any attempt to suppress thoughts of forbidden foods only increases the dieter's preoccupation with the very foods they are trying to deny themselves. As soon as food is denied, therefore, it becomes more attractive.

There is research support for this…

Soetens *et al.* found that participants who suppressed thoughts about food also showed a rebound effect, and were more likely to think about food after suppression. This might explain why denial of thoughts about food leads to greater rather than less preoccupation with it.

An alternative explanation might be…

Some people find dieting ineffective because they have high lipoprotein lipase (LPL) levels, which make the body more effective at storing calories. This would challenge the view that restraint or denial alone could be effective as a means of losing or maintaining weight.

There may be gender differences in LPL activity…

Research suggests that sex hormones play a part in LPL activity. For example, oestrogen inhibits LPL activity, which explains why women put on weight after menopause when oestrogen levels are lower.

A consequence of this is that dieting through restraint or denial may be more difficult for post-menopausal women for purely biological reasons.

Detail and dieting

Fending off boredom

Redden claims that people usually like experiences less when they have to repeat them constantly. When it comes to dieting, this makes it harder to stick to a particular regime. However, by focusing on the specific details of each meal, people get bored less easily and are better able to maintain their diet.

IDA *Real-world application*…

This has led to the development of anti-diet programmes aimed at replacing dieting with conventional eating. These emphasise regulation of eating by body hunger and satiety signals rather than the development of inappropriate attitudes to food (e.g. denial or restraint), which have been shown to be ineffective at weight control.

A meta-analysis of the effectiveness of anti-dieting programmes (Higgins and Gray) found that they could improve both eating behaviour and psychological wellbeing, and led to weight stability rather than weight change.

Neural mechanisms in eating and satiation

Homeostasis

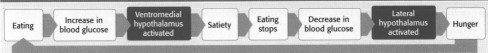

Eating → Increase in blood glucose → Ventromedial hypothalamus activated → Satiety → Eating stops → Decrease in blood glucose → Lateral hypothalamus activated → Hunger

Involves mechanisms that detect the state of the internal environment and also correct it to restore that environment to its optimal state.

The body has evolved two homeostatic mechanisms to regulate food intake, both dependent on glucose levels.

- Hunger increases as glucose levels decrease.
- A decline in glucose levels activates the lateral hypothalamus (LH) resulting in feelings of hunger.
- This causes the individual to search for and consume food, causing glucose levels to rise again.
- This activates the ventromedial hypothalamus (VMH), leading to feelings of satiation and a cessation of feeding.

There are limitations to a homeostatic explanation…

For a homeostatic hunger mechanism to have been truly adaptive, it must anticipate and prevent energy deficits, rather than just react to them. The claim that feelings of hunger and eating behaviour are only triggered when energy resources fall below their optimal level is inconsistent with the harsh environment in which this mechanism would have developed. A buffer against lack of future food availability would have been necessary in such circumstances.

IDA An evolutionary approach…

Evolutionary theorists offer an alternative explanation. They propose that the primary influence for hunger and eating is not homeostasis, but food's positive-incentive value, i.e. people eat because they develop a taste for foods that promote their survival.

Role of the hypothalamus

Lateral hypothalamus (LH)

Research discovered that damage to the LH in rats causes aphagia (absence of eating). Stimulation of the LH brings about feeding behaviour.

Neuropeptide Y (NPY) is important in turning on eating behaviour. When injected into LH of rats it causes them to immediately start feeding, even when satiated. Repeated injections of NPY cause obesity in just a few days.

There is a problem with this explanation…

Marie et al. genetically manipulated mice so that they did not make NPY, yet found no subsequent decrease in their feeding behaviour.

IDA Real-world application…

Yang et al. found that NPY is also produced by abdominal fat. This leads to a vicious cycle where NPY produced in the brain leads to more eating and the production of more fat cells, which in turn leads to the production of more NPY. By targeting individuals at risk of increased levels of NPY, it should, therefore, be possible to treat obesity.

Ventromedial hypothalamus (VMH)

Damage to VMH causes hyperphagia (overeating) in rats. Stimulation of this area inhibits feeding.

Damage to VMH also causes damage to the paraventricular nucleus (PVN). It is now believed that damage to PVN is what causes hyperphagia.

There is a problem with this explanation…

Gold claimed that lesions to the VMH alone did not produce overeating, but did so only when these lesions included the PVN; however, subsequent research studies failed to support Gold's findings.

As a result, it is now acknowledged that animals with VMH lesions eat substantially more and gain weight rapidly. However, in humans, the PVN has another function, i.e. to detect the specific foods that our body needs, which may account for many food 'cravings'.

Neural control of cognitive factors

Amygdala

The role of amygdala is to select foods on the basis of experience.

Rolls and Rolls surgically removed the amygdala in rats, which then consumed novel and familiar foods indiscriminately, whereas amygdala intact rats avoided novel (i.e. unfamiliar) foods.

IDA Real-world application…

Damage to these two areas could explain feeding abnormalities found in Klüver-Bucy patients. Research with these patients typically shows patterns of indiscriminate eating with individuals even trying to eat non-food items. The indiscriminate eating is caused by damage to the amygdala, and the 'eat anything' attitude observed in patients suggests that food cues (e.g. smell, taste) no longer represent their reward value to the individual.

Inferior frontal cortex

Receives messages from the olfactory bulb (responsible for smell). Damage to this area decreases eating because of diminished sensory information about the food, which in turn affects its taste (Kolb and Whishaw).

IDA Real-world application…

Recent research (Lutter et al.) suggests that hunger and eating may not be under purely neural control. The body produces extra quantities of the hormone ghrelin in response to stress. However, ghrelin also boosts appetite, leading to increased comfort-eating. This suggests that blocking the body's response to ghrelin may help people with a tendency to comfort-eat when stressed, to control their weight.

Chapter 5

Eating behaviour
Biological explanations of eating behaviour > Neural mechanisms in eating and satiation
Eating behaviour > Eating disorders
Evolutionary explanations for food preference

Evolutionary explanations for food preference

The EEA

The environment of evolutionary adaptation (EEA) is the environment in which a species first evolved.

The adaptive problems faced by our ancestors in the EEA would have shaped early food preferences.

For most of human history, human beings would have lived in hunter-gatherer societies, which would have led to a preference for high-calorie (for energy) and easily available foods.

IDA *Evolutionary explanations can be tested*… by studying a related species that faces similar adaptive problems. After starving for much of the year, chimpanzees go straight for the fattiest parts of their kill (Stanford).

However… Ultimate explanations of human behaviour (e.g. fatty foods because of the need for energy) may mask more proximate causes of the same behaviour (e.g. price, availability).

Not all food preferences can be traced back to the EEA…

Some modern preferences (e.g. low-cholesterol foods) could not have evolved during the EEA, because they had no beneficial effects for our ancestors. Similarly, many things that were important to our distant ancestors (e.g. high-fat foods) are more likely to be avoided by modern humans because they are now damaging to health.

Early diets

Preference for fatty foods was adaptive because harsh conditions in the EEA meant that energy resources were vital to stay alive.

Early humans evolved a preference for foods that were particularly rich in calories (fatty foods, sweet foods) because these promoted survival.

There is research that supports this…

Gibson and Wardle found the best way to predict which fruit and vegetables would be preferred by children, was to measure how calorie rich they were. Bananas and potatoes are rich in calories and were most preferred by 4–5-year-olds. This supports the claim that humans have an evolved preference for calorie-rich foods.

Bitter taste evolved to detect potentially harmful toxins in plants.

There is research that supports this…

Sandell and Breslin studied different variants of a bitter taste receptor gene making individuals more or less sensitive to glucosinolates. Being able to detect glucosinolates therefore conferred a significant adaptive advantage and so is still widespread today.

Preference for meat

Good for brain growth

A meat diet was full of densely packed nutrients and therefore provided a catalyst for the growth of the brain.

As a result, humans were able to evolve into the active and intelligent species that they became.

By supplying all the essential amino acids, minerals and nutrients needed to stay active and alive, this allowed early humans to supplement their diet with widely available, but less nutritious, plant-based foods.

However, early humans might have been vegetarian…

Cordain *et al.* claimed that early humans are more likely to have found most of their calories in sources other than saturated animal fats.

However… Evidence (e.g. Abrams) has shown that all societies show a preference for animal fats, suggesting that this is a universal evolved preference. It is also unlikely that early humans could have found sufficient calories for an active lifestyle from a vegetarian diet.

What about cultural factors?…

It is likely that many food preferences (e.g. for spicy foods) developed because of cultural tastes and preferences.

However… Although cultural differences do exist, they are usually a fine-tuning of evolved food preferences that are found in all cultures.

Taste aversion

Taste aversion was first demonstrated by Garcia *et al*. Rats made ill through radiation after eating saccharin developed an aversion to it because they formed an association between the illness and the taste of the saccharin.

Adaptive advantages

Taste aversion would have helped our distant ancestors to survive, because if they survived after ingesting poison then they could learn to avoid that food in the future.

Once learned, taste aversions are difficult to shift, an adaptation that would have helped survival.

The medicine effect describes a tendency for individuals to develop a preference for any food eaten just before recovery from an illness, which then becomes associated with feeling better.

Taste aversions can be explained by… biological preparedness. Differential learning abilities in different species means that each species has the ability to learn certain associations more easily than others, particularly associations that help them survive.

IDA *Real-world application*…

Research on the origins of taste aversion has been used to help understand the food avoidance that often occurs during chemotherapy used in the treatment of cancer.

This claim was supported in a study by Bernstein and Webster, who gave patients a novel-tasting ice cream prior to their chemotherapy and the patients subsequently developed an aversion to that ice cream.

This has led to hospitals giving patients both a novel and a familiar food prior to their chemotherapy. Aversion then forms to the novel (i.e. unfamiliar) food and not to the familiar food.

This is consistent with our evolved avoidance of novel foodstuffs (*neophobia*), which is also consistent with our survival.

Chapter 5		Psychological explanations of anorexia
	Eating behaviour	Biological explanations of anorexia
	Biological explanations of eating behaviour	Psychological explanations of bulimia
Eating behaviour	> Eating disorders	> Biological explanations of bulimia

Psychological explanations of anorexia nervosa (AN)

Sociocultural explanations

Cultural ideals
Western standards of attractiveness are thought to contribute to body dissatisfaction, a distorted body image and AN.

Gregory et al. found that in the UK, 16% of girls aged 15–18 were on a diet.

IDA Ethical issues in AN research…
Researchers are increasingly using anorexia chat rooms and newsgroups to gain qualitative data from those who actually have AN (or care for those with the disorder). This creates significant ethical issues for the researcher, particularly in relation to invasion of privacy, lack of informed consent and a breach of confidentiality.

Media influences
The portrayal of thin models on TV and in magazines is a significant contributory factor in body image concerns and the drive for thinness among Western adolescent girls.

Jones and Buckingham found people with low self-esteem are more likely to compare themselves to idealised images portrayed in the media.

There is research support…
A study of adolescent Fijian girls (Becker et al.) found that after the introduction of television to the island, these girls stated a desire to lose weight and to be like the women they saw on Western television.

However…
Other research has shown that instructional intervention *prior* to media exposure to idealised female images prevents the adverse effects of media influences (Yamamiya et al.). This suggests that the media can and does have an effect on the development of disordered eating and AN, but these effects can be avoided.

IDA Real-world application…
Because the media has such a powerful influence on eating behaviour in young people, the fashion industry in France has responded by pledging to use a diversity of body types and not to stereotype the 'thin ideal'.

Ethnicity
Other cultural groups place less emphasis on thinness in women, e.g. the incidence of AN in non-Western cultures and black populations in Western cultures is much lower.

In many non-Western cultures, there are more positive attitudes toward large body sizes, which are associated with attractiveness and fertility (Pollack).

Not all research supports ethnic differences in AN…
Cachelin and Regan found no significant differences in the incidence of disordered eating in African-American and white-Caucasian participants. Roberts et al. found that ethnic differences were only true for older adolescents.

Peer influences
Eisenberg et al. found dieting among friends was related to unhealthy weight control behaviours.

Teasing about overweight girls or underweight boys may serve to enforce gender-based ideals concerning weight.

Not all research supports the role of peer influences in AN…
Shroff and Thompson found no correlation among friends on measures of disordered eating in an adolescent sample.

Although…
Jones and Crawford did find support for the claim that overweight girls and overweight boys are more likely to be teased and so develop disordered eating patterns, these gender differences did not emerge until adolescence.

Psychological factors

Bruch's psychodynamic theory
distinguished between effective parents who respond to their child's needs, and ineffective parents who fail to respond appropriately.

Children of ineffective parents grow up confused about their internal needs and become overly reliant on their parents.

During adolescence these children strive for independence, but are unable to achieve this without taking excessive control over their body shape and developing abnormal eating habits.

There is support for this theory…
Steiner found that parents of adolescents with AN had a tendency to define their children's needs rather than letting them define their own needs. This supports the claim that children of ineffective parents become overly reliant on their parents to identify their needs.

Supporting the lack of control claim, Button and Warren examined a group of AN sufferers seven years after they were diagnosed with the eating disorder. These individuals relied excessively on the opinions of others and felt a lack of control over their lives.

Personality
Two personality characteristics commonly associated with AN are perfectionism (Strober et al.) and impulsiveness (Butler and Montgomery).

There is support for the perfectionism claim…
Halmi et al. found that women with a history of AN scored higher on a scale of perfectionism, and the extent of perfectionism was directly related to the severity of AN experienced by these women.

IDA A genetic explanation for the perfectionism/AN link…
Halmi et al. also studied the relatives of individuals with AN, and found that perfectionism as a trait appears to run in families. This suggests that perfectionism represents a genetic vulnerability (i.e. a diathesis) for the development of AN.

Chapter 5

Eating behaviour
Biological explanations of eating behaviour

Psychological explanations of anorexia
Biological explanations of anorexia
Psychological explanations of bulimia

Eating behaviour > **Eating disorders** > Biological explanations of bulimia

Biological explanations of anorexia nervosa (AN)

Neural explanations

Serotonin

Disruption of serotonin levels leads to increased anxiety, which may then trigger AN. Bailer et al. found high levels of serotonin in women with binge-eating/purging AN, with highest levels in those with the most anxiety.

A problem for the serotonin explanation…

SSRIs, which alter levels of serotonin in the brain, are ineffective when used with AN patients.

However… Some studies (e.g. Tannenhaus) report that SSRIs may help to elevate mood and reduce some of the obsessive symptoms of anorexia.

Dopamine

Increased dopamine activity in the basal ganglia alters the way people interpret rewards, so individuals with AN find it difficult to associate good feelings with things that are usually pleasurable (e.g. food).

There is research support for this…

Castro-Fornieles et al. found that adolescent girls with AN had higher levels of HVA (waste product of dopamine).

However… Wang et al. found that obese individuals had lower than normal levels of dopamine, suggesting an inverse relationship between levels of dopamine and body weight.

Season of birth

Individuals with AN are more likely to be born during spring months.

May be due to infections during pregnancy or temperature at time of conception.

There is research support for this…

Eagles et al. found that AN individuals tend to be later in birth order than healthy individuals. They may be at greater risk of being exposed to common infections from their siblings during the critical period of brain development in the second trimester of pregnancy.

Pregnancy and birth complications

Inadequate nutrition during pregnancy among mothers with an eating disorder may act as diathesis for the development of AN in child.

Lindberg and Hjern found an association between birth complications and the development of AN.

Birth complications may lead to brain damage due to lack of oxygen, impairing neurodevelopment of a child.

There is research support for this…

Favaro et al. found that the perinatal complications associated with a risk of developing AN were: obstructed blood supply in the placenta, early eating difficulties and low birth weight.

IDA Real-world applications…

An advantage of these explanations of AN is that people realise they are dealing with a dysfunctional biology (which is treatable), rather than a dysfunctional family (which isn't). This reduces the guilt felt by many parents that they caused the development of AN in their child.

IDA Biological determinism – a real-world application…

Research in this area has implications for insurance payouts for psychiatric conditions which do not regard AN as 'biologically based' and therefore not liable for a payout.

Evolutionary explanations

Reproduction suppression

Females in the ancestral environment had a delayed onset of sexual maturation when conditions were not conducive to their offspring's survival.

AN may be a variation of this adaptation, causing females to alter the timing of their reproduction when they feel unable to cope with the biological, social and emotional responsibilities of womanhood.

There is research support for this…

This explanation is supported by the observation that the onset of puberty is delayed in prepubertal girls with AN. Additionally, because amenorrhoea is a typical characteristic of AN, this means that reproduction is suspended in AN females.

IDA Gender bias…

The reproduction suppression account of AN does not explain why AN would develop in men. According to recent statistics, 25% of adults with eating disorders are male, suggesting that AN is not solely a female disorder and therefore cannot be explained just in terms of the suppression of reproduction.

'Adapted to flee' famine hypothesis

Typical AN symptoms of food restriction, hyperactivity and denial of starvation reflect evolved adaptation in response to local famine conditions.

When individuals lose weight, adaptive mechanisms usually cause conservation of energy and an increase in desire for food.

This adaptation must be 'turned off' so that individuals increase their chances of survival by moving to a more favourable environment in terms of food resources.

There are limitations of evolutionary explanations of AN…

We might question how the symptoms of AN would have been passed on through generations by natural selection, particularly as AN decreases fertility and makes reproduction more difficult, and may even kill the individual with this condition.

Ultimate versus proximate factors…

In addition, although AN may have been an effective adaptation in the harsh conditions faced by our distant ancestors (an 'ultimate factors' explanation), outside these conditions the development of AN would not be favourable to the individual, suggesting that its development nowadays is a consequence of factors that have very little to do with evolution (i.e. caused by 'proximate factors').

Chapter 5

Psychological explanations of anorexia
Eating behaviour
Biological explanations of anorexia
Biological explanations of eating behaviour
Psychological explanations of bulimia

Eating behaviour > Eating disorders > Biological explanations of bulimia

Psychological explanations of bulimia nervosa (BN)

Cognitive explanations

Cooper et al.'s cognitive model

People with BN are thought to have suffered early traumatic experiences that make them feel as though they are unlovable and worthless.

They may later experience criticisms about their shape and weight and so begin to diet in the belief that this will overcome thoughts of worthlessness.

BN maintained by 'circle of thoughts':

- Individual believes that binge-eating will make them feel better…
- Triggers a binge until thought that 'I will get fat' takes over…
- Triggers purge to avoid harm of binge-eating episode…

Leads to feelings of worthlessness followed by binge-eating and the cycle starts again.

There is research support for this…

Leung et al. found that a lack of parental bonding was linked to the development of dysfunctional beliefs (e.g. feelings of worthlessness) among individuals with BN.

Dysfunctional beliefs have been linked to bingeing and vomiting symptoms in a number of studies (e.g. Waller et al.).

Consistent with claims of Cooper et al.'s model, there is evidence that binge-eating in BN is preceded by feelings of distress, e.g. Abraham and Beaumont found that feelings of loneliness triggered bingeing.

Implications for treatment…

If BN is cognitively based then it should be possible to treat it using a cognitively based therapy.

However…

Not everybody gets better after cognitive treatment. A follow-up study of patients who had received CBT for their BN found that only half were symptom free at the end of treatment and more than one third still met the diagnostic criteria for BN (Fairburn et al.).

The functional model

People engage in binge-eating as a way of coping with problems associated with their self-image.

By overeating, an individual attributes the resulting distress to overeating rather than to low self-image.

Therefore the binge-eating associated with BN is functional for individuals trying to deal with life stressors.

Wheeler et al. propose that negative self-image and desire to escape from difficult life issues predict the onset of BN, the consequence of which is a 'diffuse-avoidant identity style'.

There is research support for this…

Polivy et al. found that, compared to ordinary dieters, stress-induced dieters consumed larger quantities of food regardless of its palatability. This lends support to the claim that the primary purpose of binge-eating is to alleviate identity-related stress, rather than because of the attractiveness of the food.

Implications for treatment…

The development of a diffuse-avoidant identity style has been shown to make individuals susceptible to a number of different health and social problems, including self-harm.

Targeting the symptoms that lead to BN (such as self-consciousness and depression) can, therefore, both prevent the development of BN and prevent the development of the potentially harmful diffuse-avoidant identity style and its associated health problems.

Explanations based on relationship processes

Insecure attachment

Women attempt to change their size and shape to meet some perceived idea of what men find attractive.

Insecure attachment in adult relationships is characterised by a strong desire for closeness and a fear of abandonment.

Evans and Wertheim found a relationship between insecure attachment and BN, as individuals try to lose weight to avoid rejection.

Bodily self-consciousness

Cash suggested that women who are dissatisfied with their physical appearance become self-conscious about their bodies and worry about being accepted by their partners.

Allerdissen et al. found that women with BN reported more fear about meeting their partners' sexual expectations than did a sample of healthy volunteers.

Bulimia or depression?

It is possible that the adverse relationship processes associated with BN may be part of a more general psychopathology that happens to accompany bulimic symptoms (e.g. depression and low self-esteem) rather than being specific characteristics of BN.

There is research support for this…

Schembri and Evans tested the link between relationship processes and bulimic symptoms. They found that self-consciousness during sexual activity was the strongest predictor of bulimic symptoms, followed by anxious attachment. These findings support the claim that adverse relationship processes are a significant risk factor for the development of BN.

However…

The findings of this study imply that adverse relationship processes have a causal relationship with the development of BN. This may not be the case as the study was a correlational design only, and so does not, for example, demonstrate a causal relationship between self-consciousness and BN.

IDA A heterosexual bias…

Most research has focused on risk factors for the development of BN in heterosexual women, although studies have shown that the incidence of eating disorders such as AN and BN among gay and bisexual men is much higher. Feldman and Meyer estimate that 15% of gay or bisexual men have suffered from an eating disorder compared to just 8% of heterosexual women.

Chapter 5

Eating behaviour
Biological explanations of eating behaviour

Psychological explanations of anorexia
Biological explanations of anorexia
Psychological explanations of bulimia

Eating behaviour   > Eating disorders   > Biological explanations of bulimia

Biological explanations of bulimia nervosa (BN)

Neural explanations

Serotonin

The fact that depression and BN often occur together suggests they have a common cause.

A study by Kaye et al. of recovering bulimics and a control group of non-bulimics found that levels of dopamine and noradrenaline were the same in both groups, but the bulimic group showed elevated levels of serotonin.

Low levels of serotonin are associated with depression and high levels with anxiety.

Binge-eating relieves feelings of depression, but may raise levels of serotonin too high, leading to feelings of anxiety. To counter these feelings the person purges, reducing levels of serotonin too low, leading to depression once more.

There is research support for this…

If BN is a product of abnormal serotonin levels, then it should be possible to treat it with SSRIs, which raise levels of serotonin in the brain and should inhibit binge-eating episodes. Walsh et al. found that patients given SSRIs showed decreased binge-eating and purging, compared to a control group given placebo treatment.

Research can explain the serotonin–BN link…

Smith et al. found that, compared to a control group, women recovering from BN who were deprived of tryptophan (which makes serotonin) for 17 hours, showed greater dips in mood, were more concerned about their body image and feared losing control over their eating.

This shows that…

Lowered brain serotonin triggers some of the characteristic features of BN, even among recovered bulimics, who remain vulnerable to the disorder.

IDA Real-world applications…

The success of drug therapies in the treatment of BN (e.g. Walsh et al.), compared to the limited success of similar drug therapies for AN, has made the case for a biological basis for bulimia more convincing.

Nitric oxide (NO)

NO is a neurotransmitter that is 'delivered' to receiving neurons by plasma nitrate.

This causes the production of cGMP.

Together, NO and cGMP regulate much of our eating behaviour. NO mediates the action of hormones involved in weight control (e.g. leptin and ghrelin).

There is research support for this…

Vannacci et al. assessed the effect of NO in bulimia. They found significantly higher levels of plasma nitrate and cGMP in a BN group compared to a control group, and the levels of both positively correlated with the degree of pathological impairment in these individuals.

IDA Age bias…

Research on the causes and development of BN has focused almost exclusively on adolescents and young women. Mangweth-Matzek et al. found that 3.8% of women between the ages of 60 and 70 met the diagnostic criteria for an eating disorder, yet this group is typically ignored.

Evolutionary explanations

The sexual competition hypothesis

Abed suggests that BN is a direct consequence of the evolved need to compete with other females in order to attract a mate.

Obsession with weight is an evolved adaptation to preserve a shape that is attractive to potential mates.

Evolution of nubility

Abed proposes that the traditional 'hourglass' female figure was designed by sexual selection, through the differential reproductive success of those who had this shape (i.e. nubile females).

Sexual competition

This adaptation enabled nubile females to differentiate themselves from lower reproductive value females, and allowed them to compete with other nubile females in the immediate vicinity.

Because of so many 'pseudo-nubile' older women, nubile females must set the desired shape much lower than it would have been in the ancestral environment to demonstrate their higher reproductive potential.

There is research support for this…

Sypeck et al. examined the covers of popular fashion magazines from 1959 to 1999 and found that they represented an increasing preoccupation with body size, particularly during the 1980s and 90s, reflecting the drive for thinness (as predicted by the sexual competition hypothesis) among their readers (mostly young women).

This explanation fits the statistics…

BN is an eating disorder where there is a particularly uneven sex ratio between males and females. A US study (Soundy et al.) found an incidence of BN in females 33 times greater than in males.

IDA Cultural bias…

Cross-cultural statistics suggest that BN is more a characteristic of Western rather than non-Western cultures (APA).

However…

Some studies suggest that BN symptoms are similar in both Western and non-Western cultures. This is important for the sexual competition hypothesis, because it suggests that BN arises because of a universal female concern for 'physical attractiveness'. If this were absent from some cultures it would pose a serious challenge to this explanation.

IDA The myth of genetic determinism…

The sexual competition hypothesis acknowledges the equally important influences of both genes (a male preference for nubile females and a female concern for attractiveness) and environment (e.g. competition with 'local' females and media influences in the development of eating disorders).

Gender

Division A Biological influences on gender
The role of genes and hormones
Evolutionary explanations of gender roles
The biosocial approach to gender development

Division B Psychological explanations of gender development
Cognitive developmental theory
Psychological androgyny and gender dysphoria

Division C Social contexts of gender role
Social influences on gender role
Cross-cultural studies of gender role

Specification
We have chosen to begin this chapter with biological influences on gender whereas, in the actual specification that is shown below, biological influences are the second division. We have made this decision because it makes it easier to understand the various explanations in the chapter.

Gender	
Psychological explanations of gender development	• Cognitive developmental theory, including Kohlberg, and gender schema theory. • Explanations for psychological androgyny and gender dysphoria, including relevant research.
Biological influences on gender	• The role of hormones and genes in gender development. • Evolutionary explanations of gender roles. • The biosocial approach to gender development.
Social contexts of gender role	• Social influences on gender role: for example, the influence of parents, peers and schools, media. • Cross-cultural studies of gender role.

Chapter 6

Biological influences on gender	>	The role of genes and hormones
Psychological explanations of gender development		Evolutionary explanations of gender roles
Gender > Social contexts of gender role		The biosocial approach to gender development

The role of genes in gender development

Chromosomes

Humans have 23 pairs of chromosomes in each cell, each carrying hundreds of genes.

One pair of chromosomes determine an individual's sex:

- XX is a female.
- XY is a male.

The role of hormones

Chromosomal sex (XX or XY) determines what hormones are produced, e.g. more testosterone is produced in XY individuals. During prenatal development hormones cause changes to:

1. External genitalia.
2. The brain.

1. External genitalia

Initially male and female embryos have the same external genitalia, but around three months gestation, testosterone causes male external genitalia (penis, testicles) to develop.

This in turn affects later behaviour, because a baby is labelled as a boy or girl at birth based on their external genitalia, and this creates their gender identity.

2. Brain development

Exposure to male hormones creates a masculinised brain (Geschwind and Galaburda).

For example, girls are generally better at understanding what people think and feel (empathisers), whereas boys are better at categorising and understanding systems (systematisers) (Baron-Cohen).

Animal studies show that female monkeys deliberately exposed to testosterone during prenatal development are more masculine (more aggressive, more rough-and-tumble play) (Quadagno et al.).

Abnormal development

Male abnormal development, e.g. *androgen insensitivity syndrome* (AIS) is a condition where genetic males are insensitive to male hormones during prenatal development and born with no penis. One case study considered members of the Batista family, who were labelled as girls at birth, but later, during adolescence, high levels of testosterone led to the development of male external genitalia (Imperato-McGinley et al.).

Female abnormal development, e.g. female embryos whose mothers took drugs containing male hormones were born with swollen labia and some mistakenly sex-typed as boys. Those identified as girls appear to show an interest in male activities, which may be due to masculinisation of the brain.

There is evidence that biological sex is not the main factor…

Money and Ehrhardt claimed that sex of rearing is more important in determining gender identity than biology (as long as sex-typing is done before the age of three). Money used the case David/Bruce/Brenda Reimer to support this.

Bruce was born an XY male with a penis that was accidentally removed during surgery when he was an infant. Money advised that Bruce's parents raise him as Brenda and later claimed that this 'experiment' was successful, supporting his view that social not biological factors determined gender identity.

However…

Diamond and Sigmundson uncovered the true story and revealed Brenda's unhappiness as a girl and eventual decision in adolescence to become a boy (taking the name David). This suggests that genetic sex is important in the development of gender identity.

This is further supported…

Reiner and Gearhart studied 16 genetic males born with almost no penis; 14 were raised as females – eight had decided by adolescence to re-assign themselves as males, further supporting the importance of biological determinism.

IDA Is biological determinism correct?…

The evidence above suggests that gender identity is mainly determined by genetic sex (which determines production of hormones, external genitalia and brain development).

However… socialisation matters too…

For example, *congenital adrenal hyperplasia* (CAH) is a condition where XX individuals have high levels of testosterone prenatally, causing varying degrees of external male genitalia at birth. Dessens et al. studied 250 cases where individuals were typed as females at birth and found that 95% were content with their role, despite prenatal exposure to male hormones. A further 33 patients were typed as males, of whom 12 experienced serious gender problems.

IDA Nature and nurture…

This research shows that biological factors (nature) are very important in determining gender identity, but socialisation and personal cognitive processes (nurture) also contribute.

IDA Real-world application…

Biological determinism is a real-world issue in sports because occasionally XY individuals have competed as females and had an unfair advantage (since males are more muscular). The Olympic Committee has tested all individuals since 1968, which meant that AIS individuals (XY genotype but raised as females) couldn't compete.

In 1991 a decision was made not to test genetic sex because of genetic abnormalities, and the only criteria that excludes anyone from female events is obvious male genitalia (Bown).

There are methodological issues with this research…

One problem with this research is the use of case studies of individuals with unique characteristics. Each individual has a special set of circumstances, e.g. the amount of testosterone they were exposed to prenatally, the availability of suitable gender role models, etc. This means it is impossible to generalise from such cases.

A second issue is that much of the research involves abnormal individuals – intersexes who are not clearly male or female (e.g. there is a mismatch between chromosomal sex and what hormones they were exposed to). Such individuals may be more vulnerable to social influences than 'normal' because their biological ambiguities mean they have to search for clues to their identity. This again threatens the extent to which the research findings can be generalised to all people.

Chapter 6

Biological influences on gender	>	The role of genes and hormones
Psychological explanations of gender development		Evolutionary explanations of gender roles
Gender > Social contexts of gender role		The biosocial approach to gender development

Evolutionary explanations of gender roles

Division of labour

Complementary division of labour was adaptive in the EEA because it enhanced reproductive success and also helped avoid starvation (by maximising food production).

- Men were hunters because, if women spent time hunting, this would reduce a group's reproductive success. Therefore men are physically and psychologically equipped to be hunters.
- Women contributed to the provision of food by growing vegetables, milling grain and producing clothing.

Lack of role division

Kuhn and Stiner propose that male and female Neanderthals both hunted (based on evidence of hunting injuries), which meant that when hunting failed the group starved because there was no backup. The evolution of a division of labour in humans (*homo sapiens*) enhanced their ultimate success over the rival Neanderthal species.

One consequence of men as hunters…

The meat-sharing hypothesis (Stanford) suggests that males use control of meat as a means of attracting female interest.

Studies of modern day hunter-gatherer societies support this (Hill and Kaplan), as do comparative studies of chimpanzees.

IDA *The evolutionary approach is speculative and lacks sound research support…*

This may be a fair criticism of some evolutionary accounts, e.g. the disappearance of Neanderthals being due to a lack of role division (an equally plausible suggestion relates to climate change).

It is not a fair criticism… Of all evolutionary accounts, which are often supported by historical records, comparative studies and cross-cultural studies (see, for example, below).

IDA *The evolutionary approach is determinist…*

In terms of gender roles the evolutionary approach suggests that men and women are constrained to behave in predetermined ways in line with selective pressures that operated in the EEA.

However…

Evolutionary psychologists actually propose that our genes only predispose us to certain behaviours and that culture and personal experience are important influences (nature and nurture).

Mate choice

Gender role behaviours are related to adaptive reproductive strategies:

- Men increase their reproductive success by mating as frequently as possible and with those females who are most fertile. To ensure this, men look for indicators of youth and healthiness (e.g. smooth skin, glossy hair, thin waist – i.e. physical attractiveness) that indicate greater fertility.
- Women seek signs of fertility in a partner, but are also interested in the ability to provide resources (e.g. partner's wealth, power and possessions) because they need to be cared for during childbearing and rearing.

There is research support…

Buss questioned men and women in 37 cultures. He found that as predicted:

- Men placed more importance on physical attractiveness in a mate, evidence of a woman's fertility and reproductive value.
- Women more than men desired mates who were good financial prospects (i.e. had resources or ambition).

Waynforth and Dunbar used personal ads to demonstrate that, as predicted:

- More men sought a physically attractive partner than did women (44% versus 22%).
- More women sought resources than did men (50% versus 34%).

One strength of this study is… That the choices represented an individual's ideal bid in the process of mate selection.

Cognitive style

Empathising-systemising (E-S) theory

Baron-Cohen proposed that women are better at empathising (understanding what people think and feel) whereas men are better at systemising (understanding and building systems).

This may have evolved because of selective pressures – women make better mothers by being empathisers and men make better hunters by being systemisers.

There is research support…

Baron-Cohen has used his own *Systemising Quotient Questionnaire* (e.g. 'When I read a newspaper I am drawn to tables of information'), and found gender differences as expected. Only about 17% of men had a female empathising brain and 17% of women had a male systemising brain.

One implication of E-S theory…

Autism may be an example of the extreme male brain (Baron-Cohen). Autistic individuals lack the ability to empathise (poor Theory of Mind) and excel at systemising.

Stress responses

Another difference between men and women that would have been adaptive in the EEA is their complementary response to situations of threat:

- Men respond with fight or flight to deal with the threat.
- Women respond with tend and befriend to protect group members (Taylor *et al.*).

There is research support…

Ennis *et al.* tested levels of cortisol (stress hormone) just before and after taking exams (a 'threatening'/stressful situation). Cortisol levels increased in males but not females.

Taylor *et al.* showed that levels of oxytocin increase in females when stressed (not males); this hormone is associated with reduced anxiety and increased sociability.

Both studies show that there are gender differences in line with the predictions from evolutionary theory.

Chapter 6

Biological influences on gender > The role of genes and hormones
Psychological explanations of gender development | Evolutionary explanations of gender roles
Gender > Social contexts of gender role
The biosocial approach to gender development

The biosocial approach to gender development

Biosocial theory (Money and Ehrhardt)

Sex of rearing is the pivotal point in gender development.

What matters is what gender you are told you are, and this must happen before the age of three.

- Biology is likely to determine sex of rearing because babies are sexed at birth on the basis of external genitalia – which are usually in accord with genetic sex.
- In ambiguous cases, a child may be raised as a gender incongruent with genetic sex.

In both cases, gender identity will be determined by subsequent socialisation based on a person's gender assignment.

The research evidence is flawed...

Most of the evidence is derived from the study of abnormal individuals, e.g. the study of genetic females exposed to male hormones prenatally because of drugs taken by their mother.

Such evidence may not be relevant to understanding gender development, as it does not reflect experiences of normal individuals.

The research evidence supports biological determinism...

Initially, the case study of David Reimer (Brenda/Bruce) supported biosocial theory as he (Bruce) accepted his gender re-assignment until reaching adolescence. However, ultimately he rejected this, suggesting that biological sex is more important than socialisation.

Reiner and Gearhart studied 16 genetic males born with almost no penis; 14 were raised as females – eight had decided by adolescence to re-assign themselves as males.

Social role theory (Eagly and Wood)

An evolutionary approach

Traditional evolutionary theory proposes that both physical and psychological sex differences are naturally selected.

- Physical sex differences e.g. men are stronger and faster, women bear children.
- Psychological sex differences e.g. men become more aggressive because they are hunters, women become more empathetic because they raise children.

The psychological differences lead to social role differences, e.g. men become hunters because they are stronger, women become homemakers because they have to be at home with children.

In contrast, Eagly and Wood suggested that only physical sex differences are naturally selected and these cause differential social roles, which in turn create psychological sex differences.

Division of labour

Social role theory predicts that:

- Physical sex differences can be related to social roles, e.g. men hunt because they don't have to stay at home for childcare.
- In societies where strength is not required for obtaining food or where childcare is shared, male/female social roles will be more similar and psychological differences will be reduced.

Mate choice

Traditional evolutionary theory: what men and women seek in a partner is related to the value of certain traits (e.g. red lips as a sign of youthfulness).

Social role theory: mate choice is related to social roles. Men and women maximise their reproductive success by seeking a mate who is a good homemaker or hunter (respectively).

Hormonal differences may be the outcome of social roles, rather than the cause.

For example, greater levels of testosterone in males occur because they engage in more athletic events and this creates higher levels of testosterone than in women.

IDA *It is also a social constructionist approach...*

Eagly and Wood's biosocial theory suggests that psychological sex differences are the outcome of social roles, which in turn are related to the behaviours of a particular society or culture. There is no objective reality, such as a real difference between men and women – or even if there is one, social factors tend to overshadow these differences. According to this approach, behaviours are best understood in terms of the social context in which they occur.

The findings from Buss's study of 37 cultures can be explained using social role theory...

Buss found that in all cultures men prefer younger, physically attractive women (because they are more fertile), whereas women seek men with resources (to make childrearing easier).

Eagly and Wood explain this as (1) men want younger women because they are more obedient, (2) women frequently earn less than men and therefore seek a partner with resources.

This is supported by...

Eagly and Wood who found, for example, that in situations where women have higher status Buss's sex differences were less pronounced. This supports the idea that social roles are the driving force in psychological sex differences.

However...

Gangestad et al. re-analysed Eagly and Wood's data, controlling for factors such as affluence and social structure. They concluded that gender equality was not related to sex differences, and therefore concluded that traditional evolutionary is adequate.

The traditional evolutionary approach may be better...

Luxen argues that traditional evolutionary theory is preferable for a number of reasons:

- It is simpler (Occam's razor).
- Selective pressure acts on behaviour as well as on physical characteristics and therefore psychological sex differences would be selected at the same time as physical ones.
- Research has shown that very young children and animals display sex differences – these must be biological rather than psychological because sex role socialisation is unlikely to have occurred.

IDA *Real-world application...*

The traditional evolutionary approach implies that sex differences are innate and cannot be changed by altering social context, whereas social role theory supports the feminist view that changes in social roles will lead to changes in psychological differences between men and women.

Cognitive developmental theory

Gender constancy theory (Kohlberg)

Cognitive development

Piaget suggested that children under the age of seven are pre-operational, lacking internal logic and conservation skills (cannot distinguish between appearance and reality, the appearance–reality distinction).

For example, McConaghy showed that children under five years judged a drawing to be a woman if it was wearing a dress, yet male genitals were also visible.

A stage theory

Changes in gender thinking occur due to maturation of a child's thinking.
- *Stage 1 Gender labelling* (2–3½ years). Children select gender label based on appearance, but can change this if appearance changes.
- *Stage 2 Gender stability* (3½–4½ years). Children understand that gender is consistent/stable over time (e.g. boys grow into men), but lack understanding of constancy, i.e. it is not stable across situations. They are still swayed by outward appearances.
- *Stage 3 Gender consistency.* Children realise that gender is constant across time and situations. Only at this point will children start to learn about gender-appropriate behaviour.

IDA *Approaches to explaining gender development*…

The cognitive developmental approach suggests that the key to gender development is the way a child thinks about their gender.
There are many other approaches:
- The social learning approach suggests we learn about appropriate gender behaviour through direct and indirect reinforcement and punishment (e.g. boys are teased for wearing girls' clothes).
- The biological approach proposes that genes and hormones determine gender behaviours.

There is research support…

- *Gender labelling* – Thompson found that 2-year-olds were less able to identify their sex than 3-year-olds (76% versus 90% correct).
- *Gender stability* – Slaby and Frey asked children: 'Were you a little girl or a little boy when you were a baby?'. There was no evidence of gender stability across time until they were three or four years old.
- *Gender consistency* – Slaby and Frey found that children high in gender constancy (stability+consistency) showed greatest interest in same-sex models i.e. gender-appropriate models.

However, the studies may lack validity…

Bem gave children aged three to five years a gender conservation task (shown a nude child and then the same child dressed gender inappropriately). Those children who assigned gender on basis of clothing (i.e. no constancy) also tended to fail a genital knowledge test. Therefore they were not failing to conserve gender because there was nothing for them to conserve.

Bem also argued that the basic task is nonsense – when children are asked to resolve a contradiction between genitals and clothing, the child goes for the cue that is most salient in our society – i.e. clothes.

Gender schema theory (Martin and Halverson)

Children start to learn about gender-appropriate behaviour *before* gender constancy is achieved.

Basic gender identity (gender labelling) is sufficient for a child to identify him/herself as boy/girl and take an interest in what behaviours are appropriate.

Gender schemas are organised clusters of information about gender-appropriate behaviour.

Children learn such schemas as a result of their interactions with people, e.g. learning what clothes to wear.

Ingroup and outgroup processes

Children focus on ingroup schemas (e.g. if you are a girl you focus on feminine schemas) and avoid behaviours that belong to outgroup schemas.

Resilience of gender beliefs

Children hold very fixed gender attitudes because they ignore information that is inconsistent with ingroup information.

For example, if a boy sees a film with a male nurse, this information is ignored (not consistent with ingroup schema) and therefore the boy doesn't alter his existing schema.

There is research support…

- *Gender stereotypes without constancy* – Martin and Little found that children under the age of four showed no signs of gender stability, but did display strong gender stereotypes.
- *Greater attention to information consistent with gender schemas* – Martin and Halverson found that children under six recalled more gender-consistent pictures (e.g. male firefighter) than gender-inconsistent ones (e.g. female chemist), as we would expect.
- *Greater attention to ingroup schema* – Children aged four to nine took a greater interest in toys labelled as belonging to the ingroup and one week later were better able to remember these (Bradbard et al.).

Gender constancy versus schemata…

The key argument is whether gender knowledge is absorbed after gender constancy (Kohlberg) or before (Martin and Halverson).
Stangor and Ruble proposed a compromise, and supported this with a study, finding that:
- Preference (motivation) for same-sex toys increased with gender constancy (supporting gender constancy theory).
- Memory (organisation) for gender-consistent pictures increased with age (supporting gender schema theory).

IDA *Limitations of the cognitive developmental approach*…

The cognitive developmental approach fails to incorporate the influence of social factors, e.g. the fact that girls are more likely to take on masculine traits but the same is not true for boys (Huston).

The way we think may not be related to behaviour, e.g. couples who agree to share domestic tasks in reality don't (Durkin).

Explanations of psychological androgyny

Androgynous individuals

Flexibility and psychological health

Traditional views of gender emphasise the differences between men and women, limiting people to inflexible gender roles.

It is psychologically more healthy to be androgynous, selecting a mixture of male and female traits as suits each individual.

Bem Sex Role Inventory (BSRI)

Found that 34% of male participants and 27% of female participants were androgynous (Bem).

Androgynous people have higher self-esteem and a greater sense of emotional wellbeing (Flaherty and Dusek).

Androgynous societies

Applied to societies

Gender schemas are created by the culture in which we live.

It is the culture rather than the individual that is gender schematic (i.e. follows traditional gender schema).

Bem proposed that society should be androgynous to increase the adjustment of the individuals within that society.

There is research support for flexibility…

Androgynous individuals (and those rated as masculine) showed lower levels of conformity to a confederate's behaviour than feminine individuals when asked to judge cartoons (Bem).

Androgynous individuals (and those rated as feminine) displayed greater warmth in interpersonal interactions (a female characteristic), whereas males were more constrained by gender roles (Bem et al.).

However…

Lippa points out that such findings are inevitable because masculinity is measured on the BSRI in terms of resisting pressures to conform and femininity is measured in terms of nurturance – therefore we are bound to find that people who are androgynous/masculine are low in conformity and that people who are androgynous/feminine show greater warmth in interpersonal interactions.

There are similar problems with psychological healthiness…

Masculinity is measured in terms of confidence and assertiveness, so people scored as masculine are likely to score high in self-esteem.

Therefore…

Androgyny is a meaningless concept because it is circular – people who display both masculine and feminine behaviours are rated as androgynous, which means they are more flexible in terms of gender orientation, which is why they select a mixture of masculine and feminine behaviours.

IDA A social constructionist view…

Sex differences may be biological but societies can de-emphasise what they expect of men and women and therefore permit individuals greater freedom to select the characteristics suited to their personality, rather than their gender.

Explanations of gender dysphoria

Psychological explanations

Gender dysphoria is related to mental illness or caused by childhood trauma, e.g. cross-gender fantasy created to resolve anxiety (Coates et al.).

Stoller found that individuals with GID (gender identity disorder) had overly close mother–son relationships.

The research evidence is poor…

Cole et al. studied 435 individuals experiencing gender dysphoria and reported that the range of psychiatric conditions displayed were no greater than found in a 'normal' population.

This suggests that gender dysphoria is generally unrelated to trauma or to pathological families.

Biological explanations

Environmental pollution

Insecticide DDT contains oestrogens, which may feminise male embryos.

Genetic conditions

AIS (androgen insensitivity syndrome) occurs in XY males who are insensitive to the male hormone androgen, so that male external genitalia don't develop.

CAH (congenital adrenal hyperplasia) occurs in XX females exposed to high levels of male hormones during development, resulting in male genitalia.

Both cause a mismatch between genetic sex, hormones, external genitalia and sex of rearing, causing intersex conditions.

There is research support…

A study in Holland found that boys born to mothers who were exposed to dioxins (which can promote oestrogen) displayed feminised play (Vreugdenhil et al.).

Prenatal hormones may change specific areas of the brain…

The BSTc (the bed nucleus of the stria terminalis) in the hypothalamus is normally larger in males, but was found to be smaller in six male-to-female transsexuals (Zhou et al.).

This suggests that transsexual tendencies may be caused by brain differences.

Sex of rearing may be most significant factor…

Dessens et al. studied 250 genetic females with CAH.

• 95% of those raised as girls were content with their gender assignment.
• 88% of those raised as boys were content with their gender assignment.

IDA Real-world application…

Research on the effects of erroneous gender assignation at birth is crucial in helping the small but significant group of individuals born with ambiguous sex.

Social influences on gender role

Social learning theory (SLT)

Social learning theory

New behaviours are acquired through observing what people do, and modelling this behaviour if it is vicariously reinforced.

When such behaviour is imitated this will then be directly rewarded or punished, which affects future behaviour.

Thus, learning is a product of both indirect (vicarious) and direct reinforcement.

Effects of modelling limited by existing stereotypes…

Perry and Bussey found that children only imitated same-sex models if the behaviour was not counter to existing stereotypes.

Direct tuition may be more important…

Martin *et al.* found that preschool boys played with toys labelled 'boys' toys' (a form of 'direct tuition') even after seeing girls playing with them, but did not play with toys labelled 'girls' toys' even when they saw boys playing with them (i.e. they did not model same-sex behaviour when it was counter to direct tuition).

Social cognitive theory

Emphasises the role of cognitive factors. Three major modes of influence:

1. Modelling involves a cognitive representation of the modelled activities, plus understanding of the underlying rules of the modelled behaviours, e.g. storing the principles of behaving in a masculine or feminine way.

2. Enactive experience occurs as children become mobile and can direct their own experiences. This leads to an increase in social interactions, which reinforce ideas about gender roles.

3. Direct tuition begins as children acquire linguistic skills and can be told what gender behaviours are appropriate or inappropriate. The impact of such 'tuition' is weakened when what is being taught is contradicted by what is being modelled (Hildebrandt *et al.*).

IDA *Contrasts with the cognitive-developmental approach…*

Cognitive-developmental theories can explain research which shows that children attend specifically to information consistent with gender (outgroup) schemas (Martin and Halverson).

Cognitive-developmental theories suggest that children take an active involvement in their gender development through self-evaluation and self-regulation, whereas SLT proposes that gender is learned passively through reinforcement.

Cognitive-developmental theories explain how children's thinking changes qualitatively as they get older, whereas SLT is an adevelopmental approach because there is no sequence (Durkin).

However…

There is some suggestion of a sequence in social cognitive theory, e.g. moving from modelling to enactive experience.

IDA *Does not ignore biological influences…*

The SLT approach is not in opposition to the biological approach. Bandura acknowledged that the starting point for a behaviour is often biological – it is the means of expressing it that is learned.

Sources of social influence

Parents

Reinforcement is differential, e.g. fathers react more negatively to sons' feminine play than do mothers (Idle *et al.*).

There is research support…

Smith and Lloyd found that mothers selected gender-appropriate toys for an infant presented as a boy or girl.

Parents who differentially reinforce gender behaviour have children who are quickest to develop strong gender preferences (Fagot *et al.*).

Peers

Peers provide gender-specific models and also reinforce gender-appropriate behaviour (Bandura).

Boys are more likely to be criticised for feminine behaviour than vice versa (Fagot).

Schools

Teachers aim to socialise children into their society, reinforcing gender-appropriate behaviour and acting as role models.

There is research support…

Peer behaviour probably doesn't create gender role stereotypes but simply reinforces existing ones,.

For example, Lamb and Roopnarine found that when male-typed behaviour was reinforced in girls, the behaviour continued for a shorter time than when male-typed behaviour was reinforced in boys. This suggests that peer reinforcement mainly acts as a reminder of what is gender-appropriate behaviour.

The media

The media communicate cultural stereotypes, e.g. males are portrayed as independent and directive, females as unambitious and emotional (Bussey and Bandura).

Individuals who watch more TV tend to display more gender stereotypic role conceptions than do light viewers (McGhee and Frueh).

The media provide role models and also enhance self-efficacy, leading males to have increased self-confidence.

There is research support…

Rare cases of communities that have no TV allow us to observe the effects of exposure to media stereotypes, e.g. Williams found that children with no TV had weaker gender stereotypes (especially girls). After exposure to TV their views became more gender stereotyped.

IDA *Real-world application…*

Such research leads to pressure on programme makers to try to use this media to alter gender stereotypes. Pingree found that stereotyping was reduced when children were shown commercials with women in non-traditional roles. However, pre-adolescent boys displayed *stronger* stereotypes after exposure to the non-traditional models.

Cross-cultural studies of gender role

Cultural similarities

Division of labour

In almost all societies women look after food and children (even when such activities are shared, it tends not to be a major male responsibility).

Aggressive behaviour

Mead studied three groups in Papua New Guinea.

Initially, she found evidence for *cultural determinism* (gender roles varied in the different groups, e.g. sometimes women were more aggressive than men or vice versa).

Subsequently, she decided the evidence pointed towards *cultural relativism* (there were cultural differences, but in all societies men were more aggressive).

Characteristics desirable in a partner

Buss questioned people in 37 cultures about what they look for in a partner. He found that gender role behaviours were related to strategies that ensure the greatest reproductive success, e.g.

- Women valued good financial prospects, ambition and industriousness in a partner more highly than did men.
- Men preferred physically attractive mates and those who were younger; both are signs of good genes and youthfulness (indicators of fertility).

Sex stereotypes

Williams and Best studied people in 30 countries, using a 300 item adjective checklist.

- Men were seen as more dominant, aggressive, autonomous.
- Women were seen as more nurturant, deferent and interested in affiliation.

IDA *Issues with cross-cultural research…*

Western research investigating non-Western cultural practices is likely to be biased even when indigenous researchers are used (as in Buss's study), e.g. because it tends to use questionnaires, methods and concepts developed in the West (imposed etics) (Berry *et al.*).

IDA *Genetic determinism…*

The fact that there are cultural similarities in gender role behaviour suggests that these behaviours are genetically determined, but is this a direct or indirect effect of inherited factors?

Eagly and Wood proposed that inherited physical differences between men and women create social role differences and these in turn create psychological differences, such as those identified by Mead and Buss.

According to Eagly and Wood, Buss's evidence on the left (see 'characteristics desirable in a partner') can be explained in terms of the fact that women generally have had less earning capacity and therefore women seek men with resources. Along with resources men have power and dominance. Men want younger women not because of their fertility, but because they will be more obedient.

This was supported by…

Eagly and Wood re-analysed Buss's data and found that when women have a higher status and male–female division of labour is less pronounced, then sex differences in mating preferences become less pronounced. This suggests that social roles (rather than genetic factors) are the driving force in psychological sex differences.

Labour divisions are not the same in all cultures…

There are some exceptions, for example Japanese men reject the American 'macho' male stereotype and prefer to be well rounded in the arts (Sugihara and Katsurada).

There are methodological criticisms of this study…

The task was a forced choice one so divisions between gender stereotypes may be exaggerated.

The task was related to stereotypes and not to actual behaviours.

Participants were university students who may share a high level of consensus across cultures.

Cultural differences

Spatial perception

Berry *et al.*'s study of 17 societies found male superiority on spatial perceptual tasks only in relatively tightly knit, sedentary societies but absent or even reversed in 'looser' nomadic societies.

This shows that sex differences on spatial perceptual tasks interact with ecological and cultural factors.

Conformity

Women are generally more conformist than men, but this difference varies with culture. Berry *et al.* report that conformity is highest in tight, sedentary societies.

Historical differences

In the UK, women continue to perform more domestic duties than men and continue to occupy less powerful positions, but this gender gap has been decreasing.

IDA *Social versus biological approach…*

The social approach: In sedentary societies men are the hunters and women stay at home, whereas in nomadic groups both men and women hunt and both therefore develop spatial perceptual abilities (Van Leeuwen).

The biological approach: In hunting societies those with poor spatial abilities die (and thus are selected against), therefore the men who remain in such societies have better spatial abilities than the women (where no selection has taken place). This doesn't happen in nomadic groups (Kimura).

This may happen because…

In nomadic societies women contribute to food accumulation and thus are more highly valued, less regarded as objects for reproduction and have more power and so less need to conform (Schlegel and Barry).

IDA *Culture or biology?…*

The existence of universal gender differences supports biology, but the decrease in these differences (such as women gaining greater power in wealthier societies) supports the role of social factors.

Intelligence and learning

Division A Theories of intelligence

The psychometric approach
The information-processing approach
Gardner's theory of multiple intelligences

Division B Animal learning and intelligence

Classical conditioning
Operant conditioning
Conditioning and the behaviour of animals
Intelligence in non-human animals

Division C Evolution of intelligence

Evolutionary factors in human intelligence
Genetic factors in intelligence-test performance
Environmental factors in intelligence-test performance

Specification

Gender		
Theories of intelligence	• Theories of intelligence, including psychometric and information-processing approaches.	
	• Gardner's theory of multiple intelligences.	
Animal learning and intelligence	• The nature of simple learning (classical and operant conditioning) and its role in the behaviour of non-human animals.	
	• Evidence for intelligence in non-human animals, for example, self-recognition, social learning, Machiavellian intelligence.	
Evolution of intelligence	• Evolutionary factors in the development of human intelligence, for example, ecological demands, social complexity, brain size.	
	• The role of genetic and environmental factors associated with intelligence-test performance, including the role of culture.	

Chapter 7

Theories of intelligence	>	The psychometric approach
Animal learning and intelligence		The information-processing approach
Intelligence and learning	>	Evolution of intelligence	Gardner's theory of multiple intelligences

The psychometric approach

General intelligence

General intelligence (g) is considered a general factor underlying performance in different types of intelligence test.

Intelligent behaviour is therefore derived from an underlying 'mental energy' (g).

Spearman's two-factor theory

Using factor analysis, Spearman found that individuals who performed well on one IQ test also performed well on other types of test. This was explained by:

- *Specific abilities* (s) – Individuals tend to perform consistently well on specific aspects of intelligence such as vocabulary and mathematics.
- *General intelligence* (g) – The positive correlation between individuals' perform-ance on different tests is explained by general intelligence (g), something that is almost entirely inherited.

Multifactor theories

Theories that focus on multiple factors in intelligence rather than one underlying 'g' are known as multifactor theories.

Cattell's Gf-Gc theory

Cattell proposed that intelligence was comprised of two distinct components:

- *Crystallised intelligence* (Gc) – Acquired knowledge and skills (e.g. vocabulary and general knowledge), which are the result of cultural and educational experiences.
- *Fluid intelligence* (Gf) – Reasoning and problem solving ability, which is not dependent on experience. This provides the 'raw material' for development of Gc.

Relationship between Gc and Gf – People with high capacity for Gf acquire Gc at faster rates and develop a greater level of Gc.

Guilford's 'structure of intellect' theory

Guilford proposed intelligence was the result of 150 abilities, in three groups:

- *Operations* – Different ways in which people process information, including *memory, cognition* and *evaluation*.
- *Contents* – Different types of material on which operations are performed, including *visual, auditory* and *semantic* operations.
- *Products* – Different forms in which information is stored, processed and used by the individual to make connections between stimuli, including *units, relations* and *transformation*.

Combining all possible operations, contents and products, results in 150 different components of intelligence.

There is neurophysiological evidence for general intelligence…

Duncan *et al.* used PET scans and presented participants with tasks that required general intelligence or did not. Regardless of the type of task, the same areas of the frontal lobes 'lit up' during 'g' tasks' but not during 'non-g' tasks.

Spearman committed the logical error of reification…

Gould claimed that Spearman gave an abstract thing (g) a 'concrete' status. This leads to circular reasoning where the explanation for a positive correlation between test performances is an underlying general intelligence, but its proof of existence is solely that correlation.

IDA *Cultural bias in intelligence testing*…

In 1921, the US army tested 1.75 million men using psychometric IQ tests. The tests showed that white Americans scored significantly higher than European immigrants and black Americans.

However, the poor scores found in the immigrant and black groups were a result of the cultural bias of the test items used to test them; these included questions relating to US sports, food and customs. Black Americans and immigrants could not answer questions relating to white, middle-class experiences.

There are advantages in Cattell's explanation of intelligence…

It appears better able to explain what typically happens over an individual's lifespan. Gc tends to rise over the lifespan, whereas Gf usually falls (McArdle *et al.*). This cannot be explained in terms of one unchanging general intelligence, which underestimates the complexity of cognitive changes throughout the lifespan.

Distinction between Gc and Gf is supported by the Flynn effect…

Flynn provided evidence that IQ scores have been increasing steadily over the last 50 years. However, the 'Flynn effect' appears only to hold for measures of fluid intelligence, and has ignored measures of crystallised intelligence. Raven confirmed Flynn's findings, but also found much smaller increases in adults (and in some cases *decreases*) in vocabulary and other measures of crystallised intelligence over the same period.

Psychometric tests may not be a fair measure of ability…

Bunting and Mooney found that pupils who were coached in how to do well in IQ tests tended to improve their 11-plus scores by 40%, giving an inaccurate measure of their true abilities. The consequence was that many then struggle to keep up with the academic demands in selective post-11 education.

Strengths of Guilford's 'structure of intellect' theory…

- *A broad view of intelligence* – Guilford was the first to define intelligence very broadly, with later theorists (e.g. Gardner) building on Guilford's initial ideas.
- *The importance of scientific testing* – Although Guilford's views on intelligence have not been supported by scientific investigation, he did create a theory that *could* be tested scientifically, something that is missing from many other explanations of intelligence.
- *Sufficiently detailed to be tested* – This is especially important within scientific psychology, where theorists must provide sufficient theoretical information to allow disconfirmation. In fact, the demise of Guilford's theory is precisely *because* it lends itself to falsifiability.

However…

Guilford's theory is dismissed by many critics as lacking parsimony (i.e. it is unnecessarily complicated and difficult to construct IQ tests to measure all the different components claimed by Guilford) and having very little practical importance in the testing of intelligence.

The information-processing approach

The triarchic theory

Sternberg identified three distinct aspects of intelligence: analytical, practical and creative intelligence.

Analytical (componential) intelligence

The ability to combine most appropriate mental mechanisms (components) when applying intelligence to a problem. Sternberg believed these to be universal.

- *Metacomponents* determine the exact nature of a problem, develop strategies and allocate resources.
- *Performance components* are cognitive processes used in solving a problem.
- *Knowledge-acquisition components* are used to acquire and learn new material.

Practical (contextual) intelligence

The ability to make a considered response that is dependent on the context in which the problem occurs.

This involves selecting a response that is most likely to bring success.

Creative (experiential) intelligence

Helps an individual identify when a problem is a new one, and so requires intelligent behaviour to solve it (*novelty*).

Automisation refers to the performance of an action that requires little thought.

There is evidence for Sternberg's theory…

Grigorenko *et al.* taught reading either triarchically or through the regular curriculum to middle and high school students. In all settings, students who were taught triarchically substantially outperformed students who were taught in standard ways, supporting the importance of identifying three aspects of intelligence.

Berg and Sternberg supported the main predictions of Sternberg's theory *and* the predicted decline in cognitive abilities associated with ageing. They found that younger adults were superior in the metacomponents and performance components associated with analytical intelligence.

However…

Cunningham and Tomer suggest that not all aspects of analytical intelligence decline with age. Knowledge-acquisition components based on experience may stay relatively stable in old age.

IDA *Real-world application…*

Sternberg's theory has been successfully applied to education at both school and university levels. Williams *et al.* assessed the impact of the *Practical Intelligence for School* (PIFS) intervention, in which all three types of intelligence are emphasised. When PIFS was used as a major part of the curriculum, significant improvements in practical intelligence were obtained.

There are criticisms of this theory…

Gottfredson claims that Sternberg has failed to provide sufficient evidence to support his claim that practical intelligence is distinct from general intelligence and that it is superior to *g* in predicting academic success.

However…

Sternberg argues that although there is, as yet, no published test of the complete theory of triarchic intelligence, it is an ongoing theory rather than a completed piece of work.

Processing speed

Processing speed refers to the speed with which we carry out mental operations e.g. retrieval from memory.

It has been found to correlate positively with IQ.

Age-related changes

Age-related changes in the speed of processing lead to changes in working memory, which in turn lead to changes in performance on tests of fluid intelligence.

Salthouse's *processing speed theory of ageing* predicts age-related declines in intellectual function are a consequence of age-related slowing in processing speed.

Processing efficiency

This refers to the efficiency with which we perform basic cognitive operations.

- By minimising brain resources required to conduct a particular cognitive process, it becomes possible to process more information at any one time.
- By maximising efficiency, we maximise speed of processing and so maximise intellectual performance.

There is evidence for a processing speed explanation…

Fry and Hale assessed processing speed, working memory capacity and fluid intelligence. About half of the increases in fluid intelligence were attributed to developmental changes in working memory, and about three-quarters of the improvements in working memory were attributed to developmental changes in processing speed.

IDA *Real-world application…*

Many computer-based applications have been developed to slow down cognitive ageing. Smith *et al.* tested 524 adults aged over 65 on the *Posit Science Brain Fitness Program*. Compared to a control group, those in the Brain Fitness group significantly increased their processing speed and reported associated positive changes in their everyday life.

Is processing speed a cause or a consequence?…

It is possible that the causal relationship between processing speed and intelligence is reversed from that described on the left.

For example, age-related changes in abilities other than processing speed (such as the ability to recognise relationships between objects or ideas) might be responsible for faster performance on information-processing tasks.

The link between processing speed and school performance is questioned…

Rindermann and Neubauera studied students aged 14–16 and found little evidence to suggest that processing speed had any direct effect on school performance. Any improvement seems to be indirect only (e.g. influencing intelligence and creativity, which in turn influenced school performance).

Chapter 7

Theories of intelligence	>	The psychometric approach
Animal learning and intelligence		The information-processing approach
Intelligence and learning	>	Evolution of intelligence		Gardner's theory of multiple intelligences

Gardner's theory of multiple intelligences (MI)

Gardner believed that many different abilities could count as 'intelligence' if they resolved genuine problems within a particular cultural setting. He originally came up with seven, but later added an eighth (natural intelligence).

Gardner believed that no two people possessed exactly the same profile of intelligences.

Criteria for inclusion as an 'intelligence'

Neuropsychological evidence – People have multiple intelligences because they have distinct neural modules. Damage to one area may impair one intellectual skill while leaving others intact.

Existence of individuals with exceptional talent – Child prodigies or autistic savants who have an exceptional ability in one area suggest that there are separate forms of intelligence.

Distinct developmental history – For example, spoken language develops quickly and to reasonably high levels of competence in most people.

Research evidence – Individuals are less able to carry out two tasks at the same time if they utilise the same *type* of intelligence. If they use different types of intelligence there is less interference.

Gardner's eight intelligences

Linguistic intelligence – Language skills, e.g. the ability to learn languages and express oneself.

Logical-mathematical intelligence – Numerical skills, e.g. the ability to carry out mathematical operations and investigate issues scientifically.

Spatial intelligence – Understanding relationships in space, e.g. the ability to read maps or transform mental images onto paper.

Bodily-kinaesthetic intelligence – Using the body, e.g. using mental operations to co-ordinate bodily movements.

Musical intelligence – Skills, e.g. playing an instrument or composing music.

Interpersonal intelligence – Understanding and relating to others, e.g. understanding the motivations and intentions of others.

Intrapersonal intelligence – Understanding oneself, including an appreciation of feelings, fears and motivations.

Natural intelligence – Showing an expertise in the recognition and classification of different species of flora and fauna in the natural environment.

IDA *Real-world application*…

A Danish experience park (Danfoss Universe) features the Explorama, with games, exercises and challenges that draw upon different intelligences. This allows visitors to learn about their own intelligences with the intention that practice will enhance the intelligence in question.

There isn't a great deal of empirical support for MI…

There have been very few studies that offer empirical support for the validity of MI as an explanation of intelligence.

However…

Some research support is starting to appear, e.g. Douglas *et al.* found that, compared to direct instruction, teaching methods that concentrated on fostering multiple intelligences produced significant increases in students' academic, social and emotional wellbeing.

IDA *MI is not a scientific theory*…

Evidence does not exist to confirm most of the hypotheses generated by Gardner's theory. Gardner admits that the theory would be difficult to test scientifically, which limits its acceptability as a 'scientific' theory of intelligence.

There is evidence for this theory…

The exceptional skills shown by autistic savants such as Stephen Wiltshire, who shows exceptional spatial intelligence, support Gardner's theory because they demonstrate exceptional ability in one area while showing deficits in others.

There are positive implications from MI theory…

MI theory suggests a whole set of ways in which children might succeed both educationally and in life generally. By assuming that there are many different ways to approach a problem, educators can help children to improve their skills and feel good about themselves in the process.

There may be other types of intelligence…

Gardner suggested that there may be other types of intelligence provided they fit the criteria. However, even those types of intelligence that do form part of the theory have their problems (in terms of lack of empirical support) and types such as 'musical' and 'bodily-kinaesthetic' intelligences might better be described as 'talents' than 'intelligences'.

Different types of intelligence may be no more than differences in cognitive style…

Morgan claims that each of Gardner's eight types of intelligence is no more than a different cognitive style, (i.e. preferred ways of solving problems) rather than a distinct type of intelligence.

For example, Morgan argues that 'spatial Intelligence' is highly compatible with the cognitive style construct of 'breadth of categorisation'.

There are implications for assessment…

Gardner claimed that the assessment of intelligence should involve multiple measures rather than relying on one single measure of IQ. A single measure provides too little information for educational intervention. As such, Gardner believes that the primary purpose of assessment in education is to help children rather than rank them.

IDA *There is a cultural bias in this theory*…

It is clear from research that some intelligences are more highly valued than others in different cultures. For example, in China, mathematical intelligence is very highly valued, whereas bodily-kinaesthetic and natural intelligence are less highly valued.

A consequence of this is that…

Individuals in some countries (e.g. China) are considered 'intelligent' if they possess particular, more highly valued, forms of intelligence. This undermines the importance of other types of intelligence proposed by Gardner in those cultures.

Chapter 7

| Classical conditioning |

Theories of intelligence | Operant conditioning
Animal learning and intelligence > | Conditioning and the behaviour of animals
Intelligence and learning > Evolution of intelligence | Intelligence in non-human animals

Classical conditioning

The nature of classical conditioning

Classical conditioning explains learning thus:

A reflex consists of an unconditioned (i.e. unlearned) stimulus and its naturally associated response. By repeatedly associating a neutral stimulus with this unconditioned stimulus, it is possible to produce the same response even in the absence of the unconditioned stimulus.

IDA *Real-world application*…

In advertising, humans can be conditioned to associate neutral stimuli (such as cars, coffee or perfume) with stimuli that already make them feel good (e.g. lifestyle, celebrity, humour etc.).

Gorn concluded that consumer attitudes and behaviour are particularly susceptible to classical conditioning. More recent studies have not provided such strong support of the value of classical conditioning in explaining the impact of advertising.

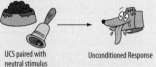
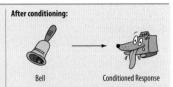
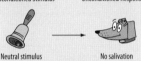

Before conditioning:

Unconditioned Stimulus — Unconditioned Response

Neutral stimulus — No salivation

During conditioning:

UCS paired with neutral stimulus — Unconditioned Response

After conditioning:

Bell — Conditioned Response

Characteristics of classical conditioning

Acquisition

Prior to conditioning, the neutral stimulus (NS) doesn't bring about a response, but after many pairings of the unconditioned stimulus (UCS) and NS, this changes.

If the NS is able to produce the same response *in the absence* of the UCS, it becomes a conditioned stimulus (CS) and produces a conditioned response (CR).

Timing

Precise timing of NS–UCS pairing is important in determining whether the NS becomes a reliable CS.

- NS precedes UCS = strong conditioning.
- The longer the delay after NS before onset of UCS = weaker conditioning.
- NS at same time as UCS = weak conditioning as cannot *predict* UCS.
- NS after UCS = ineffective conditioning.

Extinction and spontaneous recovery

Extinction – CS–CR link does not last very long after the removal of the UCS because CS no longer predicts the coming of the UCS.

Spontaneous recovery – If CS and UCS are paired together again in the future, link between them is made more rapidly, suggesting it had merely been inhibited.

Generalisation and discrimination

Stimulus generalisation – If a stimulus is presented that is similar to the CS but isn't the CS, then it still produces the CR.

Stimulus discrimination – If one NS is presented with a UCS and other NS are presented that are not associated with it, eventually only the former develops into a CS.

The neutral stimulus may not be truly neutral…

Domjan suggests that the NS cannot be totally unrelated to the UCS in the natural environment. For one to predict the other, they must occur together frequently in an animal's environment. It they didn't, there would be no predictive value in the NS and conditioning would not take place.

Taste aversion learning…

Doesn't require NS and UCS to occur closely together in time nor require many repetitions of NS–UCS association for conditioning to take place. Very resistant to extinction and persists long after withdrawal of UCS. This challenges traditional classical conditioning theory which requires:

- That the NS and UCS should be paired together many times before conditioning can take place.
- That delay between NS and UCS is critical, yet in taste aversion learning this can be several hours and still lead to strong conditioning.
- That the withdrawal of UCS means extinction sets in rapidly, yet in taste aversion this time period is far beyond what we might expect.

Is classical conditioning universal?…

Species differ in terms of their motives, cognitive capacities and the degree to which their lives depend on learning. Each species' genetic make-up would place limitations on its learning abilities, which therefore means that the principles of classical conditioning cannot be applied in the same way across all species or even all situations.

IDA An evolutionary perspective – biological 'preparedness'…

Relationships between CS and UCS are more difficult to establish for some species than others because different species typically face different challenges, therefore must learn some things more rapidly than others in order to survive. Animals are *prepared* to learn associations that are significant in terms of their survival needs; *unprepared* to learn associations that are not significant in this respect; *contraprepared* if, after many associations of NS and UCS, no learning occurs.

There is evidence for preparedness…

Mineka observed that rhesus monkeys reared in captivity experienced no fear of snakes, but monkeys captured in the wild displayed a frenzied panic when confronted by a snake. However, when the lab-reared monkeys were shown a film of wild monkeys acting fearfully in the presence of a snake, they rapidly acquired the same fearful reaction.

Operant conditioning

Operant conditioning theory explains learning thus:

Spontaneous behaviours (operants) produce reactions in other animals or in the environment, i.e. they have *consequences*.

Whether or not a particular behaviour reappears depends on these consequences, desirable consequences leading to greater frequency of response and undesirable consequences to lower frequency.

Reinforcement

A reinforcer is something in the animal's environment that is a consequence of a particular behaviour and makes that behaviour more likely to recur.

- *Positive reinforcement* – Behaviour produces a consequence that is satisfying or pleasant to the animal.
- *Negative reinforcement* – Behaviour terminates something that the animal finds unpleasant. Negative reinforcers strengthen a behaviour because they remove an aversive stimulus.
- An animal may learn to avoid an aversive stimulus completely by responding to a stimulus that precedes it (*avoidance conditioning*).

Schedules of reinforcement

Reinforcement can either be *continuous* (i.e. full) or *partial*. Partial reinforcement schedules are more effective at maintaining a behaviour.

- *Fixed-ratio* – Animal receives reinforcement for a fixed proportion of responses (e.g. every 10th response).
- *Variable-ratio* – Animal receives reinforcement for fixed percentage of responses (e.g. 60%), although the number of responses required before each reinforcement is unpredictable.
- *Fixed-interval* – Animal reinforced after fixed period (e.g. every ten minutes) provided it performs the behaviour.
- *Variable-interval* – Animal receives reinforcement at certain time intervals (e.g. four per hour) but at varying intervals between each reinforcement.

Punishment

Reinforcement increases the likelihood of a behaviour recurring, whereas punishment *decreases* it.

- *Positive punishment* means adding an unpleasant consequence (e.g. an electric shock) after a behaviour.
- *Negative punishment* means taking away something pleasant (e.g. removing a dog's food after it has growled at someone).

There is the problem of instinctive drift...

Not only are some behaviours easier to learn because the animal is biologically prepared to learn them, but they can also override more artificial conditioned behaviours.

For example, Breland and Breland trained animals to perform cute, human-like behaviours using operant conditioning techniques. Over time, however, their conditioned behaviours deteriorated as the animals' more natural behaviours intruded on their performance. Breland and Breland called this *'instinctive drift'*.

Positive reinforcement may be more influential than negative...

Lalli *et al.* compared the effects of either positive reinforcement (food) or negative reinforcement (taking a break from a tedious task) on compliance behaviour. Results showed that compliance was higher when it led to food (positive reinforcement) rather than a break (negative), suggesting that positive reinforcement is at least as influential if not more influential than negative reinforcement in conditioning.

The definition of reinforcement is circular...

The explanation of reinforcement has been criticised as being circular, as it suggests that the frequency with which a behaviour is performed is determined solely by reinforcement. Reinforcement is, in turn, then defined as something that increases the frequency with which a behaviour is performed.

However...

The correct usage of the term reinforcement is that something is a reinforcer *only* because of its effect on behaviour, therefore this breaks the circular nature of the definition.

IDA Real-world application...

The power of operant conditioning has been demonstrated in behaviour modification (replacing undesirable with desirable behaviours). Research has shown that operant conditioning techniques have been used successfully to help people avoid obesity, give up smoking and in toilet training (e.g. Azrin and Foxx).

IDA Problems with the use of non-human animals...

Skinner's reliance on rats and pigeons for his experiments on operant conditioning has led some critics to suggest that such studies can neither confirm nor refute hypotheses about *human* behaviour.

However...

Skinner's reliance on the experimental method allowed him to establish a cause and effect relationship between the consequences of a behaviour and its future frequency of occurrence.

IDA The illusion of free will...

Skinner believed that all behaviour was the result of either positive or negative reinforcement, and therefore any perception of free will was an illusion. What we may think of as behaviours chosen by free will are really behaviours that are determined by external influences (e.g. parents, educators) within our culture.

IDA There are cultural differences in reliance on conditioning...

These reflect the dangers that confront a particular society, e.g. the Gusii of Kenya have a history of tribal warfare and face constant threats from wild animals. As a result, Gusii parents make more frequent use of punishment than reward to shape appropriate behaviour in their children.

There are problems with punishment...

Because reinforcement cannot, by itself, eliminate undesirable behaviours, punishment becomes necessary. However, it is often used in ways that render it ineffective.

For example, the individual may come to fear the person doing the punishing, rather than the action that led to the punishment. If children are punished physically for their transgressions, they may learn that problems can be solved with violence, which legitimates it for them.

Chapter 7

Theories of intelligence

Classical conditioning
Operant conditioning

Animal learning and intelligence > Conditioning and the behaviour of animals

Intelligence and learning > Evolution of intelligence

Intelligence in non-human animals

Conditioning and the behaviour of animals

Classical conditioning

Training animals for release

Animals are sometimes held in captivity prior to release. This creates a problem because they become dependent on humans, e.g. learning that feeding is associated with human presence.

- *Simple conditioning* – Among captive dolphins, food (the UCS) always appears in the presence of humans (NS) and never when they are absent. This means that dolphins learn a strong association between humans and food, which puts them in danger when back in the wild.
- *Compound conditioning* – The learned association between human and food can be prevented by combining the human presence with a more appropriate stimulus (e.g. an auditory stimulus). For captive dolphins an auditory stimulus is a more reliable predictor because it *always* precedes food, whereas humans do not (i.e. they sometimes appear without food).

There is a problem with the use of compound conditioning…

It would be difficult and even undesirable to totally isolate many species completely from humans. Goldblatt, in a review of research on captive animal stress, concluded that understimulating environments, including those totally devoid of human contact, were more likely to be associated with stress responses in a wide range of species, including marine mammals.

Training animals for release is a necessity because…

A critical objective in caring for animals in captivity is to ensure that they do not learn responses that they will transfer to the wild and that will endanger them there. This means that the researcher cannot rely on learned associations between humans and food extinguishing naturally; they must prevent them from being learned in the first place.

IDA There are ethical issues with using animals for research…

The use of conditioning techniques in the training of animals while in captivity may both create and alleviate problems for these animals. Reliance on humans for food may create learned patterns of behaviour that prevent their post-release adjustment. However, the use of compound conditioning techniques may go some way to alleviating this.

Reproductive success

Researchers have puzzled over why the CR has developed. One possibility is increased reproductive success.

For example, a CS that occurs before mating (e.g. a signal from the female) serves to predict mating opportunities and therefore would increase an animal's reproductive success if they can respond appropriately to the CS.

There is evidence to support this…

The importance of classical conditioning in reproductive success is demonstrated in a laboratory study using quail. Matthews *et al.* found that male birds that received a CS signal prior to mating fertilised more than double the number of eggs compared to males who received no CS.

An arbitrary CS–UCS association is not adaptive in the natural environment… this is because the CS-UCS pairing must occur regularly in the natural environment. If it does not, this would undermine any learned association as such accidental pairings of CS and UCS would be rare.

Operant conditioning

Foraging

Animals are subject to the principles of operant conditioning as they forage in their environment.

For example, woodpeckers are reinforced for pecking a certain tree if they find insects there. They return to that spot frequently because of that reinforcement. When the supply of insects becomes exhausted, the pecking response is gradually extinguished.

There is evidence to support…

The role of operant conditioning in foraging strategies among non-human animals is supported by a study of foraging behaviour in monkeys. Agetsuma manipulated the quality of food patches frequented by monkeys by making the probability of food higher in one patch than another. Consistent with an operant conditioning prediction, subsequent visits were more frequent to the high-quality patch than the low-quality patch.

Positive reinforcement training (PRT)

Desensitisation – Pairing positive rewards with objects or procedures that cause fear so that they become less frightening and less stressful.

Cooperative feeding – Dominant animals are rewarded for allowing subordinate animals to feed and subordinate animals for being 'brave' enough to accept food in the presence of dominant animals.

The use of PRT events has been associated with enhanced psychological wellbeing of animals used in research.

There is supporting evidence for PRT…

Bloomsmith *et al.* used PRT to train dominant chimpanzees not to chase and steal subordinate's food by reinforcing behaviours incompatible with chasing and stealing (e.g. sitting in one spot while feeding). This had the desired effect of decreasing aggression from dominants and submission from subordinates during feeding periods.

Clay *et al.* used PRT with macaques to desensitise them from feeling fearful in the presence of humans. A group who received positive reinforcement whenever they were in the laboratory environment subsequently showed less fearful behaviour than a control group who were simply exposed to the same environment without reinforcement.

IDA PRT deals with ethical issues in animal research…

PRT has alleviated many of the stressors associated with research participation, and has satisfied both the requirements of the Animal Welfare Act, and the needs of the different species used in research.

Chapter 7

Theories of intelligence | Classical conditioning
Operant conditioning
Animal learning and intelligence > | Conditioning and the behaviour of animals
Intelligence and learning > | Evolution of intelligence | Intelligence in non-human animals

Intelligence in non-human animals

Machiavellian intelligence

Social problem solving

Intelligence may be an adaptation to social problem solving in large groups.

Individual animals that are able to manipulate others in their group without causing aggression are at an advantage and possess Machiavellian intelligence.

Manipulation and deception

Social-living animals can use behavioural tactics to manipulate and deceive others for their own ends. This ability is restricted to the great apes.

Manipulative tricks include:

- *Management of attention* – Target's attention is diverted to or away from something so as to profit the deceiver.
- *Creating an image* – Deception changes the way the target views the individual (e.g. grooming prior to snatching food).

Forming alliances

Power in social groups is often determined more by having the right allies than by physical strength.

Many apes form alliances based on an individual's ability to provide useful help in the future. For example, males may form alliances with more powerful individuals.

A female ape may behave in Machiavellian ways by having sex with a dominant male to increase the likelihood that he will protect her and her offspring.

There is support for the existence of Machiavellian intelligence…

Studies of agonistic buffering (Deag and Crook) showed that subordinate Barbary macaque monkeys would sometimes carry an infant monkey when approaching a high-ranking male to reduce the likelihood of being attacked by the dominant male.

Machiavellian intelligence may not be restricted to primates…

The idea that intelligence and social complexity are linked is supported by research which suggests an important role of the neocortex in the rise of Machiavellian intelligence in primates.

Burish *et al.* have also provided evidence for this relationship in birds where the degree of social complexity is positively related to the size of the *telencephalon* (equivalent to cortex) in the brain.

A consequence of Machiavellian intelligence…

More highly developed social intellect in some individuals will exert selection pressures on others, so that over evolutionary time, there will be an 'arms race' of social intelligence within a particular species.

Machiavellian intelligence alone may not be enough…

Maestripieri found evidence for many of the behaviours associated with Machiavellian intelligence (e.g. forming alliances, strategic sexual alliances with dominant males) in a colony of rhesus macaques.

However… The macaques failed on another criterion of intelligence – self-recognition. Rhesus macaques will viciously attack their own image in a mirror, suggesting that they do not recognise it as their own image.

IDA *A biological approach to Machiavellian intelligence…*

Byrne and Corp found a positive correlation between the amount of tactical deception used by a species and their typical neocortex volume. Among primate species, neocortex volume varies much more than the volume of other brain areas. Neocortical enlargement appears necessary to give individuals sufficient memory to develop the extensive social knowledge necessary for Machiavellian intelligence.

Self-recognition

Research into self-recognition

The ability of an animal to recognise itself in a mirror is usually accepted as indicating a form of intelligence.

- *Chimpanzees* – Gallup found that chimpanzees used their image in a mirror to touch a red mark placed on their forehead and ears.
- *Dolphins* – Reiss and Marino used either a black ink marker or a 'sham marker' that was just water. They found that those marked with black ink spent longer in front of reflective surfaces.
- *Killer whales* – A similar study using killer whales (Delfour and Marten) found that they also appear to possess the cognitive abilities necessary for self-recognition.

Why species differ

Self-recognition may result from large brains and advanced cognitive ability rather than species-specific characteristics.

For example, dolphins and primates have a very different evolutionary history, but both possess large brains and self-recognition.

Self-recognition may be evident in other species also…

Research by Plotnik *et al.* suggests that elephants are also able to recognise themselves in a mirror, a key criterion for 'intelligence'. The researchers found that the elephants used the mirror to guide them, touching a mark on the side of their head.

However… There remains the possibility that the elephants simply touched the mark because they felt it on their skin, therefore did not possess self-recognition. The researchers overcame this possibility by also using a transparent mark, which would have felt the same yet was largely ignored by the animals.

There is a general lack of research support for this…

Heyes argues that there is little reliable evidence that self-recognition is present in all primate species. First of all, the fact that chimpanzees may use a mirror to explore parts of their body is unconvincing as a demonstration of self-recogniton, Second, not all chimpanzees pass the mark test. Thus, Heyes claims that the evidence does not indicate the possession of a self-concept or other aspect of self-recognition that might be equivalent to the cognitive abilities of human beings.

IDA *There are ethical issues associated with this research…*

The rarity of self-recognition among non-human species and the fact that it is more common in species that help other individuals in need indicates a certain level of consciousness in these animals.

This emphasises the need to extend many of the ethical issues currently associated with humans to these species and to protect species such as the Asian elephant, which is currently on the endangered list.

Chapter 7

	Theories of intelligence	Evolutionary factors in human intelligence
	Animal learning and intelligence	Genetic factors in intelligence-test performance
Intelligence and learning >	Evolution of intelligence >	Environmental factors in intelligence-test performance

Evolutionary factors in human intelligence

Heritable characteristics such as intelligence are changeable rather than fixed, and likely to be caused by natural or sexual selection.

The measure of evolutionary success is reproductive fitness.

Ecological demands

These are aspects of the environment that must be adapted to in order to survive. Two such demands are:

• *Finding food* – Intelligence evolved because of an increased cognitive demand on frugivores to monitor a food supply that was only available at certain times and locations.

• *Extracting food* – Tool use is an indication of intelligence in non-human and human species. A study of chimpanzees by Mercader *et al.* found evidence of tool use. Successful hunter-gatherer groups (e.g. *!Kung San*) use elaborate tools, whereas less successful groups use simple tools.

Social complexity

Individuals who best dealt with the demands of group living increased their reproductive fitness. This involves:

• *Machiavellian intelligence* – Whiten and Byrne suggest the evolution of human intellect was primarily driven by the need to deal with problems posed by group members. This selective pressure led to Machiavellian intelligence (see page 64).

• *The meat-sharing hypothesis* – Meat was an important source of saturated fat for early humans. Meat could be used to forge alliances and to persuade females to mate. Strategic meat-sharing requires considerable cognitive abilities to keep a running score of debts and credits.

Brain size and intelligence

Broman found that measures of head size at birth and at age seven significantly predicted later IQ.

The use of MRI allows researchers to measure brain size more directly. Studies (e.g. Andreasen *et al.*) have found significant correlations of around +.40 using this method.

Evolutionary factors in the development of large brains

• *Innovation, social learning and tool use* provide a measure of behavioural flexibility of a species. Reader and Laland found the frequency of all three was positively correlated with brain size in 116 primate species.

• *Sexual selection* – Miller suggests that large brains evolved in humans because they enhanced reproductive success, with intelligence attractive to the opposite sex.

Ecological versus social theories of intelligence…

Dunbar found that only social complexity correlated with neocortex volume, suggesting that the social demands of group living shaped human intelligence more than the demands of the physical environment.

However… Byrne claims that group size alone cannot explain why apes are more intelligent than monkeys, as both species live in groups of similar size and complexity.

IDA *Cultural bias in the brain size and intelligence relationship…*

Beals *et al.* found significant differences in cranial volume between East Asians, Europeans and Africans. Rushton explains this in terms of the 'Out of Africa' hypothesis, in that early humans left Africa and encountered more cognitive demanding problems to stay alive. This led to larger brain sizes in East Asians.

However…

Higher levels of intelligence found in East Asians (Jensen and Rushton) may also be due to the fact that intelligence is more highly valued in East Asian cultures.

IDA *Gender differences in brain size…*

Ankney found male brains were consistently heavier than female brains, yet there is no difference in IQ levels in men and women (Peters).

This may be explained by the possibility that brain organisation is more important than brain size and female brains are better organised.

There is evidence to support the Machiavellian intelligence hypothesis…

Mitani and Watts provide support for the importance of alliances (a key aspect of Machiavellian intelligence) and the role of meat-sharing among primates. They found that male chimpanzees were more likely to share meat with other males than with females. This is important in forging alliances because hunting is more successful when carried out in groups.

Consequently, it may be 'meat for alliance' rather than 'meat for sex' that explains the strategic importance of meat-sharing.

There is evidence to support the meat-sharing hypothesis…

Hill and Kaplan found that among the *Ache* people of Paraguay, meat is frequently shared outside of the family. Skilled hunters are rewarded with disproportionate sexual favours from women in the group.

However…

Wrangham suggests a simpler explanation for this. Males must expend considerable energy defending a kill or deterring scavengers. By sharing with others, they can eat without interruption.

Brain size does not correlate with all types of intelligence…

Witelson *et al.* studied the brains of 100 adults. Before their death the adults had completed a full IQ test as part of the study. Researchers found that performance on the test correlated with brain volume, but the relationship depended on the type of intelligence studied, with only verbal intelligence having a significant relationship with brain volume.

There are problems associated with large brain size…

Large brains are extremely demanding in terms of energy, and must compete with other body organs for resources. A large brain takes longer to mature, which means that infants are heavily dependent on their parents for much longer, which in turn limits how quickly they reach reproductive age. Given these factors, we might expect there would be considerable selective pressure *against* the evolution of large brains.

Large brains are not only found in humans…

Despite the costs associated with large brains, progressively larger brains have evolved in all primates, not just in humans. Reader and Laland's research challenges the view that large brains arose in human beings because of the development of uniquely human characteristics such as language. Many other primates have brains of a similar relative size (in terms of body/brain size), yet lack language.

Chapter 7

Theories of intelligence	Evolutionary factors in human intelligence
Animal learning and intelligence	**Genetic factors in intelligence-test performance**
Intelligence and learning >	Evolution of intelligence >	Environmental factors in intelligence-test performance

Genetic factors in intelligence-test performance

Twin studies

Dizygotic twins (DZ) share 50% of their genes, monozygotic (MZ) share 100%.

Because it is difficult to disentangle the effects of genes and environment, the real value of twin studies comes from twins who are raised apart.

Bouchard and McGue found that the concordance rate (the degree to which IQ is the same for two related individuals) was 60% for DZ twins reared together, but this was higher (72%) for MZ twins reared apart, suggesting a stronger genetic component for IQ.

Malouff et al. carried out a meta-analysis that covered more than 400 twin studies. The overall finding was that approximately half of the variation in IQ test scores could be attributed to genetics.

There are problems with twin studies…

Kamin and Goldberger claim that the result of twin studies may overestimate the heritability of intelligence. They argue that MZ twins share a more similar environment than DZ twins because they are identical. Therefore, some of the estimated similarity that is attributed to genetic influences may be the product of a shared environment instead.

Twins may not be a representative group…

Voracek and Haubner carried out a meta-analysis of studies that had compared more than 30,000 twins and nearly 1.6 million singletons (non-twins). On average, twins score more than 4 IQ points lower than singletons. Consequently, this may lead to a biased estimation of the heritability of intelligence.

IDA A sub-cultural bias in the study of genetic factors…

Turkheimer et al. have identified a potential bias in the reporting of studies in this area, i.e. that the same gene can have different effects in different environments. They found that in children from affluent families, about 60% of the variance in IQ scores could be accounted for by genes. However, for children from poorer backgrounds, genes accounted for almost none of the variance in their IQ scores.

Adoption studies

Adoption studies compare the IQ of adopted children with other members of their adoptive and biological families.

If genetic factors influence intelligence, research should find a greater similarity between IQ scores of adopted children and their biological families than with their adoptive families.

The Texas Adoption Project (Horn et al.) studied adopted children on two occasions, ten years apart. When first assessed, IQs correlated more strongly with the IQs of their adoptive parents than their biological mothers. However, ten years later, correlations were higher with their biological mothers.

This suggests that the impact of family influences decreases with age, while the impact of genetic influences increases.

There is evidence to support these findings…

The conclusions for the Texas Adoption Project were supported by findings from another large-scale adoption project (the Colorado Adoption Project), which also found that adopted children have an increasing tendency to resemble their biological mother's IQ as they age and a decreasing tendency to resemble the IQ of their adoptive parents.

There are some contradictory findings…

Several studies have challenged the conclusion of the Texas Adoption Project (e.g. Schiff et al.). These studies have demonstrated substantial IQ gains in children adopted from impoverished biological parents to middle-class adoptive homes. For example, transferring an infant from a family having low socioeconomic status (SES) to a home where parents have high SES improves childhood IQ scores by 12 to 16 points.

IDA Genetic 'influences' may be due to selective placement…

Nisbett claims that children are often adopted into environments similar to the ones they came from, which would explain why correlations for IQ between adopted children and their biological family remain high.

A gene for intelligence

IGF2R gene

Hill et al. divided children into 'super-bright' and 'average' groups. Twice as many of the children in the super-bright group had a particular variant of the IGF2R gene than in the average group. They concluded that this form of the gene contributes to high intelligence test performance.

Genetic markers for intelligence

Curtis et al. studied the DNA of more than 7,000 children. They found six genetic markers that showed any sign of influencing IQ test scores. However, after subjecting the data to more stringent statistical tests, only one gene passed, and this accounted for just 0.4% of the variation in IQ scores.

The IGF2R gene cannot cause high IQ on its own…

More than half of the children in the 'super-bright' group did not have this variant of the gene. Similarly, some of the children in the 'average' group did have this variant of the IGF2R gene. This clearly indicates that many other factors, some genetic, some environmental, must contribute to the overall level of intelligence possessed by any one individual.

IDA Research into genetic markers is socially sensitive…

The discovery of any genes associated with high IQ could divide society by marginalising and discriminating against those individuals who did not possess these 'IQ genes'. This also highlights the importance of the peer review process, which aims to ensure that only properly controlled studies with appropriate conclusions are allowed to be published.

Genes can also mould the environment…

Genes may also influence behaviour in terms of how intelligence develops, by moulding the intellectual environment in particular ways. For example, genes may cause us to seek out some experiences rather than others, which in turn affects our intelligence for better or worse.

Chapter 7

| Theories of intelligence | Evolutionary factors in human intelligence |
| Animal learning and intelligence | Genetic factors in intelligence-test performance |

| Intelligence and learning > | Evolution of intelligence > | **Environmental factors in intelligence-test performance** |

Environmental factors in intelligence-test performance

Family environment

Socioeconomic status (SES)

In the UK, SES is determined by parental occupation from Class I (professional) to Class V (unskilled).

Mackintosh found that even after factors such as financial hardship and area of residence were taken into account, children of Class I fathers scored, on average, 10 IQ points higher than children of Class V fathers.

Why does SES influence intelligence?

Families with high SES are better able to prepare their children for school because they have better access to resources (e.g. the Internet) and information (e.g. from better educated parents) essential to children's cognitive and intellectual development.

IDA Real-world application…

If SES has such a strong effect on intelligence, then improvements in SES should produce a corresponding increase in IQ. Adoption studies where low SES children have been adopted into high SES families (e.g. Schiff *et al.*) have demonstrated substantial IQ gains in those children.

Birth order and family size

Belmont and Marolla studied family size, birth order and IQ in a sample of 386 19-year-old Dutch men. They found that, when SES was controlled, children from larger families had a lower IQ than children from small families, and first-born children typically had higher IQ than later-born children.

There is research evidence to support these effects…

Bjerkedal *et al.* confirmed the importance of birth order in a Norwegian sample. They found that first-born children had higher IQs than later-born children and also found that when a first-born child had died, the second-born scored closer to the IQ score of an average first-born child.

Birth order effects on IQ may be short-lived…

A study (Blake) of more than 100,000 people found that in small- and medium-sized families, birth order had no effect on how far adults progressed in education, suggesting that birth order effects do not persist.

Education

School effects

Ceci carried out a meta-analysis to see if school boosts intelligence. He found that children who attended school regularly scored higher in tests of IQ than those who attended less regularly, and that IQ scores decreased over the long summer holidays. IQ scores were also found to rise by an average of 2.7 points for each year of formal education completed.

Compensatory education

The *Perry Preschool Project* provided high-quality preschool education to African-American children living in poverty and considered at high risk of school failure. When the children started school, 67% of those in the programme group had IQs greater than 90, whereas only 28% of those not involved in the programme scored above 90.

Not everybody agrees that education has such an effect…

Herrnstein and Murray claim that intelligence is mostly genetically heritable, and that no one has been able to manipulate IQ to a significant degree through changes in environmental factors such as improved education.

As a result, they argue that attempts to raise IQ through compensatory education are doomed to failure.

Explaining contradictory viewpoints…

These contradictory claims (i.e. Ceci versus Herrnstein and Murray) can be explained in two ways.

- There is a failure to define what constitutes 'an improvement'. Both would accept that education has an effect, but disagree on the size of that effect and how it might be measured.
- Herrnstein and Murray base their view on an acceptance of the concept of '*g*' and a belief that this can be accurately measured by IQ tests. This view is challenged by theorists such as Sternberg (see page 59) and Gardner (see page 60) who both argue that intelligence is multidimensional and so any attempts to measure the success of an educational programme with a single IQ test would be meaningless.

Culture

Group socialisation theory

Harris claims that experiences outside the home may be more important in developing a child's intelligence than experiences within it. As children grow older, they are less influenced by their family life, and more influenced by life outside the home (e.g. peer groups).

The group socialisation explanation is rejected…

Pinker argues that the interaction between genes and peer group influence is a possible explanation for some behaviours (e.g. smoking), but there is little, if any, evidence for an influence on intelligence.

IDA A physiological explanation for the influence of poverty on IQ…

Kishiyama *et al.* found that children from low SES backgrounds showed a lower prefrontal cortex response to novel stimuli; possibly a consequence of a stressful and impoverished environment that is often associated with low SES.

Ethnicity and IQ

Herrnstein and Murray found that immigrants to the US had IQ levels that were significantly lower than US residents. They argued that immigration into the US created a downward pressure on intelligence levels, and an increase in the social problems typically associated with people with low IQ.

IDA IQ tests are culturally biased…

Greenfield argues that assessing the IQ of people from cultures other than the one in which the test was developed represents a cultural bias (an imposed etic). This inevitably influences any results when such tests are used and leads to invalid conclusions about the measure of IQ in such groups.

Cognition and development

Division A Development of thinking

Piaget's theory of cognitive development
Vygotsky's theory of cognitive development
Bruner's theory of cognitive development
Applications of these theories to education

Division B Development of moral understanding

Kohlberg's theory of moral understanding
Eisenberg's theory of prosocial reasoning

Division C Development of social cognition

Development of a child's sense of self
Development of a child's understanding of others
Biological explanations of social cognition

Specification

Cognition and development	
Development of thinking	• Theories of cognitive development, including Piaget, Vygotsky and Bruner. • Applications of these theories to education.
Development of moral understanding	• Theories of moral understanding (Kohlberg) and/or prosocial reasoning (Eisenberg).
Development of social cognition	• Development of the child's sense of self, including Theory of Mind (Baron-Cohen). • Development of children's understanding of others, including perspective-taking (Selman). • Biological explanations of social cognition, including the role of the mirror neuron system.

Chapter 8

Development of thinking >

Development of moral understanding

Cognition and development > Development of social cognition

Piaget's theory of cognitive development

Vygotsky's theory of cognitive development

Bruner's theory of cognitive development

Applications of these theories to education

Piaget's theory of cognitive development

Mechanisms of cognitive development

Maturation and the environment

As a child gets older (maturation), certain mental operations become possible and at the same time, through interactions with the environment, their understanding of the world becomes more complex.

Key mechanisms

Schema are self-constructed mental structures for dealing with the world. Some are innate but most are learned as a consequence of the child's interaction with the environment.

Assimilation occurs when an existing schema (such as sucking) is used on a new object (such as a toy car). It involves the incorporation of new information into an existing schema.

Accommodation occurs when a child adapts existing schema in order to understand new information that doesn't appear to fit.

Equilibration drives cognitive development. An imbalance between existing thinking and what is encountered in the child is dealt with using assimilation or accommodation until equilibrium is restored.

Operations are logical mental rules such as the rules of arithmetic.

There is little direct research support…

Inhelder *et al.* found that children's learning was helped when there was a mild conflict between what they expected to happen and what did happen, but Bryant claims that this wasn't really the sort of conflict that Piaget was talking about.

Limitations of Piaget's theory…

The research evidence given below (e.g. Samuel and Bryant) suggests that Piaget underestimated children's abilities at younger ages, and may have overestimated the ability to use abstract logic at older ages.

His theory focuses too much on logic and generally ignores social factors, such as the benefit of cooperative group work.

The research methods he used were flawed, e.g.:
- He used a biased sample of middle-class Western children who value logical thinking.
- The research designs may have confused younger children, e.g. the three mountains task was unrealistic (Hughes), younger children were confused by two questions in the conservation task (Samuel and Bryant), the conservation transformation acted as a demand characteristic (McGarrigle and Donaldson).

Strengths of Piaget's theory…

Subsequent evidence from critics (see below) still supports qualitative changes in cognitive development as a child matures.

Piaget's main contribution was in increasing our understanding of the qualitative differences between child and adult thinking.

IDA *Real-world application… to education* (see page 72)

Stages in cognitive development

Stage 1: Sensorimotor (0–2 years)

Children learn to coordinate sensory input (e.g. what they see) with motor actions (e.g. hand movements) through circular reactions. They lack an understanding of object permanence.

Nativists claim that infants have more knowledge…

Baillargeon and DeVos showed that infants as young as 3–4 months did display object permanence, using a carrot rolled on a toy train set behind a screen with a large window. A large carrot should be visible as it passes behind the window, whereas a small carrot (not as broad) should remain hidden. The infants looked longer for the large carrot when it didn't appear, presumably expecting the top half to be visible.

Stage 2: Pre-operational (2–7)

Children's thought becomes symbolic but they are not capable of *reversibility of thought* because they rely on perceptual rather than internally consistent logical reasoning (appearance–reality distinction). Children are also egocentric.

There is research evidence…

Piaget illustrated pre-operational thinking using the three mountains task. Children 3–4 years old chose their own perspective when asked for the dolls' perspective.

However…

Hughes showed that younger children could cope with the task if it was more realistic, for example, using a naughty boy doll that was hiding from a toy policeman.

Stage 3: Concrete operational (7–11)

Children acquire the rudiments of *logical reasoning*, and display skills of *reversibility* and decentration (no longer focusing on just one aspect of a task). This means that they are capable of *conservation* (e.g. recognising quantities don't change even if they look different).

There is research evidence…

Children younger than seven weren't able to conserve when tested using rows of counters, cylinders of plasticine, or beakers of water. Each display was transformed so the quantity *appeared* to have increased (e.g. the counters were spread out) i.e. if it looked bigger, it was bigger.

However…

Younger children can conserve if not confused by questions and only asked one question (after the transformation) (Samuel and Bryant).

Stage 4: Formal operational (11+)

Children can now solve abstract problems using hypothetico-deductive reasoning (e.g. testing hypotheses) and idealistic thinking (they are no longer tied to how things are, but can imagine how things might be).

There is research evidence…

Piaget and Inhelder demonstrated that younger children do not use logical thinking using the *beaker problem* (children asked to work out how to turn a liquid yellow by combining various liquids).

However…

Wason and Shapiro found that only 10% of university students could cope when given an abstract test of logical reasoning.

Dasen claims that only a third of adults ever reach this stage.

Vygotsky's theory of cognitive development

Mental processes

The importance of culture

The main theme of Vygotsky's theory is that social interaction plays a fundamental role in cognitive development.

Elementary and higher mental functions

Children are born with *elementary mental functions*, such as perception.

These are transformed into *higher mental functions* (such as use of mathematical systems) by the influence of culture. Higher mental functions are exclusively human.

What to think and how to think

Through culture, children acquire:
- The *content* of their thinking, i.e. their knowledge.
- The *processes* of their thinking, i.e. the tools of intellectual adaptation.

Process of cultural influence

The role of others: experts

A child learns through problem-solving experiences shared with an 'expert' (i.e. parent, teacher or more competent peer).

The expert guides problem solving activity, but gradually this ability to guide learning transfers to the child.

Semiotics and the role of language

Culture is transmitted by experts using *semiotics* (cultural signs and symbols such as language and mathematics).
- Language begins as shared dialogues (*preintellectual speech*).
- Around 2–3 years children use language to solve problems, often out loud (*egocentric speech*).
- About age 7, this gives way to silent or *inner speech*, which continues to be used as a way of reflecting upon and solving problems.

Zone of proximal development (ZPD)

The ZPD is the distance between what a child actually can do (determined by independent problem solving) and their potential (determined through problem solving under expert guidance).

The ZPD is the region where cognitive development is taking place. Learning between people (social) later becomes internalised (individual) i.e. 'internalisation'.

The social and individual levels

Every aspect of a child's cognitive development appears first at a social level (i.e. between the child and others), and later, at an individual level (i.e. inside the mind of the child).

Importance of culture supported by research…

Gredler cited the primitive counting system used in Papua New Guinea as an example of how culture can limit cognitive development, because using body parts alone makes it very difficult to deal with large numbers.

There is challenging research evidence…

Attempts to teach chimpanzees to use language (e.g. Savage-Rumbaugh) suggest that they can acquire higher mental functions.

Limitations of Vygotsky's theory…

This theory does not lend itself as readily to experimentation as Piaget's because the concepts are more difficult to operationalise.

Whereas Piaget underplayed social influences, Vygotsky may have overplayed the importance of the social environment – if social influence was all that was needed to advance cognitive development then learning would be a lot faster than it is.

Vygotsky's theory may lack detail because he died at such a young age and did not have time to fully develop it (Lindblom and Ziemke).

Strengths of Vygotsky's theory…

The Vygotskian approach provides a bridge between social and cognitive domains.

It is a more positive approach than Piaget's because it offers ways that others can be actively involved in assisting a learner.

In this way, Vygotsky's theory may potentially have more educational applications than Piaget's theory.

IDA *Real-world application… to education* (see page 72)

There is research evidence for the role of language in cognitive development…

The acquisition of a new word is the beginning of the development of a concept, illustrated in a study by Carmichael *et al.* where participants' recall of a drawing was influenced by the label given to it (e.g. a kidney shape labelled as a kidney bean or a canoe).

However…

Sinclair-de-Zwart tried to teach non-conserving children to use comparative terms such as bigger and shorter. She found very little improvement in their ability to conserve, a finding that does not support Vygotsky because his theory suggests that cultural tools (such as language) should lead to cognitive development.

There is research evidence…

McNaughton and Leyland observed young children working with their mothers or alone on jigsaw puzzles of increasing difficulty. The children could do more when working with their mothers than individually.
- When children were doing easy puzzles (below the child's ZPD) the mothers were mainly concerned with keeping them on task.
- When they were working within their ZPD, mothers focused on helping the children solve the puzzle themselves.
- At the third level (beyond the child's ZPD) the emphasis was on completing the puzzle by whatever means.

IDA *Comparing Piaget's approach with Vygotsky's…*

The two theories represent different styles of learning and different kinds of learner. Vygotsky was a communist believing in the power of society in the development of the individual; Piaget was a product of individualist European society. Piaget's child is an introvert, whereas Vygotsky's child is an extravert (Miller).

The theories have similarities; both emphasise the interactionist character of development, the importance of scientific thought and the learner as active rather than passive (Glassman).

Chapter 8

Development of thinking >

Cognition and development >

Piaget's theory of cognitive development
Vygotsky's theory of cognitive development
Development of moral understanding
Bruner's theory of cognitive development
Development of social cognition
Applications of these theories to education

Bruner's theory of cognitive development

Thinking

The organisation of knowledge

Thinking is based on categorisation.

People interpret the world in terms of similarities and differences, and use a coding system to store information.

This coding system consists of categories, which are organised into a hierarchy with more general categories at the top.

Culture

The categorisation structures that form the basis of knowledge reflect the views of a person's culture, e.g. the way different species of birds are culturally categorised.

Paradigmatic and narrative thinking

Paradigmatic thinking is logical thinking, which leads to the construction of categories and hierarchies.

Narrative thinking is a more interpretive approach, based on the assumption that the complicated and rich phenomena of life are better represented in stories or narratives.

Paradigmatic and narrative approaches generally complement each other, though paradigmatic thinking may block the ability to think narratively, because it makes us look for patterns and logic rather than focusing on subjective experience and creativity (Gardner).

There is research evidence for categorisation…

A century of research on human memory shows that 'unless detail is placed in a structured pattern, it is rapidly forgotten' (Bruner).

For example, Bower *et al.* showed that people remembered more when words were presented in hierarchies rather than randomly.

There is research evidence for Importance of culture…

Gredler cited the primitive counting system (using body parts) in Papua New Guinea as an example of how culture can limit cognitive development.

Carmichael *et al.*'s study showed how language affects categorisation (see facing page), another example of cultural influence on knowledge.

IDA *Different approaches…*

Bruner's theory is an example of a number of different approaches:

• A cognitive theory – explaining behaviour in terms of mental activity.

• An information-processing theory (like Piaget) – suggesting development occurs as mental structures become more elaborate and sophisticated through experience and maturation.

• A social constructionist approach (like Vygotsky) – emphasising the importance of social context in creating knowledge.

Limitations of Bruner's theory

The theory is more focused on thinking and learning than the development of these skills.

IDA *Real-world application… to education* (see page 72)

Bruner's focus on education has meant that his views have had a profound effect on education.

Modes of thinking and phases in development

Action, image and word

We represent the environment through three different modes; each one dominates particular phases of development:

• Enactive skills (early childhood), action-based skills including manipulating objects and spatial awareness, e.g. children can learn to play a musical instrument or learn to ski more quickly than an adult.

• Iconic skills (middle childhood), image-based skills, e.g. visual recognition and being able to compare and contrast items.

• Symbolic skills (dominant in adolescence), language-based skills that assist with abstract reasoning.

There is research evidence from the 'nine glasses experiment'…

• Nine glasses are placed on a 3×3 grid in order of height and diameter. A child participant is asked to describe the arrangement.

• Next, the glasses are removed and the child is asked to reproduce the pattern (a reproduction task).

• The glasses are again removed. The child is asked to transpose the display (so that the glass at the bottom left is now bottom right, etc).

The reproduction task is iconic because it involves reproducing a visual image, whereas transposition requires symbolic thinking.

Bruner and Kenney found that 60% of 5-year-olds could complete the reproduction task, but none could cope with the transposition task.

They also found that children who used words such as 'tall', 'wide', etc. in their description were more likely to be able to perform the transposition task, i.e. their ability to use language (a symbolic system) was vital to the task.

Development of thinking

Skilled behaviours act as modularised units, which can be combined in different ways to build up a repertoire of new skilled behaviours.

They also become automatic so that attention can be freed for other things.

Learning consists of 'spurts' when a number of smaller bits of knowledge accumulate (something 'clicks') and suddenly a whole new understanding is opened up.

It is the environment rather than age that slows down or speeds up learning.

Thinking develops through scaffolding…

Scaffolding is a 'process that enables a … novice to solve a problem, carry out a task, or achieve a goal which would be beyond his unassisted efforts' (Bruner).

Wood and Middleton studied scaffolding. Mothers were observed helping their 3–4-year-old children assembling a 3D pyramid puzzle, a task beyond the children's current abilities. Wood and Middleton found a positive correlation between children's independent task mastery and 'contingent regulations' – when a mother responds to her child's failure by providing more explicit instructions and responds to success by providing less explicit instructions.

Wood *et al.* produced a list of six key steps in the scaffolding process: recruitment, reduction in degrees of freedom, direction maintenance, marking critical features, frustration control and demonstration.

Chapter 8

Development of thinking >

Piaget's theory of cognitive development

Vygotsky's theory of cognitive development

Development of moral understanding

Bruner's theory of cognitive development

Cognition and development >

Development of social cognition

Applications of these theories to education

Applications of these theories to education

Applying Piaget's theory to education

Readiness

Piaget proposed that cognitive development is due to the process of ageing, therefore you can't teach a child to perform certain activities before they are biologically 'ready'.

Stages of development

Educational programmes should follow Piaget's stages of development.

Motivation to learn

Cognitive growth comes from the desire to resolve the disequilibrium caused by cognitive conflict. The teacher's role is not to impart knowledge, but to create an environment where the learner is challenged, so knowledge develops through discovery learning.

Logical thinking

Logical thinking is the spur to cognitive development and needs to be taught through maths and science.

There is research support for the notion of readiness…
Danner and Day found that students aged 10–13 showed no improvements when tutored on three formal operational tasks, whereas 17-year-olds (who were 'ready') did show significant improvements.

However…
Bryant and Trabasso showed that pre-operational children could be trained to solve logical tasks (by practising simple tasks first) and suggested that failure was due to memory restrictions rather than a lack of operational (logical) thinking (readiness).

However…
Even when practice does improve performance, this doesn't mean a child can transfer the understanding to a novel situation.

Limitations of the Piagetian approach…
Piagetian discovery activities are often at the expense of content knowledge and may lead to backwardness in reading and writing, because children spend too little time practising these skills (Modgil et al.).

IDA *Culture bias…*
The Piagetian view may be culture biased. It suggests that the child is the sole agent of his learning, which is an individualist approach.

Applying Vygotsky's theory to education

Collaborative learning

Students at various abilities work together in groups towards a common goal and shared understanding.

The more knowledgeable other (MKO)

Experts who guide learners through the ZPD can be a child's teacher or older adult, or a peer with more knowledge (*peer tutoring*).

Motivation to learn

The learner is motivated to move through their ZPD by MKOs using the process of scaffolding.

There is research support for the value of collaborative learning…
Students who participated in collaborative learning later performed better on an individual critical-thinking test than did students who studied individually (Gokhale).

There is research support for the value of peer tutoring…
Peer tutoring leads to improvements in tutees' performance (Cohen et al.); however, it is most effective for peer tutors (Cloward).

However, one confounding variable is… That experimental groups often receive peer tutoring in addition to normal lessons, thus receiving more instruction overall (Slavin).

IDA *Culture bias…*
Vygotsky's approach may be more appropriate in collectivist settings because true sharing is the basis of such cultures, whereas in individualist settings children are encouraged to be more competitive and self-reliant.

This is supported by… Stigler and Perry who found group work was more effective in Asian schools (collective culture) but not in American ones (individualist culture).

Applying Bruner's theory to education

Scaffolding

The process of offering assistance to a learner when it is necessary.

Spiral curriculum

Start 'difficult' concepts early and then revisit them repeatedly. Children may not fully understand the first time, but early learning acts as a basis for later learning.

Modes of thinking

Teachers should explain the world in a way that is appropriate to the child's mode of thinking.

Motivation to learn

The best stimulus for learning lies in the material to be learned. Academic subjects have intrinsic attraction, and don't have to be related to daily experience in order for children to be interested in learning.

There is research support…
Studies of scaffolding were described on the previous page.
Support for the value of the spiral curriculum is demonstrated by the fact that it is widely used, e.g. nursery schools, GP training.

General methodological issues…
It is difficult to assess and compare approaches because outcome measures depend on the aims of the technique and because teachers may adapt methods and they may thus not be comparable.
Scaffolding and the spiral curriculum are difficult strategies to test as they take place over a period of many years.

IDA *Comparing and contrasting the three approaches…*
All three approaches place importance on discovery (active) learning.
All approaches have influenced education practice; however, this may be because they provide 'after the fact' justifications for a new educational idea rather than being the original driving force (Walkerdine).
More traditional, formal, teacher-oriented approaches lead to higher attainment levels than active learning (Bennett). This may be because 'formal' teachers spend more time on core topics and because active learning requires more sensitivity and experience from teachers.

Chapter 8

Development of thinking
Development of moral understanding > Kohlberg's theory of moral understanding
Cognition and development > Development of social cognition | Eisenberg's theory of prosocial reasoning

Kohlberg's theory of moral understanding

General principles

Moral decisions

Kohlberg focused particularly on the way that children think about moral decisions rather than on their moral behaviour.

Stage theory

The theory was based on extensive interviews with boys aged 10 to 16. The boys were given moral dilemmas (e.g. the Heinz dilemma) and asked what should be done and why.

Each stage:
- Is invariant and universal.
- Represents a more equilibrated form of moral understanding, resulting in a more logically consistent and morally mature form of understanding.
- Forms an organised whole – a qualitatively different pattern of moral understanding applied across all situations.
- Moral maturity is achieved through (1) biological maturation, (2) disequilibrium (noticing weaknesses in existing style of thinking) and (3) gains in perspective-taking (understanding another's point of view).

Stages of moral development

I Preconventional level

Children accept the rules of authority figures and judge actions by their consequences. Actions that result in punishments are judged as bad, those that bring rewards are judged as good.

Stage 1 Punishment and obedience orientation

Stage 2 Instrumental purpose orientation

II Conventional level

Individuals continue to believe that conformity to social rules is desirable, but not out of self-interest. Maintaining the current social system ensures positive human relationships and social order.

Stage 3 Interpersonal cooperation

Stage 4 Social order maintaining orientation

III Post-conventional level

The post-conventional individual moves beyond unquestioning compliance with the norms of their own social system. They now define morality in terms of abstract moral principles that apply to all societies and situations.

Stage 5 Social-contract orientation

Stage 6 Universal ethical principles orientation

Do moral *principles* explain moral *behaviour?*...

When students could cheat on a test, only 15% at the post-conventional stage did so, whereas 70% at the pre-conventional stage did, showing that moral principles are related to moral behaviour (Kohlberg).

However...

Burton found that people only behave consistently with their moral principles on some *kinds* of moral behaviour such as cheating. Likelihood of punishment or the nature of the situation may be critical in determining whether or not someone behaves morally, rather than moral principles.

Krebs and Denton found, when analysing real-life moral decisions, that moral principles were used to justify behaviour *after* it had been performed – therefore moral behaviour isn't based on principles.

Research support for the stage theory...

Colby *et al.* re-interviewed Kohlberg's original participants regularly over 20 years, confirming that stage 1 and 2 reasoning decreases with age, while stage 4 and 5 reasoning increases.

Walker *et al.* interviewed 80 children (boys and girls). Six-year-olds were at stage 1 or 2, whereas by age 15 most children had reached stage 3.

A further sample of adults (average age 40) were tested and were mainly between stages 3 and 4, with only 3% between stages 4 and 5.

Stage 6 may be an unrealistic ideal, which is rarely achieved.

Moral dilemmas lack realism...

Kohlberg's evidence is not based on real-life decisions and the moral dilemmas may have made little sense to young children. Gilligan conducted research interviewing people about their own moral decisions.

IDA *Gender bias*...

Kohlberg's dilemmas are based on a male morality of justice and ignore female concerns with relationships (a morality of care), making women appear morally inferior.

Gilligan's stage theory is based on principles of care, intended as an expansion of Kohlberg's theory rather than an alternative (Jorgensen).

IDA *Culture bias*...

Kohlberg's moral dilemmas are rooted in Western moral principles, nevertheless evidence from Mexico, Turkey, India and Kenya, using the dilemmas, found the stages and sequence are universal (Colby and Kohlberg).

Snarey found the same using the dilemmas in 27 countries.

However...

Snarey and Keljo found cultural differences – post-conventional understanding occurs mainly in more developed, industrialised societies.

This may occur because diverse communities (found in industrialised societies) pose more conflicts, which promotes moral development because individuals have to question moral standards (Kohlberg).

Ignores emotional factors...

Eisenberg criticised Kohlberg's restricted view of morality because it ignored emotional factors.

IDA *Real-world application*...

Kohlberg set up democratic groups (*Cluster Schools*) in schools and prisons where people had the power to define and resolve disputes within their group, encouraging moral development.

Strengths of Kohlberg's approach...

The core concepts put forward by Kohlberg remain unchallenged, such as the invariant sequence of development and the importance of social interactions.

Eisenberg's theory of prosocial reasoning

General principles

Prosocial behaviour

The prosocial approach emphasises interpersonal concerns and the emotional component of moral behaviour (in contrast with Kohlberg).

Eisenberg claimed that young children are more advanced in their ability to reason than Kohlberg had suggested.

IDA *Other approaches to explaining moral development…*

Both Kohlberg and Eisenberg portray moral/prosocial development as a mix of biological and social influences (nature and nurture).

The behaviourist approach is restricted to the effects of social experience – i.e. the experience of rewards and punishments.

The evolutionary approach proposes that morality evolved because cooperative social relations maximise our survival (Krebs).

The role of empathy

The development of empathy is important in prosocial reasoning.

Young children experience personal distress when they see that someone else is unhappy, but their distress is not due to experiencing someone else's emotions; it is because seeing unhappiness is *personally* distressing (Cialdini *et al.*).

There is research support for the importance of empathy…

Childen only behave prosocially when they experience empathic concern, but not when they experience personal distress.

Caplan and Hay found 3–5-year-olds were often very upset by another child's distress, but rarely offered to help.

Hughes *et al.* showed children pictures about unhappy things (such as a dog running away). Children under 5 usually provide egocentric explanations for their sadness, reflecting their personal distress. Children aged 7–9 years old show empathic concern because they can take another person's perspective (e.g. say 'I'm sad because if he really liked his dog then he'll feel unhappy').

Perspective-taking

The development of empathy lies in being able to take the perspective of another person.

An emotional response becomes an empathic response when a child understands the distress of another *and* feels concern for them, rather than the child's own feelings of distress.

There is research support…

Eisenberg *et al.* studied Brazilian adolescents. Those with well-developed role-taking skills were more helpful and compassionate than poor role-takers. This shows that perspective-taking is fundamental for prosocial behaviour.

Offering an explanation – the felt-responsibility hypothesis…

When we feel someone else's distress, this makes us feel personally responsible for helping them. Research studies show that the likelihood of helping increases if participants are led to feel greater responsibility (Schaffer *et al.*).

Levels of prosocial reasoning

Eisenberg devised her own set of moral dilemmas to assess children's thinking about prosocial moral issues. They were specifically designed for children, unlike Kohlberg's more adult dilemmas.

Responses from cross-sectional and longitudinal studies were used to produce a 'stage' theory.

At any age children reason using several different levels. Older children are capable of more mature levels of reasoning, but may sometimes revert to earlier levels.

Levels

1 *Hedonistic, self-focused orientation* (preschool and early primary) – prosocial behaviour is motivated by benefits for self.

2 *Needs-oriented* (preschool and primary) – child understands needs of others but no empathy.

3 *Approval and interpersonal orientation* (primary and secondary) – child relies on cultural stereotypes about good and bad behaviour.

4 *Self-reflective empathetic orientation* (mainly secondary) – individual displays perspective-taking and empathic concern.

5 *Strongly internalised principles* (some adolescents and most adults) – behaving prosocially enhances self-respect and living up to one's own values.

Moral dilemmas may lack ecological validity…

Hypothetical dilemmas aren't the same as real-life decisions, which, for example, involve issues such as previous knowledge of the victim and fear of possible repercussions (Krebs and Denton).

However there is some support…

Miller *et al.* found that preschool children beyond the hedonistic level were more likely to help and spontaneously share things with their peers than were those who were still in the hedonistic stage. This suggests that such dilemmas reflect real-life behaviour.

Gender differences…

Eisenberg *et al.* found that girls aged 10–12 were more empathic than boys, but suggest this may be because girls mature earlier. By adolescence boys have caught up, and are equally empathic.

IDA *Cultural universals or differences (nature or nurture)…*

Studies conducted in West Germany, Poland and Italy have found similar changes (Eisenberg).

However…

Kibbutz-reared Israeli adolescents showed little needs orientation and were more likely to provide reasons based on communal values, as we might expect among children living in interdependent collectivist community.

IDA *Real-world application…*

Criminals lack empathy and perspective-taking skills. Socially maladjusted girls who received training in perspective-taking skills became more concerned about needs of others than age mates who received no training (Chalmers and Townsend).

Some treatment programmes used with offenders involve training them in perspective-taking skills through role reversal (Hoge *et al.*).

Chapter 8

Development of thinking | Development of a child's sense of self
Development of moral understanding | Development of a child's understanding of others

Cognition and development > Development of social cognition > Biological explanations of social cognition

Development of a child's sense of self

Subjective self-awareness

At birth, an infant is aware of basic sensations, e.g. fullness.

Age two months – shows a sense of 'personal agency' (responsibility for the movement of their limbs). Bahrick and Watson showed that 5-month-olds responded differently to a real-time video of their leg movements and one taken at an earlier time.

Age five months – they can recognise their own face. Legerstee et al. found that 5–8-month-old infants looked longer at pictures of other children than pictures of themselves (which were less novel).

Not all psychologists agree…

Freudians such as Mahler et al. argue that, at birth, an infant has no sense of separateness from his/her mother. Individuation (the infant's recognition of self as distinct from others) is something that develops over the first few months of life.

Research with infants is difficult…

Understanding children's sense of self involves inferring what is going on in their mind on the basis of outward behaviours.

Psychologists have devised some ingenious ways of doing this, such as the mirror test and the Sally Anne Test, but such measures are not perfect and may possibly underestimate what children can actually do.

Objective self-awareness

Subjective self-awareness (ability to perceive oneself as distinct) is different to objective self-awareness (the ability to reflect upon oneself) (Lewis).

Recognising your own face (subjective) is different to self-recognition (being conscious of your own existence).

The mirror test (red mark placed on face) is used to demonstrate self-recognition (Amsterdam, Gallop). Lewis and Brooks-Gunn found that 19% of babies touched their nose by 15 months and 66% did it by 24 months.

Around the same age, babies start to use personal pronouns such as 'me' and 'mine' (Slater and Lewis).

One consequence of objective self-awareness…

One consequence is the ability to display emotions. Very young children display the basic emotions of pleasure, sadness, fear and surprise, but the development of the conscious awareness of self is an important step in emotional development and leads to self-conscious emotions such as empathy, jealousy and embarrassment.

Individual differences…

Children who are securely attached develop self-recognition earlier than those who are not (Pipp et al.).

The same has been found to be true for children whose fathers encourage independence (Borke et al.).

IDA Link to intelligence in non-human animals…

Psychologists have sought to establish self-awareness in other species by using the mirror test (see page 64). Such self-awareness is evidence of intelligence, consciousness, emotions and the experience of pain – which creates ethical issues about using such animals in research.

Psychological self

Children aged 4–5 years describe themselves in terms of physical features e.g. 'I've got black hair' or 'I can ride my bike' (Damon and Hart).

Older children use psychological concepts, e.g. 'I like to play by myself'.

Children also start comparing themselves to others, e.g. 'I can run faster than my sister'.

Self-esteem begins to appear around the age of four.

Cultural differences…

Van den Heuvel et al. compared Dutch, Turkish and Moroccan children aged 10–11 years. As predicted, Western (individualist culture) children used many more psychological statements than the non-Western (collectivist) children, whereas the non-Western children used more references to the social aspects of self.

Individual differences…

Verschueren and Marcoen found that securely attached children rated themselves more favourably (higher self-esteem) than did insecurely attached children and this was stable over time (Verschueren et al.).

Theory of Mind (ToM)

Newborns can distinguish between humans and other objects, therefore displaying a knowledge of others (Legerstee).

By the age of two children display some understanding of the mental state of others, e.g. they comfort others (Dunn).

However, a distinction is made between knowing about someone else's internal state and knowing about how they feel.

About four years of age children develop ToM, as demonstrated by false-belief tasks (e.g. the Sally Anne test, where a child with ToM should recognise that Anne can hold a belief that isn't true). ToM is important in conducting social relationships and distinguishing self from others.

Link with autism…

Children with autism find social interaction difficult, which may be due to a ToM deficit. Baron-Cohen et al. found that autistic children failed the Sally Anne test, whereas children with Down's syndrome (genetic condition associated with low IQ) coped normally.

This shows that social abnormalities typical of autism are not linked to low IQ, but to a specific ToM deficit.

IDA Nature and nurture…

Baron-Cohen has proposed a ToM module (ToMM) that matures in the brain around the age of four.

ToM Is not solely determined by biology. Research has shown that discussion about motives and other mental states promotes the development of ToM (Sabbagh and Callanan).

Cross-cultural research also reveals the effect of experiential factors. Liu et al. compared more than 300 Chinese and North American children in terms of ToM. They found a similar sequence of development in both groups, but the timing differed by as much as two years in different locales supporting the role of biological and experiential factors.

Chapter 8

| Development of thinking | Development of a child's sense of self |
| Development of moral understanding | **Development of a child's understanding of others** |

Cognition and development > Development of social cognition > Biological explanations of social cognition

Development of a child's understanding of others

Early development

Imitation

Meltzoff and Moore showed that newborns less than 72 hours old will imitate facial gestures (e.g. mouth opening, tongue protrusion) and manual gestures (e.g. opening of the hand).

Intentions

This is a 'lower' mental ability than understanding the thoughts of others.

Infants of three months follow a person's gaze to nearby objects, showing an understanding of intention (D'Entrement *et al.*).

At one year, infants reliably follow gaze and pointing gestures to more distant objects (Carpenter *et al.*).

Autistic children aged 2½ – 5 years are the same as normal children, suggesting that understanding intentions is separate to ToM (Carpenter *et al.*).

Perspective-taking

Egocentricity

Piaget described the pre-operational child as 'egocentric' (see page 69).

This egocentricity concerns perceptual perspective-taking ability (tested in Piaget's *three mountains task*) as distinct from conceptual perspective-taking ability (tested by the Sally Anne test used to assess ToM).

Role-taking

Role-taking (conceptual perspective-taking) involves a child's comprehension about other people's internal experiences, leading to true ToM.

Selman used dilemmas to explore children's reasoning when faced with conflicting feelings. He constructed a stage model of the development of perspective-taking:

- Stage 0 Undifferentiated (3–6 years)
- Stage 1 Social-informational (6–8)
- Stage 2 Self-reflective (8–10)
- Stage 3 Mutual (10–12)
- Stage 4 Societal (12+)

As children grow older they develop the ability to analyse the perspectives of several people.

Role-taking and social

Eisenberg suggested that perspective-taking (role-taking) forms the basis of empathy and thus of pro-social behaviour (see page 74).

Role-taking and deception

Age three, children can plant a false belief in someone else's mind, e.g. hiding disappointment when filmed with another person but not when filmed on own (Cole).

IDA *Nature and nurture* …

The key feature of stage theories is that they describe an invariant developmental sequence, i.e. all children go through the stages in the same order. Each stage is an outcome of the previous stage, such that the behaviours associated with later stages build on behaviours developed in earlier stages.

The invariant nature of the stages implies some underlying biological mechanism. Biological maturation sets the bottom limits so that children below a certain age, for example, cannot develop ToM or abstract logical thinking.

However, nurture as well as nature is important. The speed of development is related to experience (nurture), for example, deaf children are slower to develop ToM.

Are these abilities separate or interdependent? …

Does the development of ToM depend on earlier abilities (e.g. imitation)?

Evidence for separate biological mental modules …

Neurophysiological evidence exists for a unique, innate ToM module that is activated around three years of age (see facing page).

Behavioural evidence comes from the fact that autistic children can understand the intentions of others, but do not develop ToM. Hobson found that autistic children performed 'normally' on the three mountains task (perceptual perspective-taking), but ultimately do not develop conceptual perspective-taking.

Evidence for interdependence …

Children with sensory impairments (such as hearing or visual difficulties) usually experience significant delays in the development of ToM (Eide and Eide). It is possible that their restricted sensory experiences slow down the development of perceptual perspective-taking and this, in turn, slows down the normal development of ToM.

IDA *Evolutionary approach* …

Role-taking skills produce adaptive advantages:

They are a critical component of all social behaviour, e.g. popular children have better role-taking skills (Schaffer).

The ability to deceive or manipulate others (sometimes called Machiavellian intelligence) is naturally selected. Anyone capable of deceiving their conspecifics (members of the same species) has an evolutionary advantage, because they can manipulate others for their own advantage.

IDA *Real-world applications* …

The fact that perspective- or role-taking skills can be fostered by experience has important implications for schools, therapy, the treatment of criminals and parenting.

Such training can be done with younger children through play, as it is the natural way in which role-taking skills are learned (Smith and Pellegrini).

Social skills training (SST) programmes are used with older children and in therapeutic settings with people with mental disorders.

Criminals may lack empathy and role-taking skills, which explains their 'willingness' to harm others. SST programmes teach prisoners role-taking skills to increase their empathic concern for others.

Parents may be interested in research by Sommerville *et al*. They used 'sticky mittens' to enable very young infants to manipulate objects (the mittens had Velcro on them so that infants were able to pick objects up). These infants then showed earlier-than-usual abilities to understand the intentions of others, suggesting that if you give infants earlier-than-normal experiences, this may speed up the development of understanding intentions and ultimately may speed up the development of perspective-taking.

Chapter 8

Development of thinking | Development of a child's sense of self
Development of moral understanding | Development of a child's understanding of others

Cognition and development > Development of social cognition > Biological explanations of social cognition

Biological explanations of social cognition

Mirror neurons (MNs)

Mirror neurons in macaque monkeys

Rizzolatti et al. discovered neurons in the F5 premotor cortex that were active either when the monkey performed an action (e.g. tearing up paper), or when the monkey observed another monkey or experimenter performing the task.

Mirror neurons in humans

Brain imaging studies have revealed areas of the human brain rich in MNs:

- The inferior frontal lobe is linked to emotional MNs (Wicker et al.) and Broca's area (see below).
- Areas in the temporal lobe may be related to auditory MNs (Gazzola et al.) and in the occipital, parietal and temporal lobe to visual input.
- The frontopolar cortex (in the frontal lobe) and the right inferior parietal lobule are key areas (Decety).

Explaining social cognition

Imitation

MNs are important in the acquisition of skilled behaviours (observer watches someone else perform an action and models that behaviour).

Imitation is also the beginning of the development of social cognition.

Observation should not immediately result in imitation; however, individuals who have damage to their frontal cortex (the part of the brain involved in inhibitory control) do display compulsive imitation (Lhermitte et al.).

Intentional behaviour

MNs may also encode another person's intentions. Iacoboni et al. recorded neural activity (using fMRI) while participants watched clips of a 'tea party' – context (tea cups), action (hand grasping a cup) and intention (context plus action). Highest MN activity was recorded in the inferior frontal cortex for the intention clip.

Perspective-taking

Gallese and Goldman suggest that MNs are a precursor to perspective-taking and ToM, because they enable us to experience someone else's actions and intentions as if they are our own.

Empathy

MNs could also explain empathy because they enable us to experience not just the actions of another person but also the same emotions.

Language acquisition

Binkofski et al. demonstrated MNs in Broca's area (for speech production).

MNs may assist in the imitation of speech sounds, important in language acquisition (Rizzolatti and Arbib).

MNs support simulation theory…

The discovery of MNs provided a neurological basis for simulation theory (ST) which proposes we read other people's minds by experiencing what they are experiencing and use this to predict the other's actions and feelings (Gordon, Heal).

There are alternative views…

'Theory' theory (TT) suggests that we infer mental states from observations, and construct a 'theory' about what the other person is thinking on the basis of all available information. ToM is essentially a 'theory' theory.

Borg argues that there is a difference between experiencing the actions of another person and reading their mind. Borg likens the MN approach to behaviourism where it is assumed that, for example, crying (a behaviour) is all there is to being sad (a mental state).

Is it all a myth?…

Gopnik suggests that MNs have taken on the status of a scientific myth, claiming to offer explanations of many different behaviours, e.g. ToM, empathy, altruism and moral behaviour. There are two main objections:

- The only real evidence is derived from non-human animal studies. These studies may not generalise to humans since non-human animals, arguably, do not have ToM.
- It is hard to believe that systems as complex as altruistic behaviour or ToM could be explained simply by MNs. It is likely to be more complex, e.g. Eisenberg proposed that children at first feel another person's distress (which is based on to MNs). Later, a child understands the distress of another and feels concern for them (perspective-taking), which involves more than just MNs.

IDA Nature and nurture…

The original suggestion is that MNs are an innate system, since MNs enable imitation and, as we have seen on the facing page, imitation is an ability that is present from birth.

Gopnik suggests instead that MNs might arise as a result of experience because neurons learn by association – when two events are associated the neurons for each event form a connection. An infant's first experience is to see a hand moving (its own) and at the same time experience that hand moving. This creates a mirror connection.

Mirror neurons and autism…

Williams et al. suggest that MN abnormalities may well underlie the fact that people with autism frequently have difficulty copying actions.

Dapretto et al. compared brain activity in autistic and non-autistic children as they watched faces that showed emotion or no emotion. Autistic children showed reduced activity in a part of the inferior frontal gyrus, a section of the brain identified as forming part of the mirror neuron system.

IDA Real-world application…

It might be possible to help autistic individuals by strengthening their MNs through activities that require the imitation of others (Slack).

Difficulties with gathering research evidence…

It isn't easy to gain direct evidence of human neural activity because such research requires placing electrodes inside the brain. Almost all of the human evidence so far is based on imaging studies, which can only tell us about hundreds of thousands of neurons, not individual ones.

However…

Iacoboni recently recorded the activity of almost 300 individual neurons in the frontal lobes of epileptic patients (wired up to investigate their seizures). The patients were asked to perform simple actions and to observe short films of others executing the same actions, which enabled the researchers to identify 34 mirror neurons activated by both performance and observation. They also found some MNs that suppress imitation (important for inhibitory control).

Schizophrenia

Division A Overview
Classification and diagnosis of schizophrenia

Division B Explanations of schizophrenia
Biological explanations of schizophrenia
Psychological explanations of schizophrenia

Division C Therapies for schizophrenia
Biological therapies for schizophrenia
Psychological therapies for schizophrenia

Issues, debates and approaches

In the psychopathology section (Section A) of the Unit 4 exam there is no explicit credit given to issues, debates and approaches. This doesn't mean that such material would not be creditworthy (it would) but it means it is not required. So, in this chapter we have not specifically identified IDA.

Specification

Schizophrenia	
Overview	• Clinical characteristics of schizophrenia.
	• Issues surrounding the classification and diagnosis of schizophrenia, including reliability and validity.
Explanations	• Biological explanations of schizophrenia, for example, genetics, biochemistry.
	• Psychological explanations of schizophrenia, for example, behavioural, cognitive, psychodynamic and socio-cultural.
Therapy	• Biological therapies for schizophrenia, including their evaluation in terms of appropriateness and effectiveness.
	• Psychological therapies for schizophrenia, for example, behavioural, psychodynamic and cognitive-behavioural, including their evaluation in terms of appropriateness and effectiveness.

Chapter 9

Overview >
Explanations of schizophrenia
Schizophrenia > Therapies for schizophrenia | Classification and diagnosis of schizophrenia

Classification and diagnosis of schizophrenia

Clinical characteristics

The nature of schizophrenia

Schizophrenia is characterised by a profound disruption of cognition and emotion, which affects a person's language, thought, perception, affect and even sense of self.

Diagnostic criteria (DSM-IV-TR)
- *Duration* – at least a month's duration of two or more positive symptoms, e.g. delusions and/or hallucinations.
- *Delusions* are bizarre beliefs that seem real to the person with schizophrenia but are not real. Delusions may be paranoid (i.e. fear of persecution) or may involve inflated beliefs about the person's power and importance.
- *Hallucinations* are bizarre, unreal perceptions of the environment that are usually auditory (e.g. hearing voices), but may be visual (e.g. seeing 'ghosts') or tactile (e.g. feeling insects crawling over the skin).
- The possibility of a mood disorder or organic causes (e.g. drug abuse or brain tumour) must be excluded.

Reliability of diagnosis

Reliability is the extent to which different psychiatrists can agree on the same diagnoses when assessing patients.

Existence of classification systems (e.g. DSM) is claimed to lead to a much greater agreement in diagnosis of schizophrenia.

There are different classification systems used for diagnosis. In the US the DSM is used and in the UK the ICD is also used. The issue with this is that they describe schizophrenia in different ways, which creates problems in assessing reliability.

Unreliable diagnosis

Rosenhan demonstrated the unreliability of diagnoses by arranging for 'pseudopatients' to present themselves to psychiatric hospitals claiming to be hearing voices.

All were diagnosed with schizophrenia and admitted, despite the fact they displayed no further symptoms during their hospitalisation. Throughout their stay, none of the staff recognised that they were actually normal.

The reliability of DSM is still not that high...

Recent studies (e.g. Whaley) have found inter-rater reliability correlations in the diagnosis of schizophrenia as low as +.11.

This is demonstrated in cultural differences in diagnosis...

Copeland *et al.* gave a description of a patient to US and UK psychiatrists. Of the US psychiatrists, 69% diagnosed schizophrenia, but only 2% of the UK psychiatrists gave the same diagnosis.

Blake found that psychiatrists are six times more likely to diagnose schizophrenia if the description refers to a patient as black African-American compared to a white patient with the same symptoms.

Distinguishing 'bizarre' from 'non-bizarre' lacks reliability...

If delusions are 'bizarre', this is sufficient for diagnosis of schizophrenia. Mojtabi and Nicholson found that when 50 senior psychiatrists were asked to distinguish between bizarre and non-bizarre delusions, this produced an inter-rater reliability of only +.40, suggesting that this lacks sufficient reliability for accurate diagnosis.

The implications of Rosenhan's study are...

Situational factors and expectations may be more influential when making a diagnosis of schizophrenia than are the clinical characteristics. For example, in a follow-up to this study, Rosenhan warned hospitals that he was sending out more pseudopatients. This resulted in a 21% detection rate, even though none were actually sent.

Validity of diagnosis

Comorbidity

Schneider referred to delusions, thought broadcasting and auditory hallucinations as first-rank symptoms. These could be used to distinguish schizophrenia from other psychotic disorders.

Allardyce *et al.* claim that symptoms used to classify schizophrenia do not define a *specific* disorder. Its symptoms are also found in other categories of psychosis.

First-rank symptoms don't make diagnosis more accurate...

Bentall *et al.* claim that many of the 'first-rank' symptoms of schizophrenia (e.g. delusions, thought disorders) are also found in other disorders (e.g. depression and bipolar disorder), making it difficult to separate schizophrenia as a distinct disorder.

There is an overlap with other disorders...

There is evidence (e.g. Torrey *et al.*) of overlap of bipolar disorder with schizophrenia in terms of risk factors as well as in neural abnormalities. It is therefore possible that these two disorders may form a spectrum of psychosis rather than discrete conditions.

Predictive validity

If a disorder has high predictive validity, then it should be clear how the disorder would develop and how people would respond to treatment. On this basis schizophrenia has low predictive validity.

There is little evidence that outcomes are the same...

The prognosis for people with schizophrenia varies with about 20% recovering their previous level of functioning, 10% showing significant improvement and 30% some improvement, while 40% never really recover (Bleuer). This demonstrates little predictive validity for a diagnosis of schizophrenia with so much variation in prognosis for the disorder.

Other issues

The social stigma of schizophrenia is a major obstacle in the recovery of patients with schizophrenia. The perception of individuals with a psychotic disorder as being violent has more than doubled in prevalence since the 1950s, according to one meta-analysis (Phelan *et al.*).

Stigma reduces the validity of diagnosis...

Because of the stigma associated with mental illness, clinicians may be reluctant to diagnose serious mental disorders. Kim and Berrios found that in Japan the idea of a 'disorganised mind' is so stigmatised that psychiatrists are reluctant to diagnose schizophrenia. They estimated that as a result of this, in Japan, only 20% of those with schizophrenia were actually aware of it, while the remainder are left undiagnosed.

Chapter 9

Overview
Explanations of schizophrenia   >   Biological explanations of schizophrenia
Schizophrenia   >   Therapies for schizophrenia   Psychological explanations of schizophrenia

Biological explanations of schizophrenia

Genetic factors

Family studies (e.g. Gottesman) show that schizophrenia is more common among biological relatives of a person with schizophrenia than in the general population. The greater the degree of genetic relatedness, the greater the risk.

Children with two schizophrenic parents have a 46% risk of developing the disorder, with one schizophrenic parent a 13% risk and with a schizophrenic sibling 9% risk.

A problem for genetic explanations of schizophrenia is…

Heritable traits that are maladaptive would be selected out during the process of natural selection, and so schizophrenia would no longer exist. However, Stevens and Price suggest that, among our distant ancestors, the presence of charismatic leaders with schizophrenic type symptoms (e.g. auditory hallucinations and delusions of grandeur) could have influenced other group members to follow them and form a new group (advantageous when the size of the existing group was greater than dwindling resources could sustain). Thus, the *'group-splitting hypothesis'* argues that schizophrenia is an extreme expression of an adaptive trait.

Twin studies

If MZ twins are more similar in terms of schizophrenia than DZ twins this suggests a strong genetic influence for the disorder.

A meta-analysis of twin studies prior to 2001 (Joseph) found a concordance rate of just over 40% for MZ twins and just over 7% for DZ twins, but recent studies found lower concordance rates for MZ twins.

Concordance rates may only reflect environmental differences…

It is assumed that the greater concordance rate between MZ twins compared to DZ twins is a consequence of a greater genetic similarity, rather than a greater environmental similarity for MZ twins.

However, Joseph points out that MZ twins tend to be treated more similarly, and experience more 'identity confusion'.

As a result, there is reason to believe that differences in concordance rates for MZ and DZ twins reflect nothing more than the environmental differences that distinguish the two types of twin.

Adoption studies

Such studies are valuable because it is difficult to disentangle genetic and environmental influences for those who share genes *and* environment.

Tienari *et al.* found that for adoptees whose biological mothers had been diagnosed with schizophrenia, 6.7% of these individuals also developed the disorder, compared to just 2% of adoptees born to non-schizophrenic mothers.

The problem of selective placement…

An assumption is that parents who adopt a child with a schizophrenic biological parent are no different from other adoptive parents. This is unlikely, as adoptive parents are usually informed of the genetic background of potential adoptees prior to making a decision whether to adopt.

There are methodological problems with adoption studies…

Most adoption studies have only found differences between children born to schizophrenic and non-schizophrenic biological parents by broadening the definition to include the non-psychotic *'schizophrenia spectrum disorder'* rather than restricting it to full-blown schizophrenia.

The dopamine hypothesis

The dopamine hypothesis

Neurons that transmit dopamine fire too easily or too often, leading to the symptoms of schizophrenia.

Schizophrenics have abnormally high numbers of D_2 receptors, resulting in more dopamine neurons firing. Dopamine neurons play a key role in guiding attention, so disturbances in this process might lead to the problems of perception and thought found in schizophrenia.

Dopamine alone does not cause schizophrenia…

Psychological factors (e.g. expressed emotion) influence the development of or recovery from the disorder. This suggests that for those with a biological vulnerability (e.g. high levels of dopamine), schizophrenia only develops in the presence of significant stressors.

High levels of dopamine may be consequence rather than cause…

A review of post-mortem studies (Haracz) found that most who showed elevated dopamine levels received antipsychotic medication shortly before death. This suggests that high dopamine levels may just be a consequence of its treatment.

Evidence for the dopamine hypothesis

Amphetamines are dopamine agonists, stimulating nerve cells containing dopamine, causing the synapse to be flooded with dopamine. Large doses cause hallucinations and delusions.

Antipsychotic drugs are dopamine antagonists, blocking the activity of dopamine in the brain, and so reducing the symptoms of schizophrenia.

The dopamine hypothesis is reductionist…

If schizophrenia was caused solely by excess dopamine activity, then antipsychotic drugs should be effective for *all* schizophrenics. This is not the case, suggesting that the dopamine explanation alone cannot explain the development of schizophrenia.

Evidence from neuroimaging research is inconclusive…

The development of PET scans has led to more accurate measurement, but has failed to provide evidence of altered dopamine activity in brains of individuals with schizophrenia (Copolov and Crook).

Enlarged ventricles

Brain scans have shown that the ventricles of a person with schizophrenia are 15% bigger than normal in individuals (Torrey). These may be the result of poor brain development or tissue damage, which lead to the development of schizophrenia.

Evidence on importance of enlarged ventricles is inconsistent…

A meta-analysis (Copolov and Crook) of more than 90 CAT scan studies revealed a substantial overlap between the schizophrenic and control populations. A possible explanation for why some schizophrenics have enlarged ventricles may be the use of antipsychotic medication, e.g. Lyon *et al.* found that as the dose of medication increased, the density of brain tissue decreased, leading to enlarged ventricles.

Chapter 9

Overview	
Explanations of schizophrenia >	Biological explanations of schizophrenia
Schizophrenia >	Therapies for schizophrenia
	Psychological explanations of schizophrenia

Psychological explanations of schizophrenia

Psychological theories

Psychodynamic explanation

- Regression *to a pre-ego state* – If parents are cold and uncaring, a person regresses to an earlier stage before the development of the ego or a realistic awareness of the world.
- *Attempts to re-establish ego control* from this infantile state fail and can lead to symptoms of schizophrenia (e.g. delusions and narcissism), the product of a weak and confused ego.

There is little evidence to support the psychodynamic view…

Studies have shown that parents of schizophrenics do behave differently from parents of other kinds of patient, particularly in the presence of their disturbed offspring. However, this is likely to be the consequence rather than the cause of their illness.

Psychodynamic treatment is not effective…

If the psychodynamic explanation is correct, then psychodynamic therapy should be effective in the treatment of schizophrenia. However, Malmberg *et al.* found that patients given psychodynamic therapy showed less recovery than those given antipsychotics.

Cognitive explanation

This explanation acknowledges the role of biological factors in schizophrenia but claims that further features emerge as people try to understand their condition.

When schizophrenics first hear voices and have other sensory symptoms, they turn to others to validate these experiences. If others fail to confirm their validity, the person believes the others are hiding the truth and so the schizophrenic develops delusional beliefs.

There is physiological evidence to support this…

Meyer-Lindenberg *et al.* found a link between excess dopamine in the prefrontal cortex and working memory. Working memory dysfunction is associated with the cognitive disorganisation typically found in schizophrenics. Meyer-Linderberg *et al.* also found that treatment with antipsychotics significantly improved cognitive functioning.

There are implications for treatment…

Yellowlees *et al.* have trialled a machine that can deliver 'virtual' auditory and visual hallucinations. The intentions of this are to show schizophrenics that their hallucinations aren't real.

Socio-cultural factors

Life events

Discrete stressors, such as the death of a close relative, have been associated with a higher risk of schizophrenic episodes.

Brown and Birley found that prior to a schizophrenic episode, patients reported twice as many stressful life events compared to a healthy control group, who reported a low and unchanging level of stressful life events over the same period.

Prospective studies (e.g. Hirsch *et al.*) found that life events have a cumulative effect preceding relapse rather than a concentrated effect just before a schizophrenic episode.

Not all evidence supports the importance of life stressors…

Van Os *et al.* reported no link between life events and the onset of schizophrenia. In the retrospective part of this study, patients were not more likely to have experienced a major life event in the three months prior to an episode of schizophrenia. In the prospective part of study, patients who had experienced a major life event went on to have a *lower* incidence of relapse rather than an increased risk as predicted.

Research on the link is correlational only…

Therefore we cannot infer a causal relationship between stressful life events and schizophrenia. It could be that the early symptoms of the disorder (e.g. erratic behaviour) were the cause of the major life events (e.g. divorce, loss of a job). As a result, it is possible that the stressful major life events that are evident in the lives of some schizophrenics might be the consequence rather than the cause of the disorder.

Family relationships

Double bind theory – Bateson *et al.* suggest that children who frequently receive contradictory messages (e.g. of affection *and* animosity) from their parents are more likely to develop schizophrenia.

This prevents the development of an internally consistent construction of reality, which can manifest itself as schizophrenic symptoms (e.g. withdrawal).

Expressed emotion (EE) is a family style of communication that involves criticism and emotional over-involvement. High levels of EE are likely to influence relapse rates. The negative emotional climate in these families leads to stress beyond the person's impaired ability to cope and triggers a relapse into schizophrenia.

Evidence supports the importance of family relationships…

Tienari *et al.* found that adopted children who had schizophrenic biological parents were more likely to develop schizophrenia than children of normal biological parents, but only when the adopted family was rated as disturbed, in other words, the illness only manifested itself under appropriate environmental conditions, genetics alone were not enough.

Double-bind theory has mixed support…

Berger found that schizophrenics reported a higher recall of double-bind statements by their mothers than did non-schizophrenics (although the accuracy of their recall may be affected by their schizophrenia). Other research (e.g. Liem) found no difference in patterns of parental communication in families of schizophrenics and non-schizophrenics.

Expressed emotion has led to successful therapy…

High EE relatives are taught how to reduce levels of expressed emotion. Hogarty *et al.* found that such therapy can significantly reduce relapse rates among schizophrenics.

Labelling theory

If a person displays unusual behaviours associated with schizophrenia, they are considered deviant by society. Once this diagnostic label is applied, it becomes self-fulfilling, leading to further symptoms.

There is evidence to support this…

In a review of the evidence, Scheff evaluated 18 studies explicitly related to labelling theory. He judged 13 to be consistent with the theory and five to be inconsistent. On balance, therefore, Scheff concluded that labelling theory was supported by the available evidence.

Chapter 9

		Overview	
		Explanations of schizophrenia	
			Biological therapies for schizophrenia
Schizophrenia	>	Therapies for schizophrenia	>	Psychological therapies for schizophrenia

Biological therapies for schizophrenia

Antipsychotic medication

Antipsychotic drugs block the action of neurotransmitters that bring about the symptoms of schizophrenia and consequently help the person with schizophrenia function more effectively.

Conventional antipsychotics

These drugs reduce the effects of dopamine and so reduce the symptoms of schizophrenia. They bind to dopamine receptors but do not stimulate them, thus blocking their action.

By reducing stimulation of the dopamine system in the brain, conventional antipsychotics can eliminate the hallucinations and delusions experienced by people with schizophrenia.

Atypical antipsychotics

These also act on the dopamine pathway but only temporarily occupy the D_2 receptors and then rapidly dissociate to allow normal dopamine transmission. It is this characteristic which is thought to be responsible for the lower levels of side effects associated with atypical antipsychotics (e.g. tardive dyskinesia).

Effectiveness of conventional antipsychotics…

Most studies of the effectiveness of conventional antipsychotics have compared the relapse rates of those on medication with those on a placebo. Davis *et al.* reviewed 29 studies and found that relapse occurred in 55% of those whose drugs were replaced by a placebo, and 19% of those who remained on the drug.

Effectiveness of atypical antipsychotics…

A meta-analysis of studies (Leucht *et al.*) revealed that the superiority of these drugs compared to conventional antipsychotics in the treatment of the negative symptoms of schizophrenia is only moderate.

However…

Ross and Read argue that placebo studies are not a fair test of the effectiveness of an antipsychotic, as under a placebo condition, the patient is in a drug withdrawal state and is overwhelmed by dopamine.

Appropriateness of antipsychotics…

About 30% of people taking conventional antipsychotics develop tardive dyskinesia, which is irreversible in 75% of cases. Jeste *et al.* found that 5% of those treated with atypical antipsychotics developed this. The fact there are fewer side effects with atypical antipsychotics means patients are more motivated to continue with their medication.

Ross and Read argue that being prescribed medication reinforces the view that there is 'something wrong with them', which reduces their motivation to look for other possible causes (e.g. life stressors) and then take steps to deal with these to reduce their suffering.

Electroconvulsive therapy (ECT)

ECT in practice

Using ECT in the treatment of schizophrenia is usually restricted to certain forms of the disorder (e.g. *catatonic schizophrenia*) that do not respond to other kinds of treatment. Although relatively rare today, catatonic schizophrenia is responsive to ECT, which can bring about a rapid alleviation of its symptoms.

- In unilateral ECT, an electrode is placed on the non-dominant side of the brain and another on the forehead.
- The patient is injected with a barbiturate to make them unconscious during ECT. They are then given a nerve-blocking agent to prevent fractures during the seizure.
- A small amount of current is passed through the brain for half a second.
- This creates a seizure, which affects the whole brain.

Research into ECT and schizophrenia

Tharyan and Adams carried out a review of 26 studies in order to assess whether ECT resulted in any meaningful benefit for schizophrenic patients. They found:

- When 'real' ECT was compared with 'simulated' ECT, more people improved with 'real' ECT.
- When ECT was compared with antipsychotic medication, results favoured patients who received the antipsychotic medication.
- There was some evidence that ECT *plus* medication produced a superior outcome to either used alone.

Effectiveness of ECT…

A meta-analysis of studies that used ECT in the treatment of schizophrenia (Greenhalgh *et al.*) found that ECT (either combined with antipsychotic medication or as a therapy on its own) is no more effective than antipsychotic medication.

An Indian study (Sarita *et al.*) found no difference in the reduction of symptoms between 36 schizophrenia patients given either ECT or simulated ECT.

Khalilian *et al.* studied the effectiveness of ECT combined with atypical antipsychotic medication. They found that patients responded quickly to this combination treatment, which resulted in a significant reduction of both positive and negative symptoms. They found no evidence of any significant adverse effects.

Appropriateness of ECT…

As a conclusion of their meta-analysis, Tharyan and Adams concluded that ECT may be appropriate when rapid reduction of symptoms is required, or when patients show limited response to medication alone.

The APA task force on ECT states that ECT is an effective treatment during the acute onset of symptoms, when the catatonic subtype of schizophrenia is present and where there is a history of positive response to ECT treatment.

ECT can also offer a lifesaving intervention for patients who suffer from 'neuroleptic malignant syndrome', a life-threatening adverse reaction to antipsychotic medication.

However…

Because there are significant risks associated with ECT, including cognitive dysfunction, brain damage and even death, the use of this technique as a treatment for schizophrenia has declined. In the UK, the decline between1979 to 1999 was 59% (Read) and it is no longer recommended as a treatment for schizophrenia.

Some difficulties with memory are noted in almost everybody who receives ECT. It is not clear how much of this is due to the ECT and how much to the illness.

Chapter 9

Overview
Explanations of schizophrenia
Biological therapies for schizophrenia

Schizophrenia > Therapies for schizophrenia > Psychological therapies for schizophrenia

Psychological therapies for schizophrenia

Cognitive-behavioural therapy (CBT)

Distorted beliefs alter the person's behaviour in maladaptive ways.

In schizophrenia, the person may believe that their behaviour is being controlled by somebody or something else.

Delusions are thought to result from faulty interpretations of events. CBT is used to help the patient identify and correct these.

CBT techniques

Patients are encouraged to:
* Trace the origins of their symptoms to see how they might have developed.
* Evaluate the content of any delusions or voices and consider ways in which they might test validity of their faulty beliefs.
* Develop their own alternatives to previous maladaptive beliefs and develop appropriate coping strategies.

Outcome studies

Outcome studies of CBT suggest that patients who receive cognitive therapy experience fewer hallucinations and delusions and recover their functioning to a greater extent than those who receive antipsychotic medication alone.

Effectiveness of CBT...

Research has shown that CBT has a significant effect on improving the symptoms of schizophrenia, e.g. Gould *et al.* found that all seven studies in their meta-analysis reported a significant decrease in the positive symptoms of schizophrenia after treatment.

Kuipers *et al.* found a significant reduction in positive symptoms following CBT combined with antipsychotic medication, and also found that there was a lower rate of patient drop-out and greater patient satisfaction when these two types of treatment were combined.

However...

Most of the studies of the effectiveness of CBT have combined CBT with antipsychotic medication. As a result, it is difficult to assess the effectiveness of CBT independently of antipsychotic medication.

Appropriateness of CBT...
For negative symptoms...

CBT for schizophrenia works by generating less distressing explanations for negative experiences rather than trying to eliminate them completely. Negative symptoms may well serve a useful function for the individual, so may be understood as 'safety behaviours'.

Who benefits from CBT?...

It is commonly believed within psychiatry that not everybody with schizophrenia would benefit from CBT. For example, in a study of schizophrenic patients in the UK (Kingdon and Kirschen), it was found that many patients were not deemed suitable for CBT (e.g. older patients) because they 'would not engage fully with the therapy'.

Psychodynamic therapy: Psychoanalysis

Psychoanalytic therapy is based on the assumption that individuals are often unaware of the influence of unconscious conflicts on their psychological state.

The psychoanalytic approach to schizophrenia assumes that all symptoms are meaningful and reflect unconscious conflicts that must be brought into the conscious mind to be resolved.

Other psychodynamic therapies

What these have in common with Freudian psychoanalysis is the belief that the first task of psychodynamic therapy is to win the trust of the patient and to build a relationship with them.

The therapist achieves this by replacing the harsh and punishing conscience (based on patient's parents) with one that is less destructive and more supportive.

As the patient gets healthier, they take a more active role (and the therapist a less active role) in their own recovery.

Psychodynamic therapy takes a long time to complete, therefore many patients withdraw without completing their therapy.

Outcome studies

Gottdiener reviewed 37 studies where psychological therapies had been used in the treatment of schizophrenia.

Results showed that psychodynamic and cognitive-behavioural therapies produced similar levels of therapeutic benefit.

There was no difference in improvement when psychological therapy was accompanied by antipsychotic medication.

Effectiveness of psychodynamic therapy...

Gottdiener's meta-analysis of psychological treatment for schizophrenia concluded that psychodynamic therapy was effective for schizophrenia.

However... The relatively small number of studies used meant it was difficult to assess the impact of variables such as therapist training on the outcome for patients. Also, half the studies in this analysis did not randomly allocate patients to treatment conditions, thus introducing a treatment bias that may have affected the results.

Contrary evidence...

Malmberg and Fenton argue that it is impossible to draw definite conclusions for or against the effectiveness of psychodynamic therapy in the treatment of schizophrenia. In fact, research (*Schizophrenia Patient Outcome Research Team*) has even suggested that some forms of psychodynamic therapy are harmful for schizophrenics (many find the experience of psychodynamic therapy traumatic).

There are also contradictory findings...

May found that patients treated with psychodynamic therapy plus antipsychotic medication had better outcomes than those treated with therapy alone. Antipsychotic medication alone was better than therapy alone. Other research (e.g. Karon and VandenBos) found the opposite, with patients receiving therapy alone improving more than those receiving medication alone.

Appropriateness of psychodynamic therapy...

Despite the uncertain nature of the effectiveness of psychodynamic therapy in the treatment of schizophrenia, the APA recommends 'supportive interventions' such as psychodynamic therapy when used in conjunction with antipsychotic medication.

A costly therapy?...

One argument against the use of psychodynamic therapy is the expense involved (therapy takes a long time). As it is no more effective than antipsychotic medication, the extra expense is not justified.

However... A counter argument is that the extra expense is worth it because the overall cost of treatment decreases with time as patients are less likely to seek inpatient treatment and are more likely to gain employment (Karon and VandenBos).

Chapter 10

Depression

Division A Overview
Classification and diagnosis of depression

Division B Explanations of depression
Biological explanations of depression
Psychological explanations of depression

Division C Therapies for depression
Biological therapies for depression
Psychological therapies for depression

Specification

Depression	
Overview	• Clinical characteristics of depression.
	• Issues surrounding the classification and diagnosis of depression, including reliability and validity.
Explanations	• Biological explanations of depression, for example, genetics, biochemistry.
	• Psychological explanations of depression, for example, behavioural, cognitive, psychodynamic and socio-cultural.
Therapy	• Biological therapies for depression, including their evaluation in terms of appropriateness and effectiveness.
	• Psychological therapies for depression, for example, behavioural, psychodynamic and cognitive-behavioural, including their evaluation in terms of appropriateness and effectiveness.

Classification and diagnosis of depression

Clinical characteristics

The nature of depression

Depression is classified under DSM-IV-TR as a mood disorder. Mood disorders affect a person's emotional state and include *major depressive disorder* (MDD). Depression is a low emotional state characterised by significant levels of sadness, lack of energy and of feelings of self-worth, and feelings of guilt.

Diagnostic criteria

A diagnosis of MDD using DSM-IV-TR requires the presence of five of the following symptoms *including* either depressed mood or loss of interest and pleasure plus: difficulties in sleeping, shift in activity level, change in appetite and weight, loss of energy and great fatigue, negative self-concept, feelings of worthlessness and guilt, difficulties in concentrating and recurrent thoughts of death or suicide.

Symptoms should cause considerable distress, be present all or most of the time and persist for longer than two weeks. The severity of depression is measured by the *Beck Depression Inventory* (BDI).

Reliability of diagnosis

Reliability is the extent to which different psychiatrists can agree on the same diagnoses when assessing patients.

Existence of classification systems (e.g. DSM) is claimed to lead to a much greater agreement in diagnosis of depression.

There are different classification systems used for diagnosis. In the USA the DSM is used and in the UK the ICD is also used. The issue with this is that they describe depression in different ways, which creates problems in assessing reliability.

Unreliable diagnosis

Research on the diagnosis of depression using the DSM classification system has found that inter-rater reliability tends to be reasonably good, but test–retest reliability tends to be poor. Zanarini *et al.* found an inter-rater reliability of +.80 but a test–retest reliability over one week of just +.61.

The reliability of DSM is still not that high…

Keller *et al.* interviewed 524 depressed individuals. Each was interviewed again six months later to establish reliability. Results across the five sites showed that inter-rater reliability was 'fair to good', but test–retest reliability was only poor to fair.

There are cultural differences in diagnosis…

Members of some ethnic minority groups are less likely to seek professional treatment for depression, which gives rise to the stereotype that these groups are less prone to depression. For example, Karasz gave a vignette describing depressive symptoms to South Asian and European Americans. Only the latter group identified the problem as being biological and requiring 'professional' help.

There are a number of reasons for this low reliability…

These include the fact that for a diagnosis of depression to be given on DSM, a minimum of five out of nine symptoms must be present. When the severity of the disorder is such that it is at the diagnostic threshold, a disagreement between clinicians of just one item (e.g. whether an individual is sufficiently lethargic to denote a shift in activity levels) could mean the difference between giving a diagnosis of MDD or a less serious disorder.

Validity of diagnosis

Types of depression

The diagnosis of depression requires clinicians to differentiate between several distinct subtypes of the disorder. These include *major depressive disorder* (MDD) and dysthymia (a less severe form of depression that shares some of the symptoms of MDD).

Who carries out the diagnosis?

For most people, a diagnosis of depression is given by their local GP rather than by a psychiatrist. A study by Stirling *et al.* found that the average consultation time for a GP to diagnose depression was just over eight minutes, whereas for a psychiatrist it was one hour. A 50% increase in GP consultation time resulted in a 32% increase in the accuracy of diagnosis for depression.

There may not be distinct types of depression…

McCullough *et al.* compared 681 patients who had been diagnosed with various types of depression, including MDD and dysthymia. They found considerable overlap in their symptoms, responses to treatment and other variables that made it difficult to justify distinct forms of depressive illness.

Are GP diagnoses valid?…

Van Weel-Baumgarten *et al.* suggests that diagnoses made by GPs (as opposed to those made by secondary care specialists such as psychiatrists) may be less objective because they are based on previous knowledge of the patient and family history, rather than the actual presenting symptoms (necessary for DSM diagnosis).

Some GPs are better than others at accurate diagnosis…

Millar and Goldberg found that those GPs who are more skilled in the detection of mental disorders such as depression are able to elicit more cues from distressed patients than are GPs who are less experienced and who may conduct a more hurried and less effective interview.

Other issues

The social stigma of mental illness is a

major obstacle in the treatment of patients with depression. Some people (mostly males and people with a low level of education) are afraid to acknowledge they have a mental disorder because of the stigma they perceive is attached to it.

Stigma interferes with the effectiveness of treatment…

Many cultures have stereotypes about depression, with some viewing a mental disorder as something that will brand a family for generations. Latinos (e.g. Puerto-Ricans) in particular value resilience and believe depression is a sign of weakness. Vega *et al.* found that in the USA, depressed Latinos were less likely than others to take medication, keep scheduled appointments or attempt to control their condition.

Chapter 10

Overview		
	Explanations of depression	> Biological explanations of depression
Depression	> Therapies for depression	Psychological explanations of depression

Biological explanations of depression

Genetic factors

Family studies
Having a first-degree relative with depression appears to be a risk factor for depression. Research has found that around 20% of first-degree relatives of a proband with depression also have depression compared to 10% of general population (Harrington et al.).

There is research to support a genetic explanation...
A mutant gene that starves the brain of serotonin has been found to be ten times more common in depressed patients than in normal individuals (Zhang et al.), resulting in an 80% reduction of normal serotonin levels in the brain.

Caron et al. found this mutant gene in nine out of 87 depressed patients but only three out of 219 healthy controls. Patients with this mutation failed to respond to SSRI medications, which work by increasing serotonin levels in the brain.

Twin and adoption studies
McGuffin et al. studied 177 probands with depression and their same-sex twins. They found 46% concordance rates for MZ twins and 20% for DZ twins, suggesting that depression has a substantial heritable component.

Wender et al. found a much higher incidence of severe depression in the biological relatives of adopted individuals hospitalised for severe depression compared to biological relatives of a non-depressed group.

Low concordance rates explained in terms of comorbidity...
It is possible that people inherit a vulnerability for a wider range of disorders than depression alone, which would explain the relatively low concordance rates for depression alone.

For example, Kendler et al. found a higher incidence of mental disorders in twins of depressed probands when looking at depression and generalised anxiety disorder than when looking at just depression.

Depression may have an evolutionary significance...
The fact that depression is so widespread suggests that it may have some adaptive significance. As depression is costly for the individual, it serves as an 'honest' signal of need, so that others in the social network respond by providing much-needed help and support for the individual.

Genes as diatheses
Genetic factors are thought to act as diatheses (predispositions), which interact with environmental stressors (diathesis-stress) to produce a depressive reaction.

There is research support for this...
Kendler et al. found that among the siblings of depressed probands, the highest level of depression was found in those who, together with this genetic predisposition (diathesis), had also been exposed to significant negative life events (stressors).

Neurotransmitter dysfunction

Noradrenaline
Depression can be caused by a deficiency of noradrenaline in the brain.

Evidence for this link comes from research that shows waste products associated with noradrenaline are low in depressed individuals (Bunney et al.).

Post-mortem studies show increased densities of noradrenaline receptors in brains of depressed suicide victims (caused by process of up-regulation).

There is research support for the role of noradrenaline...
Leonard showed that drugs that lowered noradrenaline levels bring about depressive states, while those that increase noradrenaline levels show antidepressant effects.

Successful treatments with SNRIs support this link...
Kraft et al. treated patients with major depression for six weeks with a dual serotonin-noradrenaline re-uptake inhibitor (SNRI). The patients showed a significantly more positive response than those treated with a placebo, thus strengthening the link between the depletion of these neurotransmitters and the development of depressive symptoms.

Serotonin
Depression can be caused by a deficiency of serotonin in the brain.

Evidence comes from the discovery that SSRIs, which selectively block the reuptake of serotonin from the synaptic gap, reduce the symptoms of depression.

Delgado et al. gave depressed patients a diet that lowered tryptophan (precursor of serotonin) levels – the majority experienced a return of their symptoms.

There is evidence to support the importance of serotonin...
Amr et al. found an association between high-level exposure to pesticides and an increased risk of depression. Animal studies have shown that exposure to pesticides leads to serotonin disturbances in the brain and therefore depression.

A problem for the serotonin explanation is... that tryptophan depletion studies have used patients who are in remission from depression. Individuals who have no history of depression tend not to show any mood changes following tryptophan depletion, despite the fact that it alters the same mood regulating areas of the brain.

Cortisol hypersecretion

Cortisol
Levels of cortisol rise in depressed individuals, but reduce to normal once depression disappears.

Cortisol levels reduce brain serotonin levels, which in turn leads to depression.

Dexamethasone suppresses cortisol secretion in normal people, but in depressed people this suppression is not maintained.

There is conflicting research evidence...
Strickland et al. found no evidence of increased cortisol levels in a large group of women with depression or in the majority of those who were vulnerable to depression through adverse life stressors.

However... They did find elevated cortisol levels in some individuals who had experienced recent severe life events, yet were not depressed.

It appears that stressful life events can result in elevated cortisol levels, but this does not necessarily lead to the development of depression.

Chapter 10

Overview	
Explanations of depression	> Biological explanations of depression
Depression > Therapies for depression	Psychological explanations of depression

Psychological explanations of depression

Psychodynamic explanations

Mourning and melancholia

Freud claimed melancholia (depression) was a pathological reaction to the loss of a loved one (or loss of their affection).

Following a loss, there is a mourning period after which life returns to normal.

In some people, this mourning never ends.

There is research support for this explanation...

Barnes and Prosen found men whose fathers died when they were boys scored higher on depression than those who had not lost their fathers.

Bifulco et al. found that individuals who lost their mothers during childhood were more likely to experience depression later in life.

Shah and Waller found that many depressed people described their parents as 'affectionless' supporting Freud's claim of 'loss of affection'.

The pathology of depression

Freud believed that we unconsciously harbour some negative feelings towards those that we love.

When we lose a loved one, these feelings are turned inwards and we continue a pattern of self-abuse and self-blame.

Depression is 'anger turned upon oneself'.

However...

Paykel and Cooper argue that 'loss' only explains a relatively small percentage of cases of depression. Possibly only 10% of those who experience an early loss of this sort go on to become depressed.

Psychodynamic therapies don't work with depression...

Psychoanalysis is not particularly effective as a treatment for depression. However, this may be because people with depression find it hard to communicate in the way required by psychoanalytic therapy.

Cognitive explanations

Beck's theory of depression

Depressed individuals feel as they do because their thinking is biased towards negative interpretations of the world.

Depressed people acquire a negative schema early on, which is activated when a situation is encountered that resembles the original one that led to the schema.

These schema are subject to irrational thinking, which lead to a *negative triad*, i.e. a pessimistic view of the self, world and future.

Cognitive therapies do work with depression...

Butler and Beck reviewed 14 meta-analyses and concluded that 80% of adults benefited from cognitive therapy (compared to control groups), lending support to the claim that depression has a cognitive basis.

There is research support for this explanation...

Hammen and Krantz found depressed women made more logical errors, and Bates et al. found that depressed participants who were given negative automatic thought statements became more depressed.

However... Although research such as this demonstrates a link between negative thoughts and depression, this does not mean that the link between the two is a causal one.

Learned helplessness

Depression may be learned when a person tries but fails to control unpleasant experiences. As a result, they acquire a sense of being unable to exercise control over their life, and so become depressed.

Depressed people show a depressive attributional style, i.e. failures considered to be *internal, stable* and *global* (Abramson et al.).

There is research support for this explanation...

Hiroto and Seligman compared three groups. One received an unpleasant loud noise, controlled by pressing a button. A second received a noise that they could not control, and a third no noise. Later, all three groups received a controllable noise, which they could turn off by pressing a button. The 'no control' group took the noise without responding, while the other two groups escaped it by pressing the button.

This finding supports the claim that people may develop the view that they can't control unpleasant life events and so develop depression.

Hopelessness

Abramson et al. explains depression in terms of pessimistic expectations of the future. The 'hopeless' person expects bad rather than good things to happen in important areas of their life.

There is research support for this explanation...

Kwon and Laurenceau found that people with a negative attributional style also showed more of the symptoms of depression when stressed.

This may be more common in women in men, as during their social development they may be taught to think negatively about themselves, which may explain why more women suffer from depression than men.

Sociocultural explanations

Life events and depression

Life events may act as a trigger in individuals who have a genetic vulnerability for depression.

A depressive attributional style acts as a diathesis that predisposes the person to interpret events in ways that bring about depression.

There is evidence to support this explanation...

Brown and Harris found that episodes of depression were almost always preceded by a major life event. Vulnerability factors such as the lack of a close confiding relationship make depression more likely.

However, there is a problem with this explanation...

Depression may be a consequence of negative life events, but may also be their cause. When depressed, a person may become overwhelmed by life stressors, which are a direct result of their illness.

Social networks and social skills

Depressed individuals often report having sparse social networks (making them less able to handle negative life events).

They may also lack social skills (which means they may elicit rejection from others) (Joiner et al.).

There is evidence to support this explanation...

Research suggests that poor social skills may play a causal role in the development of depression.

Low social competence has been found to predict the onset of depression in primary age children (Cole).

Poor interpersonal problem-solving skills have been found to lead to an increased incidence of depression among adolescents (Davila et al.).

Chapter 10

Overview
Explanations of depression
Depression > Therapies for depression > Biological therapies for depression
Psychological therapies for depression

Biological therapies for depression

Antidepressants

How do they work?

Depression is caused by insufficient amounts of neurotransmitters (serotonin and noradrenaline) available in the brain.

Antidepressants work either by reducing the rate of re-absorbtion or by blocking the enzyme which breaks down these neurotransmitters in the synapse.

This increases the amount of the neurotransmitters available to excite neighbouring nerve cells.

Tricyclics (TCAs)

These block the transporter mechanism that reabsorbs serotonin and noradrenaline into the presynaptic cell after it has fired.

As a result, more neurotransmitters are left in the synapse, prolonging their action.

SSRIs

Instead of blocking the reuptake of different neurotransmitters, they block mainly serotonin and so increase the availability of serotonin at the synapse.

Evidence comes from the success of SSRIs such as *Prozac,* which reduce the symptoms of depression.

Phases of treatment

• Treatment of current symptoms takes place during the *acute phase.*

• Once symptoms have diminished, treatment enters a *continuation phase.*

• A *maintenance phase* is recommended for individuals with history of depression.

Effectiveness of TCAs versus SSRIs…

Both TCAs and SSRIs have been shown to produce a more significant reduction in depressive symptoms compared to a placebo (Arroll *et al.*.

SSRIs may only be effective in cases of severe depression…

Kirsch *et al.* reviewed clinical trials of SSRIs and concluded that only in cases of the most severe depression was there any significant advantage to using SSRIs over a placebo.

However…

This may be because among moderately depressed individuals, even the placebo appeared to offer them *some* hope, which contributed to a lessening of symptoms. For the severely depressed, the expectation of anything working was absent, thus removing any placebo effect.

Appropriateness of TCAs and SSRIs…

SSRIs have an important advantage over TCAs with respect to tolerability. SSRIs are better tolerated than TCAs, therefore patients are more likely to continue with treatment and recover (Montgomery *et al.*).

Antidepressants are not suitable for children and adolescents…

Double blind studies (e.g. Geller *et al.*) have consistently failed to demonstrate the superiority of antidepressant medications over placebos when given to children and adolescents, which may have something to do with developmental differences in brain chemistry.

There may be an increased risk of suicide…

A review of studies (Barbui *et al.*) found that, although the use of SSRIs increased the risk of suicide among adolescents, the risk was decreased among adults, and particularly so for adults aged 65+ where it appeared to have a protective effect against the risk of suicide.

There is a publication bias…

Turner *et al.* claim that research that shows a positive outcome of antidepressant treatment is more likely to be published, thus exaggerating the benefits of antidepressant drugs.

The implication of this is that doctors may be led into inappropriate treatment decisions that may not be in the best interests of patients.

Electroconvulsive therapy (ECT)

ECT is generally used in severely depressed patients for whom psychotherapy and medication have proved ineffective.

It is used when there is a risk of suicide, because ECT often has much quicker results than antidepressant drugs.

ECT in practice

• In unilateral ECT, an electrode is placed on the non-dominant side of the brain and another on the forehead.

• The patient is injected with a barbiturate to make them unconscious during ECT, then given a nerve-blocking agent to prevent fractures during the seizure.

• A small amount of current is passed through the brain for half a second.

• This creates a seizure, which affects the whole brain.

The mechanism of ECT

It is the seizure rather than the shock that produces an improvement in symptoms.

The seizure appears to restore the brain's ability to regulate mood. It may do this by enhancing the transmission of neurochemicals, or by improving blood flow in the brain.

Effectiveness of ECT…

Research (e.g. Gregory *et al.*) has shown that when ECT is compared to 'sham' ECT, there tends to be a significant difference in outcome in favour of real ECT.

ECT has also been shown to be effective in cases of treatment-resistant depression (Folkerts *et al.*) although other studies have found no significant improvement following the administration of ECT for treatment-resistant depression (Hussain).

ECT versus antidepressants…

A review of 18 studies with 1,144 patients comparing ECT with antidepressant medication showed that ECT is more effective in the short-term treatment of depression (Scott).

However… None of these trials compared ECT with the newer types of antidepressants such as the SSRIs.

Appropriateness of ECT…
Side effects…

Rose *et al.* concluded that at least one-third of patients complained of persistent memory loss after ECT. A Department of Health report in 2007 found that, among those receiving ECT in the previous two years, 30% reported that it had resulted in permanent fear and anxiety.

ECT may help the elderly…

Benek-Higgins *et al.* claim that depression in elderly people is often misdiagnosed because its symptoms are masked by natural changes in these individuals. However, ECT can be effective and is well-tolerated in the elderly. A meta-analysis (Mulsant *et al.*) found a significant improvement in 83% cases where ECT was used with elderly patients.

Chapter 10

Overview
Explanations of depression
Biological therapies for depression

Depression > Therapies for depression > Psychological therapies for depression

Psychological therapies for depression

Cognitive-behavioural therapy (CBT)

Maladaptive cognitions

CBT emphasises the role of maladaptive thoughts and cognitions in the origins and maintenance of depression.

The aim of CBT is to identify and alter these maladaptive cognitions, as well as any dysfunctional behaviours that may be contributing to the depression.

CBT is focused on current problems and current dysfunctional thinking.

Thought catching

Individuals are taught to see the link between their thoughts and their feelings.

During CBT they are taught to challenge this association between emotion-arousing events and the 'automatic' negative thoughts that accompany them.

By challenging these dysfunctional thoughts, and replacing them with more constructive ones, clients may reduce the symptoms of their depression.

Behavioural activation

This is based on the commonsense idea that being active leads to rewards that act as an antidote to depression.

A characteristic of depression is that depressed people no longer participate in activities that they previously enjoyed.

In CBT, therapist and client identify potentially pleasurable activities and deal with any cognitive obstacles.

Effectiveness of CBT…

A meta-analysis by Robinson et al. found that CBT was superior to no-treatment control groups. However, when these control groups were divided into waiting list (i.e. no treatment at all) and placebo groups, CBT was not significantly more effective than placebos at reducing depressive symptoms.

The problem of attrition…

Hunt and Andrews examined five meta-analyses and found the median drop-out rate was 8%. If participants drop out because they feel therapy isn't helping, then the outcomes for the remaining participants will appear artificially positive, as they are more highly motivated.

Effectiveness depends on therapist competence…

Therapist competence appears to explain a significant amount of the variation in CBT outcomes. Kuyken and Tsivrikos lend support to this claim, concluding that as much as 15% of the variation in outcome can be attributed to therapist outcome.

Appropriateness of CBT…

CBT has been successfully applied to elderly populations, juveniles and depressed adolescents. When combined with antidepressants, CBT is particularly effective at reducing the symptoms of depression and reducing suicidal thoughts and behaviour (March et al.).

The appropriateness of computer- and phone-based therapies…

The cognitive aspect of CBT has been shown to be as effective as other forms of psychotherapy when administered by computer programs, such as 'Beat the Blues' (Selmi et al.).

Mohr et al. carried out a meta-analysis of 12 studies and found that psychotherapy conducted over the phone significantly reduced the symptoms of depression compared to a non-treatment control group, although it was only half as effective as face-to-face psychotherapy.

A particular advantage of computer-based and phone-based psychotherapy is the low drop-out compared to face-to-face CBT.

Psychodynamic interpersonal therapy (PIT)

The nature of PIT

Hobson emphasised that the mutual task of therapist and client was to engage in a therapeutic 'conversation'.

In this 'conversation', problems are relived in the present and resolved within the therapeutic relationship.

Hobson believed that depression arises from disturbances in personal relationships, and can only be modified effectively within another relationship – the therapeutic relationship.

Components of PIT

There are seven interlinking components:

- *Exploratory rationale* – Interpersonal difficulties identified and links with current problems explored.
- *Shared understanding* – Therapist tries to understand what client is feeling.
- *Staying with feelings* – Feelings are recreated within the therapeutic environment.
- *Focusing on difficult feelings* – Client may not display appropriate emotion.
- *Gaining insight* – Therapist points out patterns in different types of relationship.
- *Sequencing of interventions* e.g. context of feelings is established before sharing insights.
- *Change during therapy* is acknowledged and encouraged by therapist.

Effectiveness of PIT…

Paley et al. showed that, as a treatment for depression, outcomes for PIT were at least equivalent to those achieved with CBT. However, they acknowledged that changes in significant life events were not monitored during the study, therefore any observed reductions in depressive symptoms could not be attributed solely to the therapeutic effects of PIT.

The *Collaborative Psychotherapy Project* (Barkham et al.) found PIT was effective in reducing the severity of depressive symptoms, but after 12 months, patients showed a tendency for symptoms to recur, thus limiting its long-term effectiveness.

Appropriateness of PIT…
The importance of relational processes…

Guthrie argues that PIT is particularly important in the treatment of cases of depression that result from dysfunctional relationships (e.g. between parent and child).

Research has consistently shown that the quality of the relationship between therapist and client is an important determinant of the outcomes of therapy. For example, Horvath and Bedi found that the better the quality of the relationship between therapist and client, the greater the client change.

A maintenance therapy…

PIT is used effectively as a preventive measure by focusing on the period after the acute depression has passed. Once the individual is in remission and is relatively symptom-free, he or she begins to take on more responsibilities and has increased social contact.

PIT helps individuals to reduce the stresses associated with remission and thereby lower the risk of recurrence.

Phobic disorders

Division A Overview
Classification and diagnosis of phobic disorders

Division B Explanations of phobic disorders
Biological explanations of phobic disorders
Psychological explanations of phobic disorders

Division C Therapies for phobic disorders
Biological therapies for phobic disorders
Psychological therapies for phobic disorders

Issues, debates and approaches
In the psychopathology section (Section A) of the Unit 4 exam there is no explicit credit given to issues, debates and approaches. This doesn't mean that such material would not be creditworthy (it would) but it means it is not required. So, in this chapter we have not specifically identified IDA.

Specification

Phobic disorders	
Overview	• Clinical characteristics of the phobic disorders.
	• Issues surrounding the classification and diagnosis of phobic disorders, including reliability and validity.
Explanations	• Biological explanations of phobic disorders, for example, genetics, biochemistry.
	• Psychological explanations of phobic disorders, for example, behavioural, cognitive, psychodynamic and socio-cultural.
Therapy	• Biological therapies for phobic disorders, including their evaluation in terms of appropriateness and effectiveness.
	• Psychological therapies for phobic disorders, for example, behavioural, psychodynamic and cognitive-behavioural, including their evaluation in terms of appropriateness and effectiveness.

Classification and diagnosis of phobic disorders

Clinical characteristics

The nature of phobic disorders

DSM category of anxiety disorders includes agoraphobia (fear of being in a place where escape is difficult), specific phobia (e.g. of animals, aeroplanes, water) and social phobia (fear of situations involving social interaction).

Diagnostic criteria

- *Fear* – Marked and persistent fear that is excessive or unreasonable.
- *Self-awareness* of the excessive nature of the fear, which distinguishes phobia from delusional mental illness (e.g. schizophrenia) where the individual is not aware of the unreasonableness of their behaviour.
- *Interferes with normal functioning* – The avoidance of or distress in the feared situation interferes with the person's normal routine, occupation or relationships.
- *Duration* – In individuals under age 18 years the duration of symptoms is at least six months.

Reliability of diagnosis

Inter-rater reliability

Skyre *et al.* assessed inter-rater reliability for diagnosing social phobia by asking three clinicians to assess 54 patient interviews obtained using the *Structured Clinical Interview* (SCID-I). There was high inter-rater agreement (+.72). SCID is a semi-structured interview requiring extensive training to administer, which may explain the high reliability.

Hiller *et al.* reported satisfactory to excellent diagnostic agreement in a test–retest study using the *Munich Diagnostic Checklist* (MDC).

There is some evidence of poor reliability…

Kendler *et al.* interviewed phobic individuals (face-to-face or over the telephone). Over a one-month interval (test–retest) there was a mean agreement of +.46. Reliability over eight years was even lower (+.30).

This may be explained…

Kendler *et al.* suggest that low reliability might be due to the poor recall by participants of their fears (sometimes over-exaggerating fears and sometimes under-exaggerating them).

Or it might be because interviewers differ in their interpretation of the severity of symptoms, so that some interviewers might conclude that a symptom is clinically significant, whereas others might conclude that the severity does not exceed the clinical threshold and therefore a diagnosis is not made.

Unreliable diagnosis

Rosenhan demonstrated that situational factors may be more influential when making a diagnosis of mental illness than clinical characteristics (see page 79). This can be applied to diagnosis of phobic disorders.

Later research has not supported this…

Spitzer *et al.* gave 74 emergency room psychiatrists a detailed case description and found that only three offered a diagnosis of psychotic depression and only one third recommended medication.

Validity of diagnosis

Comorbidity

If two (or more) conditions co-occur, this suggests that they are not separate entities and therefore the diagnostic category is not very useful, e.g. when deciding what treatment to advise.

Research has found high levels of comorbidity between social phobias, animal phobias, generalised anxiety disorder and depression (e.g. Kendler *et al.*).

This is supported by…

Up to 66% of patients with one anxiety disorder are also diagnosed with another anxiety disorder (Eysenck). The implications are that the diagnosis should simply be 'anxiety disorder' rather than phobia or obsessive-compulsive disorder (OCD).

Validity may be increased using computer diagnosis…

Computerised scales for assessing phobic disorders may be preferable because the presence of another person can create fears of negative evaluation.

Computerised scales also mean there is less of an effect of interviewer bias on the patient's answers (Kobak *et al.*).

Concurrent validity

Mattick and Clarke showed that their *Social Phobia Scale* (SPS) correlated well with other standard measures (varying between +.54 and +.69).

Gender bias…

Women are more likely to be diagnosed with specific phobias, possibly because clinicians are influenced by gender stereotypes (Worrell and Remer).

Construct validity

Beidel *et al.* found the *Social Phobia and Anxiety Inventory* (SPAI) correlates well with behavioural measures of social phobia (e.g. ease of public speaking) and lacks association with behaviours unrelated to social phobia.

Culture differences…

Taijin-kyofusho (TKS) is a culturally distinctive phobia recognised in Japan. This is a social phobia where an individual has a fear of embarrassing others in social situations. In the UK a person exhibiting such symptoms would not be diagnosed with a social phobia, indicating the effect of cultural experiences on the diagnosis of a disorder.

Other issues

Labelling

Labelling is an issue because the diagnosis 'phobic' sticks with a person even after symptoms disappear.

Idiographic techniques may be preferable…

Labelling occurs when using diagnostic systems (e.g. DSM). Such systems are nomothetic and focus away from the individual, whereas idiographic techniques highlight an individual's unique characteristics.

Chapter 11

Overview	
Explanations of phobic disorders	>	Biological explanations of phobic disorders
Phobic disorders	>	Therapies for phobic disorders	Psychological explanations of phobic disorders

Biological explanations of phobic disorders

Genetic factors

Family studies

Fyer *et al.* found that probands had three times as many relatives who also experienced phobias compared to normal controls.

Solyom *et al.* found that 45% of phobic patients had at least one relative with the disorder compared to 17% of normal controls.

Relatives usually have the same disorder as the proband, e.g. Ost found that 64% of blood phobics had a least one relative with the same disorder.

Twin studies

Torgersen compared MZ and same-sex DZ twin pairs (85 pairs) where one twin (the proband) had an anxiety disorder with panic attacks. Such disorders were five times more frequent in MZ twin pairs.

Inherited tendencies

Various suggestions include:

- *High levels of arousal* in the ANS, which creates increased amounts of adrenaline and this leads to an oversensitive fear response *(adrenogenic theory)*.
- *Dopamine pathways* in the brain may predispose some people to be more readily conditioned, so that they are more likely to acquire phobias easily.
- *Abnormal serotonin activity* modulates those areas of the brain involved in the fear response, such as the amygdala.

Some phobias have a greater genetic component than others…

Kendler *et al.* estimated a 67% heritability rate for agoraphobia, 59% for blood/injury, 51% for social phobias and 47% for animal phobias.

Torgerson actually only found 31% concordance (which is very low) for MZ twins in terms of anxiety disorders and almost no concordance for DZ twins.

Cultural differences…

Brown *et al.* found that phobic disorders were more common among African-American than white American participants, even when socioeconomic factors were controlled. This shows that environmental/ social factors are important.

The diathesis-stress model…

It is likely that genetic factors predispose an individual to develop phobias, but experience plays a role in triggering such responses.

One of the problems with family and twin studies…

They fail to control for shared experiences. MZ twins are likely to share more similar experiences (environments) than DZ twins because, for example, they are likely to have more similar interests even when reared apart (interests often are related to inherited tendencies).

There is research support…

Children with signs of behavioural inhibition at birth (dislike of unfamiliar situations) were found later to have higher ANS activity and develop significantly more anxiety disorders (Biederman *et al.*).

Successful drug therapies for phobics include drugs that block activity of the adrenergic system (beta-blockers), reducing anxiety.

Brain scanning techniques have been used to measure the density of dopamine reuptake sites. Tiihonen *et al.* found a significantly lower number of such sites in patients with social phobia than in normal controls, which would lead to abnormally low levels of dopamine.

However…

This does not show that such differences actually cause phobias in the first place, e.g. drugs may be treating symptoms that have arisen as an effect rather than the cause of phobias.

An evolutionary approach

Ancient fears and modern minds

Ancient fears (e.g. snakes, heights) were dangers to our distant ancestors. Modern phobias are often related to these ancient fears rather than modern dangers (e.g. guns, electricity) because these have not been around enough to have influenced adaptive selection (Marks and Nesse).

Prepotency

Experiencing anxiety after an event has happened would not be an adaptive response, therefore animals have evolved a response to potential threats.

Prepotency refers to the tendency to respond prior to direct experience, e.g. to respond anxiously to snake-like movement.

Preparedness

An innate readiness to learn about dangerous situations is more flexible than inheriting rigid behavioural responses to specific situations.

Seligman argued that animals, including humans, are biologically prepared to rapidly learn an association between particular (i.e. potentially life-threatening) stimuli and fear, and once learned this association is difficult to extinguish.

Biological preparedness may be linked to ancient fears…

Rhesus monkeys rapidly develop a fear of snakes if they see another rhesus monkey showing fear towards a snake, but the same doesn't happen if fear is shown towards a flower (Mineka *et al.*).

The evolutionary approach doesn't explain clinical phobias…

Merckelbach *et al.* found that most of the clinical phobias in their survey of phobias were rated as non-prepared rather than prepared.

There is research support…

Öhman and Soares showed that people who were fearful of snakes or spiders showed a greater fear response (SNS activity measured by GSR) when shown masked (not immediately recognisable) pictures of snake/ spiders. This shows that people respond to prepotent signals.

Bennett-Levy and Marteau asked participants to rate animals (e.g. for sliminess), and found that fear was due to discrepancy with the human form and aversive stimulus configuration (e.g. hissing), i.e. prepotent signals.

There is mixed research support…

McNally reviewed laboratory studies (participants were conditioned to fear prepared and unprepared stimuli). The participants showed resistance to extinction of fear responses conditioned by 'prepared' stimuli, but evidence for rapid acquisition was, at best, equivocal.

A simpler, non-evolutionary explanation…

Davey proposed that fears are based on an expectancy bias – the expectation that fear-relevant stimuli (e.g. past experience of unpleasantness) will produce negative consequences in the future. There is no need to invoke past evolutionary history. This explains the acquisition of 'modern' phobias (e.g. phobia of hypodermic needles).

Chapter 11

Overview	
Explanations of phobic disorders	>	Biological explanations of phobic disorders
Phobic disorders	>	Therapies for phobic disorders	Psychological explanations of phobic disorders

Psychological explanations of phobic disorders

Psychodynamic approach

Freud proposed that a phobia was the conscious expression of repressed conflicts. The ego deals with conflict by repressing the undesirable emotions into the unconscious mind. Such repressed thoughts can be expressed by projecting them onto a neutral object or situation, e.g. a dog or social situation. Therefore the individual displays a fear of dogs or social situations, rather than expressing their real fear.

For example, the case study of Little Hans concerned a boy who had become terrified of horses. Freud suggested that Hans' phobia developed because Hans projected a real fear (that his mother would leave him) onto horses (because he heard a man say 'Don't put your finger to the white horse or it'll bite you' and Hans also once asked his mother if she would like to put her finger on his penis).

The Little Hans case study has been criticised...

A case study concerns one unique individual and therefore can't be generalised to the wider population.

The Little Hans study lacked objectivity because both Hans' father and Freud interpreted the evidence according to their expectations about the origins of phobias.

Hans' phobia could be explained in terms of classical conditioning (Hans associated horses with feeling scared).

However there is other research support...

Bowlby found that agoraphobics often had early experiences of family conflict. He suggested that such conflict leads a young child to feel very anxious when separated from their parents (separation anxiety). Such fears are suppressed but later emerge as agoraphobia.

Whiting et al. studied the occurrence of phobias in other cultures and concluded that they were more common in societies that had a structured form of child-rearing. The reason may be because stricter, structured parenting might lead to children having to repress desires.

The fact that therapies that simply target the symptoms of phobia (such as systematic desensitisation) are not 100% successful may be because they fail to deal with the underlying causes of the phobias.

Behavioural approach

Classical conditioning

Little Albert developed a fear of white furry objects because he experienced:

- A furry rat (neutral stimulus, NS) being associated with a loud noise (unconditioned stimulus, UCS).
- UCS produced an unconditioned response (UCR) of fear.
- The furry object (now a CS) acquired the same properties (CR) so that when Albert saw it he cried, presumably because he was scared.

Operant conditioning

Two-process theory (Mowrer) suggests that phobias are (1) acquired through classical conditioning and (2) maintained through operant conditioning, where the avoidance of the phobic stimulus reduces fear and is thus reinforcing (negative reinforcement).

There is research support...

People with phobias often do recall a specific incident when their phobia first appeared, e.g. being bitten by a dog (Sue et al.).

However...

Not everyone who has a phobia can recall such an incident, though it may be that such traumatic incidents have been repressed (Öst).

Not everyone who is bitten by a dog develops a phobia of dogs (Di Nardo et al.), though perhaps only those with a genetic vulnerability for phobias would be affected by such events (diathesis-stress model).

Biological preparedness...

Bergman failed to condition a fear response in infants by pairing a loud bell with wooden blocks. It may be that fear responses are only learned when the neutral stimulus is an 'ancient fear' (e.g. an animal).

Cultural differences...

The behaviourist approach can account for cultural differences because, for example, each society offers its own culture-specific role models that influence which phobias might be acquired.

Social learning

Phobias may also be acquired through imitating the behaviour of others, e.g. seeing a parent responding to a spider with extreme fear may lead a child to acquire a similar behaviour because the behaviour appears rewarding.

There is research support...

In one study (Bandura and Rosenthal) an observer watched a model apparently experiencing pain every time a buzzer sounded. The observer later demonstrated an emotional reaction to the sound.

We can conclude that...

Different phobias may be the result of different processes, e.g. Sue et al. found that agoraphobics were most likely to explain their disorder in terms of a specific incident, whereas arachnophobics were most likely to cite modelling as the cause.

Cognitive approach

Phobias may develop as the consequence of irrational thinking, e.g. a person in a lift may think 'I could become trapped in here and suffocate' (an irrational thought).

Beck et al. proposed that such irrational thoughts create anxiety and it is the fear of being in a situation of high anxiety that creates a phobia. Phobics tend to overestimate their fears, increasing the likelihood of phobias.

There is research support for dysfunctional assumptions...

Gournay found that phobics were more likely than normal people to overestimate risks, suggesting that they are predisposed to develop phobias because of their cognitive style.

The success of CBT as a treatment for phobia...

It can be argued that, if a therapy changes the dysfunctional assumptions a person has and this leads to a reduction to their phobia, then the dysfunctional assumptions may originally have caused the disorder.

Chapter 11

Overview
Explanations of phobic disorders
Phobic disorders   >   Therapies for phobic disorders   >
Biological therapies for phobic disorders
Psychological therapies for phobic disorders

Biological therapies for phobic disorders

Chemotherapy

Antianxiety drugs – Benzodiazepines

Benzodiazepines (BZs) (e.g. *Valium, Diazepam*) slow down the activity of the central nervous system by enhancing the activity of GABA, a neurotransmitter that has a general quietening effect on many of the neurons in the brain.

They do this by locking into GABA receptors on the outside of receiving neurons, which opens a channel to increase the flow of chloride ions into the neuron. Chloride ions make it harder for the neuron to be stimulated by other neurotransmitters.

Antianxiety drugs – Beta-blockers

Beta-blockers (BBs) reduce the activity of adrenaline (part of SNS response to stress).

BBs bind to receptors on the cells of the heart and other parts of the body that are usually stimulated during arousal. By blocking these receptors, it is harder to stimulate these cells, so the heart beats slower and blood vessels do not contract so easily, resulting in a fall in blood pressure, and less feeling of anxiety.

Antidepressants

SSRIs (e.g. *Zoloft, Prozac*) are currently the preferred drug for treating anxiety disorders (Choy and Schneier). They increase levels of the neurotransmitter serotonin that regulates mood/anxiety.

MAOI (monoamine oxidase inhibitor), an older class of antidepressants, is more effective with some patients (Lader and Petursson). *Monoamine oxidase* (MAO) is the enzyme responsible for breaking down monoamine neurotransmitters (e.g. serotonin and dopamine) so an inhibitor prevents this happening, leading to higher levels of monoamines in the synaptic gap.

The effectiveness of antianxiety drugs…

Kahn *et al.* found that BZs were more effective than placebos in reducing anxiety.

Hildalgo *et al.* found that BZs were more effective than antidepressants in reducing the anxiety associated with phobic reactions.

Research studies (e.g. Liebowitz *et al.*) have shown that BBs can also provide an effective means of anxiety control.

However…

Some studies have shown that the benefits may be largely explained in terms of placebo effects, e.g. Turner *et al.* found no difference between BBs and placebo groups in terms of reduced heart rate, feelings of nervousness and so on.

The effectiveness of antidepressant drugs…

MAOIs have been found to be more effective than placebos and more effective in the reduction of anxiety than BBs (Liebowitz *et al.*).

SSRIs led to improved levels of self-rated anxiety when compared to a placebo treatment (Katzelnick *et al.*).

Aouizerate *et al.* concluded that SSRIs provide relief for social phobics in 50%–80% of cases, a level fairly similar to BZs, but SSRIs are preferable because there are fewer side effects.

Appropriateness of chemotherapy…

Not a cure…

Drugs can't provide a complete treatment as they focus on symptoms.

Side effects…

BZs may cause increased aggressiveness and long-term impairment of memory – though recent research (Kindt *et al.*) has proposed that such negative effects might be used to remove anxiety-causing memories.

BBs have few side effects.

SSRIs are linked to increased suicides in adolescents (Barbui *et al.*).

MAOIs have a number of side effects, e.g. dizziness, insomnia.

Addiction…

BZs may become addictive, even when only low doses are given. A maximum use of four weeks is recommended (Ashton).

Ethical issues…

The issue of informed consent concerns the extent to which patients are not informed about the fact that drugs may not actually be much better than placebos.

Psychosurgery

Capsulotomy and cingulotomy

These surgical interventions sever connections to malfunctioning parts of the brain to reduce anxiety levels.

The *capsule* and the *cingulum* are both parts of the limbic system, the region of the brain that is associated with emotion.

The surgeon inserts a probe through the top of the skull and pushes it to the capsule or cingulum, which is located deep in the brain. The leading tip of the probe burns away small portions of tissue.

Such operations are irreversible and only performed as a last resort.

Deep brain stimulation (DBS)

Wires are placed in target areas (capsule and cingulum) and connected to a battery in the patient's chest. When the current is on the target circuits are interrupted.

Deep brain stimulation involves no tissue destruction, though the wires are permanent.

Effectiveness of psychosurgery…

Ruck *et al.* studied 26 patients with long-term non-obsessive anxiety disorders (e.g. panic disorder, social phobia). Following a capsulotomy, the patients showed significant reductions in anxiety.

However…

The negative symptoms were greater than expected, e.g. seven patients attempted to commit suicide after surgery.

Appropriateness of psychosurgery…

Psychosurgery is rarely suitable for phobias and then only for extreme cases that have proved otherwise untreatable and that interfere with normal day-to-day functioning.

Deep brain stimulation may offer a better, non-permanent solution.

Szasz criticised psychosurgery generally because the psyche is not something that is physical and therefore it is illogical to suggest that it can be operated on.

Ethical issues…

The irreversible nature of psychosurgery and the difficulties with providing informed consent raise ethical concerns.

Chapter 11

Overview
Explanations of phobic disorders
Biological therapies for phobic disorders

Phobic disorders > Therapies for phobic disorders > Psychological therapies for phobic disorders

Psychological therapies for phobic disorders

Behavioural therapy: Systematic desensitisation (SD)

Key principle

Phobias are perpetuated because the anxiety created blocks any attempt to re-experience the stimulus. Wolpe developed a technique where the feared stimulus is reintroduced gradually.

Counterconditioning

The patient is taught relaxation techniques and then given the opportunity to experience the feared stimulus while relaxed, forming a new association that runs counter to the original association. Wolpe also called this 'reciprocal inhibition' because the relaxation inhibits the anxiety.

Desensitisation hierarchy

Therapist and patient construct a series of imagined scenes, each one progressively more fearful. They then work through this hierarchy, relaxing and mastering each stage before moving on to the next.

Different forms of SD

In vivo desensitisation – confronting feared situations directly.

Covert (also known as in vitro) desensitisation – imagining the feared stimuli.

Flooding – no hierarchy or relaxation, just exposure to the feared stimulus.

Effectiveness of SD…

Research has found that SD is successful for a range of phobic disorders, e.g. McGrath et al. found about 75% success rates.

Capafóns et al. found overall success for 41 aerophobics receiving two one-hour sessions per week over a 12–15 week period, using in vivo and covert techniques, but SD was not 100% effective.

In vivo techniques are more successful than covert ones (Menzies and Clarke), though often a number of different exposure techniques are involved – in vivo, covert and also modelling where the patient watches someone else who is coping well with the feared stimulus (Comer).

However…

Öhman et al. suggest that SD may not be as effective in treating phobias that have an underlying evolutionary survival component (e.g. fear of the dark or dangerous animals) than in treating phobias that have been acquired as a result of personal experience.

Appropriateness of SD…
Strengths…

SD requires less effort from the patient than other psychotherapies (such as REBT, below).

SD can be self-administered, a method that has proved successful with, for example, social phobia (Humphrey).

Symptom substitution…

SD may appear to resolve a problem but suppressing symptoms may result in other symptoms. However, there is no evidence of this (Langevin).

Are the ingredients of SD necessary?…

Positive expectancies may be the most important ingredient, e.g. Klein et al. found SD and supportive psychotherapy equally effective for patients with either social or specific phobias.

Rational-emotive behaviour therapy (REBT)

Key principle

Ellis proposed that phobias occur because of irrational thinking.

Therefore treatment should make thinking rational (R) and also address emotional (E) and behavioural (B) problems (= REB).

ABC model (Ellis)

A = activating event (situation that results in feelings of frustration and anxiety) e.g. friend ignores you in the street.

B = irrational beliefs arising from A, e.g. your friend must have decided he doesn't like you; no one likes you, you are worthless.

C = self-defeating consequences, e.g. avoid social situations in the future.

Disputing

Beliefs (not activating events) lead to self-defeating consequences. Therefore REBT focuses on disputing the beliefs, e.g.:

• Logical disputing – e.g. 'Does thinking this way make sense?'.

• Empirical disputing – (evidence based) e.g. 'Where is the proof that this belief is accurate?'.

• Pragmatic disputing – (usefulness) e.g. 'How is this belief likely to help me?'.

The phobic moves from catastrophising ('All spiders will kill me') to more rational interpretations ('It is rare to encounter a poisonous spider'). This helps the phobic become more self-accepting.

Effectiveness of REBT…

REBT has generally done well in outcome studies (i.e. studies designed to measure responses to treatment), e.g. a meta-analysis by Engels et al.

Ellis claimed a 90% success rate, taking an average of 27 sessions to complete.

NICE identified CBT (of which REBT is an example) as the first-line approach in treating anxiety disorders.

However…

Emmelkamp et al. concluded that REBT was less effective than in vivo exposure treatments, at least for agoraphobia.

Appropriateness of REBT…
Not suitable for all…

Ellis believed that sometimes people who claimed to be following REBT principles were not putting their revised beliefs into action and therefore the therapy was not effective.

Ellis also suggested that some people simply do not want the direct sort of advice and cognitive effort associated with REBT.

There is research support…

Research has found that people who hold irrational beliefs form inferences that are significantly less functional than those that are formed by people who hold rational beliefs (Bond and Dryden).

On the other hand, it may be that irrational beliefs are counterproductive but realistic, e.g. Alloy and Abrahmson found that depressed people gave more accurate estimates of the likelihood of a disaster than 'normal' controls (calling it the 'sadder but wiser' effect).

Ethical issues…

REBT is regarded as one of the most aggressive CBTs (Rosenhan and Seligman) and, in addition, it is judgmental. These aspects of the therapy raise ethical concerns because of the psychological harm that may be caused to a person's self-esteem.

Obsessive-compulsive disorder (OCD

Division A Overview
Classification and diagnosis of OCD

Division B Explanations of OCD
Biological explanations of OCD
Psychological explanations of OCD

Division C Therapies for OCD
Biological therapies for OCD
Psychological therapies for OCD

Issues, debates and approaches
In the psychopathology section (Section A) of the Unit 4 exam there is no explicit credit given to issues, debates and approaches. This doesn't mean that such material would not be creditworthy (it would) but it means it is not required. So, in this chapter we have not specifically identified IDA.

Specification

Obsessive-compulsive disorder	
Overview	• Clinical characteristics of the obsessive-compulsive disorder.
	• Issues surrounding the classification and diagnosis of obsessive-compulsive disorder, including reliability and validity.
Explanations	• Biological explanations of obsessive-compulsive disorder, for example, genetics, biochemistry.
	• Psychological explanations of obsessive-compulsive disorder, for example, behavioural, cognitive, psychodynamic and socio-cultural.
Therapy	• Biological therapies for obsessive-compulsive disorder, including their evaluation in terms of appropriateness and effectiveness.
	• Psychological therapies for obsessive-compulsive disorder, for example, behavioural, psychodynamic and cognitive-behavioural, including their evaluation in terms of appropriateness and effectiveness.

Classification and diagnosis of OCD

Clinical characteristics

The nature of OCD

In OCD anxiety arises from both the obsessions and the compulsions.

- Obsessions are recurrent, intrusive thoughts or impulses that are perceived as inappropriate or forbidden (DSM-IV-TR), e.g. the idea that germs are everywhere or the impulse to shout out. Obsessions create anxiety.
- Compulsions are repetitive behaviours or mental acts that aim to reduce the anxiety that accompanies an obsession (DSM-IV-TR), e.g. hand washing (overt behaviour) or counting (mental act). OCD patients believe that something terrible will happen to them if they don't perform the compulsions and thus the compulsions also create anxiety.

Diagnostic criteria

- *Distress* – The obsessions and compulsions cause marked distress.
- *Obsessions* are more than excessive worries about real-life problems.
- *Compulsions* aim to neutralise or prevent obsessions, and are time-consuming and applied rigidly.
- *Compulsions* do not have any realistic effect to reduce obsessions and are clearly excessive.
- *Product of patient's own mind* – The obsessions or compulsions are recognised as a product of the patient's own mind (i.e. not placed in their mind, as in schizophrenia).
- *Child OCD* sufferers may not recognise that their behaviour is unreasonable.
- *A clinical diagnosis* of OCD is only made if there is no other possible physiological cause (e.g. substance abuse) or if the symptoms cannot be better accounted for by another disorder.

Reliability of diagnosis

Unreliable diagnosis

Rosenhan demonstrated that situational factors may be more influential when making a diagnosis of mental illness than clinical characteristics (see page 79). This can be applied to diagnosis of OCD.

Y-BOCS

The Yale-Brown Obsessive-Compulsive Scale is a semi-structured interview that can be used to assess symptom severity.

Woody et al. used Y-BOCS to assess 54 OCD patients and found good internal consistency. Inter-rater reliability was excellent but test–retest after about 50 days was lower than desirable.

Other studies (e.g. Kim et al.) have found good test–retest reliability over the short term (two weeks).

The children's version (CY-BOCS) has been shown to have good inter-rater reliability (Scahill et al.).

Online versions of Y-BOCS yield reliability scores similar to interviewer-administered versions (Baer et al.).

Later research has not supported this…

Spitzer et al. gave 74 emergency room psychiatrists a detailed case description and found that only three psychiatrists offered a diagnosis of psychotic depression and only one third recommended medication.

Problems assessing reliability and validity of OCD scales…

OCD patients may be embarrassed or feel afraid that an interviewer will take symptoms as a sign of a deeper psychosis, and therefore might not produce honest answers to questionnaires and this reduces the validity of any such questionnaire.

OCD patients may be fearful of handling questionnaires because they are contaminated (Anthony and Barlow).

Some OCD patients may lack awareness of the severity and frequency of their symptoms, which means that the validity of any diagnosis is likely to be improved by interviewing close friends/ partners.

Validity may be increased using computer diagnosis…

Computerised scales for assessing OCD may be preferable because the presence of another person creates fears of negative evaluation.

Computerised scales also mean there is less effect of interviewer bias on the patient's answers (Kobak et al.).

Validity of diagnosis

Comorbidity

Rosenfeld et al. found that patients diagnosed with OCD had higher Y-BOCS scores than patients with other anxiety disorders and normal controls, i.e. it does distinguish OCD patients from others.

However…

Woody et al. found poor discrimination with depression, i.e. patients diagnosed with OCD were also often diagnosed with depression.

This suggests that the diagnostic category is not very useful, e.g. when deciding what treatment to advise.

Other issues

Cultural differences

The incidence of OCD tends to be about the same in most countries/cultures (about 2–3% lifetime prevalence – source: OCD Centre).

Symptoms might also be similar across cultures, e.g. one study (Matsunaga et al.) studied Japanese OCD patients and found symptoms remarkably similar to those in the West, concluding that this disorder transcends culture.

However…

There is also evidence that symptoms differ, e.g. 'normal' black Americans were found to produce higher scores on contamination obsessions that 'normal' white Americans because, for example, they interact less with animals and thus have a greater concern about the contamination from animals (Williams et al.).

The problem of cultural differences may lead to difficulties when using diagnostic scales because symptom checklists tend to be culturally based (despite cross-cultural similarities, there are still some differences). This would then increase the likelihood of an OCD diagnosis in some cultural groups (a culture bias).

Chapter 12

Overview	
Explanations of OCD >	Biological explanations of OCD
Obsessive-compulsive disorder (OCD) >	Therapies for OCD	Psychological explanations of OCD

Biological explanations of OCD

Genetic factors

Family studies

Nestadt et al. found that people with a first-degree relative with OCD had a five times greater risk of having OCD at some time in their lives, compared to the general population.

OCD patients and their relatives found it difficult to control repetitive responses on a reaction test, suggesting such behaviours might be inherited (Menzies et al.).

Twin studies

A meta-analysis of 14 twin studies found that MZ twins were twice as likely as DZ twins to develop OCD if their co-twin had the disorder (Billett et al.).

The COMT gene

COMT (catechol-O-methyltransferase) terminates dopamine activity. Karayiorgou et al. found that a variation in the COMT gene occurred in 50% of the male OCD sufferers tested, 10% of the females and only 16% of the normal population.

Inherited tendencies

Various suggestions include:

• The worry circuit (frontal cortex) – The caudate nucleus suppresses 'worry' signals from the orbitofrontal cortex (OFC) to the thalamus. If the caudate nucleus is damaged the thalamus is 'worried'.

• Low levels of serotonin – Antidepressant drugs that increase serotonin reduce OCD symptoms (Pigott et al.), whereas those drugs that don't affect serotonin don't reduce OCD symptoms (Jenicke).

• High levels of dopamine – Drugs that increase dopamine induce stereotyped movements in animals resembling the compulsive behaviours found in OCD patients (Szechtman et al.).

There is evidence for a strong genetic component...

Concordance rates are higher for OCD than many other disorders, e.g. 87% concordance for MZ twins for OCD (Carey and Gottesmann) compared with 46% for schizophrenia (McGuffin et al.).

However... Concordance rates are not 100%, which means that environmental factors must play a role too – particularly when it comes to determining specific symptoms (it is obsessive behaviours that run in families rather than the manifestation e.g. hand washing).

Comorbidity...

OCD symptoms are also found in other disorders, e.g. autism (stereotyped behaviours), anorexia nervosa (obsessive behaviour).

In particular OCD appears to be one form of expression of the same gene that determines Tourette's syndrome, as both conditions appear to run in the same families (Pauls and Leckman).

There is research support...

Schindler et al. confirmed the link between OCD and the COMT gene, but not the gender differences found by Karayiorgou et al.

Other candidate genes are being discovered all the time, e.g. a gene involved in serotonin production (SLC6A4) (Wendland et al.) and a gene (SAPAP3) absent in mice that compulsively groom themselves (Welch et al.).

There is research support...

• PET scans show greater activity in the OFC-caudate nuclei loop in OCD patients (compared with controls) and this increase is correlated with the severity of OCD (Schwartz et al.).

• SSRIs reduce dopamine levels in the basal ganglia and this is positively correlated with a reduction of OCD symptoms (Kim et al.).

• OCD patients (and their close relatives) have reduced grey matter in key regions of the brain including the OFC (Menzies et al.).

However... A recent study (Moritz et al.) found that OCD patients did not perform abnormally on cognitive tasks related to the OFC.

Links between the worry circuit and serotonin and dopamine...

Serotonin plays a key role in the OFC and caudate nuclei, therefore low serotonin would cause these areas to function poorly (Comer).

Dopamine is the main neurotransmitter of the basal ganglia. High levels of dopamine lead to overactivity of this region (Sukel).

An evolutionary approach

Adaptive basis

Obsessions and compulsions might be an exaggeration of behaviours that are adaptive. Marks and Nesse suggest:

• Grooming behaviour reduces parasitism and smoothes social interaction. OCD patients often wash and groom endlessly.

• Concern for others decreases ostracism from the group. OCD patients are often concerned with fear of harming others.

• Hoarding guards against future shortages. OCD patients excessively store things.

Harm-avoidance strategies

Abed and de Pauw suggest that a particular mental module evolved (the Involuntary Risk Scenario Generating System, IRSGS), which allows individuals to imagine certain potential risks before they happen and thus be able to deal more effectively with them when they do happen. An exaggerated IRSGS could lead to OCD.

There is supporting evidence...

The fact that OCD is so widespread across cultures (see previous page) suggests that it may have some evolutionary significance, i.e. it may be adaptive.

Limitations of evolutionary explanations...

Evolutionary explanations are often criticised for being determinist, but this is a misunderstanding of such explanations – in the case of OCD the suggestion is that our evolutionary past simply predisposes us to worry which, when excessive, leads to abnormal behaviour (an ultimate explanation) but the disorder only develops if there are proximate triggers.

Predictions from the theory have research support...

Obsessional patients should be less prone to risk taking because overactivity of IRSGS would warn them of the dangers associated with such activities and thus lead to risk avoidance. Evidence from Osborn suggests that this is the case.

There should be an increased risk of OCD at biologically critical life stages because that would be the time when the IRSGS would be generating lots of new risks. There is evidence to support this, such as increased risk for OCD during pregnancy (Buttolph et al.).

Psychological explanations of OCD

Psychodynamic

Freud's explanation

OCD arises when unacceptable wishes and impulses from the id are only partially repressed and so provoke anxiety.

People with OCD use defense mechanisms to reduce their anxiety:

- *Isolation* from undesirable wishes and impulses, but sometimes the id dominates and the impulses intrude as obsessional thoughts.
- *Undoing* unacceptable id impulses (symbolically) using compulsive acts, e.g. compulsive hand washing, to undo.
- *Reaction formation* – Adopting behaviours that are exactly the opposite of the unacceptable impulses.

There is research support...

Freud analysed the case study of the Rat Man who had obsessive fears about harm coming to his fiancée and her father. In order to fend off his obsessional fantasies, the Rat Man felt compelled to commit certain acts such as moving a rock from the path of a carriage. Freud explained this in terms of the patient's conflicting thoughts about his fiancée and her father, e.g. he loved the father but also wished him dead so he could inherit his money.

Negative effects on OCD recovery...

Salzman suggests that the therapy derived from Freud's explanation, psychoanalysis, may actually have a negative effect on OCD recovery, which challenges the Freudian explanation.

An alternative is to use a short-term psychodynamic therapy. These tend to be more direct and action-oriented and therefore reduce the tendency in OCD patients' to 'think too much'.

Behavioural

Obsessions

Mowrer explained the acquisition of fears in two-process theory:

Classical conditioning – NS (neutral stimulus) becomes associated with anxiety, e.g. child is told that eating food from the floor (NS) is disgusting and thereafter all dirty items create anxiety.

Operant conditioning – Avoiding a feared stimulus (negative reinforcement) leads to positive outcomes and is thus reinforced.

There is research support...

Mowrer's theory predicts that OCD patients are predisposed to rapid conditioning. This was demonstrated in a study (Tracy *et al.*) where participants were tested for OCD symptoms and divided into an 'OCD-like' group and a control group. The OCD-like participants were conditioned more rapidly (using an eye blink task).

Problems with using a non-clinical population...

OCD-like participants (a 'non-clinical') group are sometimes used in research on OCD for ethical and practical reasons (because of difficulties using people with OCD). It may not be appropriate to generalise the data from such studies to understanding clinical cases of OCD.

Compulsions

If a behaviour becomes associated with reduction of anxiety, this behaviour is reinforced and repeated in future.

Compulsive rituals are learned from accidental associations.

There is research support...

OCD patients were asked to carry out a 'prohibited' activity (e.g. touching something dirty) and allowed to either carry out their compulsive act or delay this. If they delayed, their anxiety levels were found to persist for a while, but then gradually decline.

Rachman concluded that compulsive behaviours serve an important function, because they provide quicker relief from anxiety than waiting.

Cognitive

Obsessions – Intrusive thoughts

People with OCD find it difficult to dismiss 'normal' intrusive thoughts (e.g. harming others, danger from germs). This leads to self-blame and an expectation that terrible things will happen as a result (Salkovskis).

Such individuals also often have depression, which weakens their ability to distract themselves from these intrusive thoughts (Frost and Steketee).

Compulsions – Neutralising anxiety

In order to avoid the anticipated consequences of intrusive thoughts, the individual must 'neutralise' them, e.g. washing their hands after feeling contaminated by dirty objects.

However, such behaviours provide only temporary relief and then anxiety builds up again. Every time a neutralising thought or act is repeated it becomes harder to resist because of the relief it provides, and it becomes a compulsion.

This is like an addiction – the more you do it, the more you have to do it again.

There is research support...

People with OCD do have maladaptive thought patterns, e.g.

- They believe that they can and should have total control over their world (Bouchard *et al.*).
- They have more intrusive thoughts than 'normal' people (Clark).
- They report trying to do things that will neutralise unwanted thoughts (Freeston *et al.*).

Gender issues...

In males, it appears that early brain injury may be associated with OCD and Tourette's.

In females, OCD and *trichotillomania* (pulling hair out) often appear after childbirth and pregnancy.

This suggests that *obsessive-compulsive spectrum disorders* may have different triggers in men and women (Lochner and Stein).

Reductionism...

There is a tendency in all these psychological (and biological) explanations to suggest that anxiety disorders can be reduced to a simple set of principles, such as repressed anxieties or classical conditioning. It is important to recognise that the 'real' explanations are likely to consist of a combination of a number of different explanations.

Chapter 12

Overview
Explanations of OCD   Biological therapies for OCD
Obsessive-compulsive disorder (OCD)   > Therapies for OCD   > Psychological therapies for OCD

Biological therapies for OCD

Chemotherapy

Antidepressants

Antidepressant drugs (e.g. SSRIs and tricyclics) increase levels of serotonin, which may normalise the 'worry circuit' (a possible cause of OCD (see page 98).

SSRIs block the transporter mechanism that re-absorbs serotonin into the pre-synaptic cell after it has fired, resulting in more serotonin at the synapse. Tricyclics block noradrenaline as well.

Antianxiety drugs

Benzodiazepines (BZs) reduce anxiety by enhancing the activity of GABA (*gamma-amino-butyric-acid*). GABA locks onto receptors on the outside of receiving neurons and this opens a channel that increases the flow of chloride ions into the neuron. Chloride ions make it harder for the neuron to be stimulated by other neurotransmitters, thus slowing down its activity and making a person feel relaxed.

Other drugs

D-Cycloserine is an antibiotic used in the treatment of tuberculosis, which appears to enhance the transmission of GABA and thus reduce anxiety (Kushner *et al.*). It is particularly effective when used in conjunction with psychotherapy.

Effectiveness of chemotherapy...

Tricyclics are regarded as more effective than SSRIs in the treatment of OCD (Koran *et al.*) but tricyclics tend to have more side effects (e.g. hallucinations and irregular heartbeat) so they are more likely to be used as a second-line treatment.

However, some studies have found SSRIs are comparable in effectiveness to *clomipramine* (a tricyclic) (Zohar and Judge). Soomro *et al.* reviewed 17 studies of the use of SSRIs with OCD and found them to be more effective than placebos in reducing the symptoms of OCD as measured with Y-BOCS.

However...
Most treatment studies are only of three to four months duration and therefore little long-term data exists (Koran *et al.*).

Appropriateness of chemotherapy...
Strengths and limitations of chemotherapy...

Chemotherapy requires little effort and is effective in the short term, but it does not provide a lasting cure, e.g. Maina *et al.* found that patients relapsed within a few weeks if medication was stopped.

There are considerable side effects even with SSRIs, e.g. nausea, headache and insomnia are common side effects (Soomro *et al.*).

Psychotherapy may be preferable...

Koran *et al.* conducted a comprehensive review of treatments for OCD concluding that, although drug therapy is more commonly used, psychotherapies such as CBT should be tried first.

Psychotherapy is particularly useful in reducing compulsions. In fact, behavioural therapy can have the same effect on the brain as drugs – reducing activity in the caudate nucleus (Schwartz *et al.*).

Psychosurgery

Capsulotomy and cingulotomy

These surgical interventions sever connections to malfunctioning parts of the brain to reduce anxiety levels.

The *capsule* and the *cingulum* are both parts of the limbic system, the region of the brain that is associated with emotion. The cingulum links the orbitofrontal cortex (OFC) to the caudate nucleus. The capsule is part of the limbic system involved with emotion and anxiety.

The surgeon inserts a probe through the top of the skull and pushes it to the capsule or cingulum, which is located deep in the brain. The leading tip of the probe burns away small portions of tissue.

Such operations are irreversible and only performed as a last resort.

Deep brain stimulation (DBS)

Wires are placed on target areas of the brain. The wires are connected to a battery in the patient's chest. When the current is on this interrupts the target circuits in the brain, such as the 'worry circuit'.

Transcranial magnetic stimulation (TMS)

TMS, like DBS, avoids destruction of brain tissue. A large electromagnetic coil is placed above the scalp near the forehead. This creates painless electric currents that stimulate the frontal cortex, a region of the brain associated with the worry circuit and mood regulation.

Effectiveness of cingulotomy...

Dougherty *et al.* found that up to 45% of patients studied (total 44) who were previously unresponsive to medication and behavioural treatments for OCD, were at least partly improved after a cingulotomy.

However...
Such findings may be biased because they are 'unblinded' i.e. the researchers know the treatment received by patients and their expectations may influence their judgment (Koran *et al.*).

A further criticism is that...
Psychosurgery may affect behaviour more globally, e.g. reducing motivation levels (Sachdev and Hay) and this (rather than surgery) may explain reduced OCD symptoms.

Effectiveness of TMS...

Greenberg *et al.* used 20 minutes of TMS to treat 12 OCD patients, resulting in a reduction of compulsive urges lasting at least eight hours.

However...
When OCD patients were given either TMS or sham TMS there was no measurable difference afterwards, as assessed using Y-BOCS (Rodriguez-Martin *et al.*). This suggests that the earlier success might be due to a placebo effect.

Appropriateness of psychosurgery...

Szasz criticised psychosurgery; a psychological state of mind is not physical and thus it is illogical to suggest that it can be operated on.

Permanent psychosurgery is associated with severe side effects ranging from personality changes and seizures to transient mania.

However...
Nyman *et al.* followed up OCD patients who received a capsulotomy at a hospital in Sweden between 1978 and 1990. Their IQ test performance, in general, remained intact.

Ethical issues...

The irreversible nature of psychosurgery and the difficulties with providing informed consent raise ethical concerns, as in the case of Mary Lou Zimmerman, who had both a capsulotomy and cingulotomy resulting in loss of function (e.g. she couldn't walk). Her family sued the clinic (and won) because they had not been sufficiently informed of the dangerous and experimental nature of the surgery.

Psychological therapies for OCD

Behavioural therapy

Exposure and response prevention therapy (ERP)

The behaviourist approach suggests that obsessions and compulsions are acquired through conditioning and therefore, in order to recover, patients must unlearn these behaviours. ERP aims to provide opportunities for re-conditioning.

1. Exposure

Anxieties persist because of negative reinforcement. This can be unlearned by forcing a patient to experience the stimulus and learn, using relaxation, that it no longer produces anxiety.

The patient is presented with the feared stimulus repeatedly until anxiety subsides ('habituation'). Exposures may move gradually from least to most threatening, in vivo or in vitro (covert) as in systematic desensitisation (see page 95).

2. Response prevention

At the same time, the patient is prohibited from engaging in the usual compulsive response. This is important for the patient to recognise that anxiety can be reduced without the compulsive ritual.

Mode of action

Typically ERP consists of 13–20 weekly sessions (March et al.). Patients are then encouraged to continue using the ERP techniques and to apply them to new situations as they arise.

Effectiveness of ERP…

Albucher et al. report that between 60% and 90% of adults with OCD have improved considerably using ERP.

For people with mild OCD, self-directed ERP may be an effective alternative to therapist-led ERP. One computer-based program, BT STEPs, was found to be more effective than relaxation training alone, but less effective than therapist-guided ERP (Greist et al.).

ERP is most effective when combined with other therapies…

Drug therapy – Foa et al. found that a combination of *clomipramine* (a tricyclic) and ERP were more effective than either alone. Wilhem et al. also found that simultaneous administration of *d-cycloserine* (see facing page)substantially improves the effectiveness of ERP.

Cognitive therapy (e.g. discussing dysfunctional beliefs) improves the effectiveness of ERP, especially in preventing relapse (Huppert and Franklin). In fact, Koran et al. point out that in many instances ERP inevitably involves some informal cognitive techniques.

However… One review of research (Foa and Kozak) concluded that ERP alone was found to be equally effective to ERP with drugs. In both conditions (without or with drugs) patients were doing equally well at a two-year follow-up.

Appropriateness of ERP…
Not suitable for all…

Not all patients are helped by ERP, e.g. it has not been found to be successful with patients who are too depressed (Gershuny et al.), nor with patients who have certain types of OCD, such as patients with severe hoarding behaviour (Steketee and Frost).

Success depends on effort…

The success of ERP depends on the effort made by the patient and their willingness to do the 'homework' – not all patients are willing to commit to this kind of effort. This leads to a substantial refusal rate that may artificially elevate the apparent success of ERP because only those patients who are willing to 'be helped' may agree to participate.

Cognitive therapy (CT)

Obsessions

A CT therapist questions patients about their obsessions, e.g. asking a patient why they think shaking hands will pass on germs. Such beliefs can then be challenged and re-interpreted so that shaking hands is no longer experienced as an anxiety-producing activity.

Compulsions

A CT therapist also questions patients about the value of their compulsive behaviour(s), e.g. challenging the belief that hand washing guards against infection. When this belief is challenged and confronted as false, it can help control the behaviour.

Thought records

Patients are required to keep a daily record of their intrusive thoughts (e.g. where they were when they had the thought, what they felt) and about what they did to challenge the intrusive thoughts and compulsive responses.

This helps patients consider their dysfunctional beliefs. The therapist challenges unrealistic beliefs so that the patient will come to recognise the irrational nature of their beliefs and responses.

Effectiveness of CT…

CT is rarely used on its own, although Wilhelm et al. found a significant improvement in 15 patients who used CT alone over 14 weeks.

Ellis believed that sometimes people who claimed to be following the principles of CT were not putting their revised beliefs into action and therefore the therapy was not effective.

Appropriateness of CT…
Not suitable for all…

CT, like ERP, involves patient effort and is therefore not suitable for all patients. Ellis suggested that some people simply do not want the direct sort of advice that CT practitioners tend to dispense. They prefer to share their worries with a therapist, without getting involved with the cognitive effort that is associated with recovery.

There is research support…

Research has found that people who hold irrational beliefs form inferences that are significantly less functional than those that are formed by people who hold rational beliefs (Bond and Dryden).

On the other hand, it may be that irrational beliefs are counterproductive but realistic. For example, Alloy and Abrahmson found that people with depression (and some people with OCD are depressed) gave more accurate estimates of the likelihood of a disaster than 'normal' controls.

Ethical issues in research…

Ideally, research should involve a comparison between treatment and no treatment, e.g. O'Kearney et al. reported on four studies where ERP combined with CT was compared either to a placebo therapy or waiting list (two of the studies found no benefit). The issue is that it is unethical to withhold effective treatment, which makes research difficult.

Chapter 13

Media psychology

Division A Media influences on social behaviour
Explanations of media influences on prosocial behaviour
Explanations of media influences on antisocial behaviour
The effects of video games and computers

Division B Persuasion, attitude and change
Persuasion and attitude change
The influence of attitudes on decision-making
Explanations for the effectiveness of television in persuasion

Division C The psychology of celebrity
The attraction of celebrity
Research into intense fandom

Specification

Media psychology	
Media influences on social behaviour	• Explanations of media influences on pro- and antisocial behaviour. • The effects of video games and computers on young people.
Persuasion, attitude and change	• Persuasion and attitude change, including Hovland-Yale and Elaboration Likelihood models. • The influence of attitudes on decision-making, including roles of cognitive consistency/ dissonance and self-perception. • Explanations for the effectiveness of television in persuasion.
The psychology of celebrity	• The attraction of 'celebrity', including social psychological and evolutionary explanations. • Research into intense fandom, for example, celebrity worship, stalking.

Chapter 13

Media influences on social behaviour	>	Media influences on prosocial behaviour
Persuasion, attitude and change		Media influences on antisocial behaviour
Media psychology	> The psychology of celebrity	Effects of video games and computers

Media influences on prosocial behaviour

Explanations

Exposure to prosocial behaviour

There is clear evidence of prosocial content in children's TV programmes. Greenberg *et al.* analysed popular children's programmes in the US and found the same number of prosocial and antisocial acts in any hour.

There is research support for this…
Woodard found that US programmes for preschool children did have high levels of prosocial content; 77% of the programmes surveyed contained at least one prosocial lesson.

However…
The survey also found that only four of the top 20 most watched TV programmes for under-17s contained any prosocial lessons.

Acquisition of prosocial behaviours and norms

We learn by observation how to do things and when it is acceptable to do them.

Prosocial acts are likely to *reinforce* established social norms rather than contrast with them.

We are more likely to be rewarded for imitating prosocial than antisocial acts.

There is research support for this…
Research (e.g. Mares and Woodard) has found that children are most affected when they are shown the exact steps for a prosocial behaviour. This most probably is because young children are better able to remember concrete acts than abstract lessons of 'niceness'.

However…
Learning prosocial *norms* (rather than specific behaviours) from the media appears to be less common, except when viewing is accompanied by follow-up discussion.

Developmental factors

Research suggests that many of the skills involved in prosocial behaviour (e.g. perspective-taking, empathy) develop in later childhood.

This means that younger children may be less affected by prosocial portrayals in the media than older children.

Research challenges this view…
Despite the expectation that younger children would be least affected by prosocial programming, the meta-analysis by Mares (see below, left) found that the weakest effect was for adolescents and the strongest effect for primary school children.

However…
The expectation that the media has an effect on young children may be unrealistic because they are likely to be more strongly affected by home experiences than by media exposure.

Parental mediation

For many children, the effect of television viewing is mediated by the presence of a parent (as co-viewer).

Austin argued that effective mediation involves the parent discussing the programme with the child, explaining ambiguous or disturbing material and following up concepts from the TV.

IDA *Real-world application…*
Sesame Street aimed to use prosocial programming to nurture prosocial behaviour in inner city children. However, it was children from higher socioeconomic backgrounds who benefitted the most from this series, presumably because of parental mediation with this group.

However, not all forms of parental mediation work…
Valkenburg *et al.* suggest that only 'instructive mediation' is effective in enhancing prosocial messages in television programmes. They argue that when engaging in 'social co-viewing', parents and children might watch together but would not discuss the content.

Behavioural effects

A meta-analysis (Mares)

Mares examined research published between 1966 and 1995. She discovered four main behavioural effects of prosocial television:

- *Altruism* (e.g. sharing, offering help). Children who viewed prosocial content behaved more altruistically than those who viewed neutral or antisocial content.
- *Self-control* (e.g. resistance to temptation, task persistence). When exposed to a model demonstrating self-control, children subsequently showed higher levels of their own self-control.
- *Positive interaction* (e.g. friendly, peaceable conflict resolution). Children who watched prosocial programmes behaved more positively towards other children.
- *Anti-stereotyping*. Programmes which featured counter-stereotypical themes resulted in children becoming less stereotyped or prejudiced in their attitudes.

Television is not the only source of prosocial messages…
Although most research has focused on television, Mares and Woodard argue that other forms of media have prosocial effects, e.g. children's stories have traditionally carried prosocial messages. Young children are fond of reading these stories over and over again, which reinforce the message.

There are limitations in the effectiveness of prosocial messages…
Mares also found that children tend to imitate prosocial acts directly with little evidence of generalisation to other forms of prosocial behaviour, whereas aggressive acts are generalised (to other forms of antisocial behaviour). This lack of generalisation therefore limits the overall effectiveness of prosocial messages in the media.

Antisocial messages can overshadow prosocial messages…
Mixing prosocial and antisocial messages appears to reduce the effectiveness of the prosocial message. Mares and Woodard found that children who watched mixed messages behaved more aggressively than those who watched aggressive content only.

IDA *Real-world application…*
The Walt Disney Corporation has produced a set of DVDs specially aimed at babies, yet Zimmerman *et al.* claim that watching such DVDs can actually lead to poorer developmental outcomes. The *American Academy of Pediatrics* recommend no television at all for children under two, as it is associated with attention and behaviour problems later in life.

Chapter 13

Media influences on social behaviour	>	Media influences on prosocial behaviour
Persuasion, attitude and change		Media influences on antisocial behaviour
Media psychology >	The psychology of celebrity	Effects of video games and computers

Media influences on antisocial behaviour

Observational learning and imitation

Children observe actions of media models and may later imitate these behaviours, especially if they admire and identify with the model.

Television may also inform viewers of the positive and negative consequences of violent behaviour.

The more real that children perceive violent televised scenes to be and the more they believe the characters are like them, the more likely they will be to try out the modelled behaviours.

There is research support…

Bandura's Bobo doll studies (see page 33) support the view that children learn specific acts of aggression and also learn when aggressive behaviour is likely to be reinforced.

However…

Such imitation is actually quite rare outside of Bandura-style studies using specially prepared videos.

IDA Ethical issues with such research…

Laboratory experiments such as Bandura's began to die out in the 1980s, largely because of ethical concerns about subjecting children to violent media content which might then have increased aggressive behaviour in the child.

Cognitive priming

Immediately after watching a violent programme, a viewer is primed to respond aggressively because a network of memories involving aggression is retrieved.

Frequent exposure to scenes of violence may lead children to store scripts for aggressive behaviour, and these may be later recalled if any aspect of the original situation is present.

There is research support…

The importance of cognitive priming was demonstrated in a study by Josephson, where hockey players were deliberately frustrated and then shown a violent or non-violent film where an actor held a walkie-talkie. In a subsequent hockey game, the boys behaved most aggressively if they had seen the violent film and the referee in their game was holding a walkie-talkie. Presumably the walkie-talkie acted as a cue for a network of aggressive memories to be retrieved.

Desensitisation

Under normal conditions, anxiety about violence inhibits its use. Media violence, however, may stimulate aggressive behaviour by desensitising children to the effects of violence.

The more televised violence a child watches, the more acceptable aggressive behaviour becomes for that child.

Frequent viewing of television violence may cause children to be less anxious about violence and perceive it as normal.

There is research support…

Cumberbatch argues that people might get 'used' to screen violence but there is no evidence that a person will also get used to violence in the real world. He claims that screen violence is more likely to make children 'frightened' (anxious and afraid of violence) than 'frightening'.

IDA Gender bias in media effects research…

Effects research tends not to use representative samples (e.g. male students) but then makes generalisations about all viewers.

The inherent gender bias in these studies is often hidden behind gender-neutral terms such as 'college students' or 'viewers' when describing the population from which the sample is drawn.

Lowered physiological arousal

The arousal stimulated by viewing violence is unpleasant at first, but children who constantly watch violent television become used to it, and their emotional and physiological responses decline.

As a result, they do not react in the same way to violent behaviour, and so are less inhibited in using it.

Huesmann and Moise report that boys who are heavy television watchers show lower than average physiological arousal in response to new scenes of violence.

There is an alternative explanation for the role of arousal…

Zillman's excitation-transfer model explains the role of physiological arousal in a different way. According to this model, arousal creates a readiness to aggress in real-life situations because the excitation from one situation (watching violence on TV) is transferred to another (e.g. a response to provocation in real life).

Some theorists (e.g. Feshbach and Singer) believe that watching violence has positive rather than negative effects. They suggest that arousal allows one to release pent-up aggression (i.e. it is cathartic).

There is research support for justification…

Many TV programmes have mixed pro- and antisocial messages, for example the 1980s television series The A-Team portrayed good guys behaving violently, thus, justifying the use of violence.

Justification

Violent behaviours on television may provide a justification for a child's own violent behaviour or it may provide moral guidelines concerning what is acceptable and what is unacceptable.

Children who behave aggressively may watch violent television to relieve their guilt and justify their own aggression.

When violence is justified or left unpunished, the viewer's guilt or concern about consequences is also reduced.

Viewing television violence may also produce attitude change and suggest that problems can be solved through aggressive behaviour.

Liss and Reinhardt suggest that the negative effects of such programmes support the concept of justification. The use of aggression by prosocial characters lends an aura of moral justification to their violence, with which children readily identify.

The anti-effects lobby…

There is growing concern that the media are unreasonably the focus of blame for violent behaviour. The evidence does not always support the hypothesis that media violence leads to violent behaviour.

Belson, for example, interviewed more than 1,500 adolescent boys, and found that those who watched least television when they were younger were also least aggressive in adolescence. However, boys who watched most television were less aggressive (by about 50%) than boys who watched moderate amounts. This suggests that the link between watching television and aggression is unpredictable.

Chapter 13

| Media influences on social behaviour | > | Media influences on prosocial behaviour |
| Persuasion, attitude and change | | Media influences on antisocial behaviour |

| **Media psychology** | > | The psychology of celebrity | | **Effects of video games and computers** |

Effects of video games and computers

Research into video games and aggression

Experimental studies

These have demonstrated short-term increases in hostile feelings and aggressive behaviour following sessions of violent game play (Gentile and Stone).

Anderson and Dill found participants blasted their opponents with white noise for longer after playing a violent game compared to those who played a slow-paced puzzle game.

The major strength of experimental studies…

Causal relationships between exposure to violent game play and subsequent aggressive behaviour can be determined, although such studies are only used to measure short-term effects.

The major weakness of experimental studies…

Researchers cannot measure 'real-life' aggression (e.g. it would be unethical to allow participants to hit each other as a way of measuring changes in aggressive behaviour). Instead, researchers must use measures of aggressive behaviour that have no relationship to real-life aggression (e.g. noise blast).

Correlation studies

Gentile et al. found that time spent playing violent computer games was associated with aggressive feelings, arguments with teachers and a greater incidence of fights.

Children with low levels of trait hostility who spent more time playing violent video games were more likely to get into physical fights than were high trait hostility children who played less violent games.

The strength of correlational studies is…

Correlational studies overcome the primary weakness of experimental studies because they can use a range of 'real-world' measures of aggression. Because they can relate exposure to violent media to subsequent real-life aggressive behaviour, correlational studies can also be used to measure long-term effects of violent game playing rather than the short-term effects observed in the laboratory.

The major weakness of correlational studies is…

Causality cannot be determined, a problem addressed by the 'bi-directional model' below left.

Longitudinal studies

Anderson et al. found children who had high exposure to violent video games over a school year became more aggressive and less prosocial over the year.

This study indicates that repeated exposure to violent video games does not only increase aggressive behaviour, it also decreases prosocial behaviours.

The strength of longitudinal studies…

Longitudinal studies allow researchers to overcome the shortcomings of both experimental and correlational studies. By studying the same people over a period of time, researchers are able to observe patterns of behaviour and document both short-term and long-term effects.

A problem for most longitudinal studies in this area…

Participants may be exposed to other forms of media violence (e.g. on television) during the course of the study, meaning that the effect from violent video game exposure alone is uncertain.

Meta-analyses have found a link between violent games and aggressive behaviour. This association holds for both children and adults (Gentile and Anderson).

They also found a larger effect size with more recent studies (because violent video games have become more violent).

Publication bias…

The tendency to preferentially publish positive results means that published research may provide a biased view of all of the studies actually carried out. Ferguson analysed 17 studies published between 1995 and 2007. Once he had corrected for publication bias, studies provided no evidence for the hypothesis that violent game playing was associated with higher levels of aggression.

Explanations

The 'bi-directional model' (Gentile et al.)

Playing violent video games may cause an increase in aggressive behaviour, but it is just as likely that people who possess personality traits that orientate them towards aggressive behaviour prefer to play violent video games.

Desensitisation

People who are repeatedly exposed to violent video games become desensitised to violence and therefore are less likely to show an aversive response (e.g. disgust) towards violence in real life and show a greater propensity towards violent behaviour.

Interactive and passive video games

Porter and Starcevic suggest that 'interactive' media violence in video games may exert a greater influence than 'passive' media violence in TV and films, as games reward violent actions and convey a message that violent responses are appropriate and effective.

Not everybody plays games in the same way…

Research suggests that people with a more aggressive personality engage in a more aggressive style of game playing. Unlike exposure to violent content in television and films, the same game can present different content to different players on the basis of how the they choose to play.

For example, sensation-seeking players can activate game features to show more 'gore' and use more gruesome weapons. Wei et al. found that participants who had previously scored highly on a questionnaire on physical aggressiveness played more aggressively, with more frequent violent interactions, punching, kicking and shooting.

IDA A physiological perspective…

Mathiak et al. placed male participants in an fMRI machine and had them play a violent video game. During a fight in the game, parts of the brain that usually deal with emotional regulation (e.g. the amygdala and the ACC) were less active. The ACC is especially used to generate empathy, allowing an individual to imagine how others are feeling. In the case of violence, ACC activity is suppressed, which allows us to perform violent acts without emotion.

Other research (e.g. Matthews et al.) has previously found that individuals who self-reported high exposure to violent media showed reduced ACC function compared to clinically normal individuals who self-reported low exposure to violent media.

Chapter 13

Media influences on social behaviour | Persuasion and attitude change
Persuasion, attitude and change > | The influence of attitudes on decision-making
Media psychology > The psychology of celebrity | Explanations for the effectiveness of television in persuasion

Persuasion and attitude change

The Hovland–Yale model

Hovland et al. found effective persuasion could be achieved by focusing on *who* (communicator) says *what* (persuasive message) to *whom* (audience).

Source factors

Credible experts are a powerful source.

Bochner and Insko found students were swayed far more by an expert source, even when the discrepancy between their beliefs and the 'expert's' were extreme.

Attractive sources can be effective in attitude change, particularly as part of the 'peripheral route' (see below) to persuasion.

Message factors

As children age so they better understand the persuasive intent of advertisements and are less influenced by them (Martin).

Low fear and high fear messages are not as effective as moderate fear messages.

High levels of fear can rebound as they create so much anxiety in the audience that it interferes with ability to process information in the message (McGuire).

Audience factors

Low intelligence audiences are less likely to process the content of a message and so less likely to be influenced by it (McGuire).

Intelligent audiences are likely to process a message in more depth, therefore reject one-sided arguments, which are more effective for less intelligent audiences.

Methodological problems with the Hovland–Yale research…

The experimenters in these studies were in a position to cut off other stimuli and demand the complete attention of study participants, something that real-life communication sources rarely have.

It is inappropriate to generalise from the samples typically used in these studies (e.g. students). These groups had an age, wealth and education profile which was untypical of the general public.

There is research support for source factors…

Morton and Campbell examined the effects of information source on peers' attitudes towards an unfamiliar child with autism. When children received information from a 'doctor' (an expert source) they reported more favourable attitudes towards the child than when the information was provided by a parent or teacher (i.e. 'non-experts').

There is research support…

Lewis et al. provided support for the effectiveness of fear-arousing messages in a drink-driving campaign. Participants viewed two advertisements and completed two questionnaires. The first assessed pre-exposure attitudes and behaviour and immediate-post exposure attitudes and intentions. The second, two to four weeks later, assessed attitudes and behaviour.

They found that fear-arousing messages were more persuasive in the period immediately after exposure to a message, but long-term attitude change was more likely with positive (e.g. humorous) campaigns.

IDA *Gender bias in research…*

A number of studies have concluded that women are more susceptible to persuasive communications than are men.

However…

Sistrunk and McDavid claim that the gender differences in persuasion typically found in studies are actually due to methodological bias in the investigations. The materials used in research on persuasion have been chosen without due consideration of whether they might interest or involve one gender more than the other, and usually are biased towards males.

Elaboration-likelihood model

If an audience is likely to focus on the arguments, then a central route to persuasion is more appropriate.

If they focus more on the *context* of the message than the message itself, then a peripheral route is more likely to be effective (Petty and Cacioppo).

The central route to persuasion

Cacioppo and Petty suggest that some people have a high need for cognition and are more likely to focus on the *quality* of the arguments than their *context*.

Attitudes changed in this way are more lasting and less susceptible to subsequent attempts to change them.

The peripheral route to persuasion

Fiske and Taylor claim most people rely on simple and time-efficient strategies to evaluate information and make decisions.

When processing by this route, individuals are more likely to be influenced by contextual cues (such as celebrity endorsement of a product or the mood created).

Messages processed in this way tend to be less personally important and attitude change more transient.

There is support for central route processing…

Di Blasio and Milani investigated the possibility that computer-mediated communication (CMC) was more likely to activate central route processing than face-to-face interaction.

Groups of students discussed a reorganisation of the university refectory. Halfway through the discussion the experimenter introduced a new piece of information from an influential ('credible') source that was in contrast to the prevailing opinion in the group.

There were fewer opinion changes in the CMC condition than in the face-to-face condition, where participants had changed their mind because of the 'credibility' of the source (i.e. they were influenced by the peripheral route). The CMC group had not been distracted by the credibility of the source and had stuck to their original opinions.

There is evidence for need for cognition (NC)…

Haugtvedt et al. provided support for the claim that the central route for persuasion is more effective for high NC individuals. Attitude change in high NC individuals was based more on an evaluation of product attributes in adverts. For low NC individuals, simple peripheral cues were more important in shaping attitudes.

IDA *Real-world application…*

NC has not only been demonstrated under laboratory conditions. Vidrine et al. showed how it is a relevant factor in real-life health campaigns. Students were exposed to a fact-based (central route) or emotion-based (peripheral route) smoking risk campaign. Those with higher NC were more influenced by a fact-based message whereas participants with low NC more influenced by emotion-based message.

Chapter 13

Media influences on social behaviour | Persuasion and attitude change
Persuasion, attitude and change > | The influence of attitudes on decision-making
Media psychology > | The psychology of celebrity | Explanations for the effectiveness of television in persuasion

The influence of attitudes on decision-making

Cognitive dissonance theory (Festinger)

Cognitive dissonance is a mental tension caused by contradictory perceptions of a person's attitude and their actual behaviour.

Individuals are motivated to reduce any dissonance caused by inconsistent cognitions by modifying their attitudes to fit their perceptions of their behaviour.

This can be achieved by changing the attitude, changing the behaviour or adding a third cognition (e.g. that the behaviour is out of the person's control). Each strategy is aimed at reducing dissonance and restoring consistency between attitudes and behaviour.

We may also experience dissonance if, after having made a choice, we feel we may have made the wrong decision (*post-decisional dissonance*). Dissonance can be avoided by selective exposure to subsequent information.

Choice and incentive

Variables that determine the likelihood of dissonance being experienced are the perception of choice and the size of any rewards or punishments.

Behaviour that is coerced is less likely to create dissonance because it is behaviour that is not engaged in willingly.

Larger incentives, such as the threat of punishment for non-compliance or significant rewards for behaving in a counter-attitudinal manner do not lead to dissonance because there is sufficient external justification for the behaviour.

People have some tolerance for inconsistency…

Festinger believed inconsistency in attitudes and behaviour inevitably leads to a state of dissonance. However, Cooper and Fazio argued most people are content to be only partly consistent in their cognitions. They claim an individual would only experience dissonance under conditions of cognitive inconsistency if they perceive the inconsistency as unpleasant and if they take personal responsibility for this inconsistency.

There is evidence for disengagement beliefs…

Support for the prediction that people may justify a behaviour by suggesting it is out of their control comes from a study by Kleinjan et al. They found that adolescent smokers reduced their cognitive dissonance regarding their smoking through the use of justifications (e.g. nicotine dependence) to continue. These 'disengagement beliefs' were strongly and negatively correlated with motivation to quit.

Is dissonance reduction a conscious process?…

If dissonance reduction requires conscious awareness of an inconsistency between attitudes and behaviour, then individuals suffering from amnesia should show little dissonance reduction when faced with dissonant information. However, Lieberman et al. found that people with amnesia showed more dissonance reduction rather than less when compared with those with intact memories, suggesting that dissonance occurs automatically without conscious reflection.

IDA *A challenge to behaviourism*…

Dissonance theory presents a challenge to the underlying behaviourist assumption that people's actions are governed by reward and punishment.

Tavris and Aaronson predicted that if people go through a great deal of pain, effort, or embarrassment to get something, they will be happier with that 'something' than if it came to them easily. To a behaviourist it would make no sense that someone would like doing something associated with pain. However, this all makes sense within the context of cognitive dissonance theory.

Self-perception theory (Bem)

Attitude change follows observation of behaviour

An alternative explanation, *self-perception theory*, argues that people infer their attitudes by observing their own behaviour.

If behaviours change (and there is no obvious external reason for the change), then this indicates to the individual that their attitude must also have changed.

Attitude change therefore follows, and is informed by, behavioural change.

Research evidence

Holland et al. studied the association between attitudes to the environmental group *Greenpeace* and willingness to donate money to the cause.

The researchers found that individuals with relatively weak attitudes towards Greenpeace who donated money subsequently strengthened their attitudes towards Greenpeace far more than those who did not donate money or those who already had strong attitudes.

IDA *Self-perception and therapy*…

Self-perception theory has been used therapeutically in the treatment of *heterosocial anxiety*, where an individual assumes that because they had no dates with a member of the opposite sex, it must mean they have poor social skills.

Haemmerlie et al. showed that males with heterosocial anxiety who engaged in a short interaction with a 'willing' female confederate inferred that their anxiety was reduced after this apparently 'successful' interaction. This resulted in a significant increase in dates over the next six months.

'Foot-in-the-door' requests…

Han et al. have shown that the ideas behind self-perception theory can be applied in market research. Respondents are first asked to comply with a small request (e.g. answering a couple of questions over the telephone), prior to being asked to participate in the main study.

This works because of an individual's self-perception of being responsible and cooperative as a result of responding to the first request.

Cognitive dissonance or self-perception?…

Research suggests that cognitive dissonance theory better accounts for situations where behaviours are inconsistent with attitudes that are well established and important to the individual.

Self-perception theory, on the other hand, appears to be more appropriate where behaviours are associated with attitudes that are weak and/or less important.

Chapter 13

Media influences on social behaviour | Persuasion and attitude change
Persuasion, attitude and change > | The influence of attitudes on decision-making
Media psychology > | The psychology of celebrity
Explanations for the effectiveness of television in persuasi

Explanations for the effectiveness of television in persuasion

Television and advertising

Hard sell and soft sell advertising

Hard sell = presenting factual information about a product.

Soft sell = using subtle and creative persuasive techniques.

Snyder and de Bono found that hard sell and soft sell approaches had different effects on different types of people. People high in self-monitoring had more favourable attitudes to soft-sell adverts. People low in self-monitoring preferred more factual hard-sell approaches.

Product endorsement

Giles suggests that celebrities provide a familiar face, a reliable source of information that we feel we can trust because of the parasocial relationship that we have built up with that celebrity.

Celebrities are also seen as a neutral source of information and so perform the function of 'rubber stamping' the advertiser's claims.

Meenaghan found celebrity endorsements were not overly convincing or believable, with perceived credibility and expertise of the endorser being the 'source' characteristics with the greatest influence on consumer purchase intentions.

Children and advertising

Martin, in a meta-analysis of studies, found a strong positive correlation between age and understanding of persuasive intent. Older children better understood the persuasive intent of the commercials (compared to factual programmes) and trusted them less.

Does product endorsement work?…

Research suggests that celebrity product endorsement is not that effective. Martin *et al.* found that their student participants were more convinced by a television endorsement from a fictional fellow student when buying a digital camera than by one from a celebrity.

In a study of the 'persuasiveness' of more than 5,000 TV commercials, Hume concluded that celebrity endorsement did not significantly increase the persuasive communication of the advert.

The impact of advertising…

Giles points out that television and cinema advertising is successful because adverts generally have a captive audience. However, unlike cinema audiences, television audiences have more options open to them, which may limit the effectiveness of television advertising.

Comstock and Scharrer found that 80% of viewers left the room during adverts, and when programmes were recorded, viewers tended to fast-forward through the adverts, thereby minimising their impact, which may limit the effectiveness of TV advertising.

IDA *Gender bias in advertising and its consequences*…

Gender stereotypes in television advertising reinforce the traditional role of women as caretakers, wives or subordinates (Scharrer *et al.*).

As a result, gender stereotyped television advertisements promote acceptance of current social arrangements, no matter how biased or inappropriate these representations might be.

Disentangling media and other effects…

The influence of peers inevitably shapes the subsequent buying (or pestering) behaviour of children. Consequently, it becomes difficult, if not impossible, to confidently predict a direct causal relationship between exposure to advertisements and subsequent consumer behaviour among children.

Measuring the effectiveness of advertisements…

For an advert to be effective, it should lead to an actual purchase of the product being advertised. What is measured in research, however, is not the actual behaviour (product purchase) but the related attitude (liking, intention) that may or may not lead to an actual purchase.

Television and health-related behaviour change

Health campaigns

Research suggests that the media can be an effective tool in health promotion.

French suggests media is most appropriate in situations such as:
• When wide exposure is desired.
• When the timeframe is urgent.
• When the behavioural goal is simple.

The role of fictional drama

Medical messages within television drama are likely to have an impact on the knowledge of the general public.

O'Connor *et al.* found that viewers of a *Casualty* episode registered and retained information about paracetamol toxicity, despite other distracting story lines.

Philo and Henderson investigated the effects of viewing an episode of *Casualty*, which highlighted the issue of unnecessary hospital attendance. They found that a large proportion of those who had seen the episode and who had previously attended A&E would no longer go with the same complaint.

Research support for television health campaigns…

The Health Development Agency reported a number of significant changes in health-related attitudes and behaviour that could be directly attributed to television health campaigns. These included:
• *Alcohol*, knowledge of units in popular drinks: up 300% (1989–94).
• *HIV/AIDS*, belief that a condom protects against HIV: 66% in 1986; 95% in 1997.
• *Skin cancer*, proportion of the public who thought a suntan was important: 28% in 1995; 25% in 1996.

The effectiveness of fictional drama may be short-lived…

In the O'Connor *et al.* study, one week after the episode of *Casualty* was broadcast, significantly more of those who had seen the episode than those who hadn't (85% versus 45%) correctly identified paracetamol as having hepatotoxic effects (i.e. on the liver). By 32 weeks, however, this knowledge had dropped to 73% in those who had seen the episode yet had risen to 50% in those who hadn't.

How effective is fictional drama?…

There is considerable debate over whether audiences are able to tell the difference between 'fact' and 'fiction' in television programming.

Philo argues that audiences are aware that medical programmes such as *Casualty* are fictional, but nonetheless such programmes are regarded as a source of 'hard information' by many people. Such programmes are seen by many as inherently trustworthy and informative and so can have a profound effect on real-life behaviour.

Chapter 13

Media influences on social behaviour
Persuasion, attitude and change | The attraction of celebrity
Media psychology > The psychology of celebrity > Research into intense fandom

The attraction of celebrity

Social psychological explanations

Parasocial relationships

An individual is attracted to another individual, but the target individual is usually unaware of the existence of the person who has created the relationship.

A parasocial relationship is particularly appealing to some individuals because it makes few demands. They do not run the risk of criticism or rejection, as might be the case in a real relationship.

What determines the likelihood of a parasocial relationship?

Schiappa et al. concluded that parasocial relationships were most likely to form with television celebrities who were seen as attractive and similar in some way to the viewer.

If the celebrity acted in a believable way, viewers were able to compare how they would behave in similar situations.

The 'absorption–addiction model'

Maltby et al. identified three levels in people's attraction to celebrities:

- *Entertainment-social.* Fans are attracted to a celebrity because of their perceived ability to entertain and to become a source of social interaction and gossip.
- *Intense-personal.* This aspect of celebrity worship reflects intensive and compulsive feelings about the celebrity,
- *Borderline-pathological.* Typified by uncontrollable behaviours and fantasies about the celebrity, with the person believing there is a real relationship between themselves and the celebrity.

Parasocial relationships may not be dysfunctional…

It is commonly believed that parasocial relationships with celebrities are dysfunctional (i.e. based on loneliness). However, Schiappa et al. found that loneliness was not a predictor of parasocial relationships.

Benefits of parasocial relationships with celebrities…

Such relationships provide media models of social behaviours (e.g. generosity) and an opportunity to learn cultural values (e.g. importance of marriage) from them.

Perse and Rubin studied parasocial relationships with soap opera characters and found that, because people are exposed to the same characters over and over again, one benefit of parasocial interaction is a perceived reduction in uncertainty about social relationships.

The absorption–addiction model: links to mental health…

Maltby et al. used the *Eysenck Personality Questionnaire* to assess the relationship between level of celebrity worship and personality. The *entertainment-social level* was associated with extraversion and the *intense-personal level* was associated with neuroticism.

As neuroticism is related to anxiety and depression, this explains why higher levels of celebrity worship are related to poor mental health.

IDA Attachment style and parasocial relationships…

Cole and Leets reported that individuals with anxious-ambivalent attachment were most likely, and avoidant individuals least likely to enter into parasocial relationships. Coles and Leets claim individuals with anxious-ambivalent attachment style turn to TV characters as a means of satisfying 'unrealistic and unmet relational needs'.

IDA Parasocial relationships and eating disorders…

Maltby et al. found that parasocial relationships with celebrities influenced body image among female adolescents. Teenage girls who had parasocial relationships with celebrities who were slim and were seen as having a 'good body shape' tended to have a poor body image, which consequently predisposed them to eating disorders.

Evolutionary explanations

Attraction to creative individuals

Humans have a love of novelty (*neophilia*). Therefore, mate choice in the EEA could well have favoured creative courtship displays from males, which would have evolved through the process of sexual selection, favouring minds prone to creativity and fantasy.

This would explain characteristics that are uniquely developed in humans, e.g. art, music and humour. Because musicians, artists and actors display these talents in abundance, we are drawn to them.

Celebrity gossip

The exchange of social information about group members might have been adaptive for early humans living in social groups.

DeBacker suggests 'gossip' served to create bonds within groups, manipulate the reputation of rivals, and exchange information about potential mates.

Barkow suggests that our minds are fooled into regarding media characters as being members of our social network, thus celebrities trigger the same gossip mechanisms that have evolved to keep up with the affairs of ingroup members.

Evidence for an evolved love of creativity…

Shiraishi et al. discovered an enzyme correlated with novelty-seeking tendencies. Genetic differences mean that people produce different variations of the enzyme MAOA. The researchers found that one form of this enzyme was significantly associated with higher scores of novelty seeking, suggesting that there may be a genetic origin for neophilia and our attraction to creative people.

The arbitrary nature of sexual selection explanations…

Suggesting that a love of novelty, and therefore an attraction to creative people, arose because early females preferred creative behaviour in potential mates tells us nothing about *why* they would prefer it. Sexual selection explanations are arbitrary because they argue that traits are preferred simply because they would have been 'attractive'. Such explanations do not provide an adequate adaptive reason why traits such as creativity in music, art and humour would have been attractive to ancestral members of the opposite sex.

Research support for the adaptive role of celebrity gossip…

De Backer et al. surveyed more than 800 participants to test evolutionary explanations for celebrity gossip. Participants reported that gossip was seen as a useful way of acquiring information about social group members. Media exposure was also found to be a strong predictor of interest in celebrities.

De Backer et al. concluded that media exposure would lead to the misperception that celebrities were actually a part of the social network, thus explaining the interest in celebrity gossip.

Research on intense fandom

Celebrity worship

Measuring celebrity worship

Most research on celebrity worship has used the *Celebrity Attitude Scale* (CAS).

Maltby *et al.* used this scale to produce the three levels of parasocial relationships described on page 109: *entertainment-social, intense-personal* and *borderline-pathological*.

How common is celebrity worship?

Maltby *et al.* found that, in a sample of 372 people aged 18–47:

• 15% were at the 'entertainment-social' level of celebrity worship.
• 5% at the 'intense-personal' level.
• Less than 2% would be considered 'borderline pathological'.

Developmental problems

Celebrity worship is associated with less desirable developmental outcomes.

Maltby *et al.* found celebrity worshippers have lower levels of psychological wellbeing than non-worshippers.

Scores on the 'entertainment-social' subscale of the CAS predicted patterns of social dysfunction and scores on the 'intense-personal' subscale predicted both depression and anxiety scores.

The possible benefits of celebrity worship…

Cheung and Yue found that teenagers who 'worshipped' key family members, teachers and other individuals with whom they came into regular contact, tended to demonstrate higher levels of self-esteem and educational achievement than teenagers who worshipped television stars.

This is understandable given that the admiration of those who are able to provide tangible benefits and inputs to the adolescents' lives would be more likely to provide a greater positive impact than those celebrities with whom they enjoy only a parasocial relationship.

Negative consequences of celebrity worship…

Research (e.g. Phillips) has shown that high-profile celebrity suicides are often followed by increased numbers of suicides among the general population.

Sheridan *et al.* claim that pathological worshippers are often drawn to more entertaining, even antisocial celebrities. We might, therefore, expect fans of more rebellious celebrities to seek to emulate them with negative consequences for the worshipper.

IDA An evolutionary explanation for celebrity worship…

Evolutionary psychologists suggest that it is natural for humans to look up to those individuals who receive attention because they have succeeded in our society. Gill-White claims that it makes a good deal of evolutionary sense to value individuals according to how successful they are, because whoever is getting more of what everybody wants is probably using above-average methods to get them, therefore would serve as a valuable role model.

Stalking

Stalking involves repeated and persistent attempts to impose unwanted contact or communication on another person.

Types of stalker

About one in five stalkers develops a *love obsession* or fixation on another person with whom they have no personal relationship. Since most are unable to develop normal personal relationships through more conventional means, they retreat to a life of fantasy relationships with individuals they hardly know, if at all.

The *simple obsessional* stalking-type is distinguished by some previous personal or romantic relationship having existed between stalker and victim before the stalking behaviour began.

Cyberstalking

Modern technology has created a new medium for stalking unsuspecting victims, e.g. sending unwanted texts and e-mails, or 'spamming' the target individual.

Fisher found that 13% of undergraduates reported having been stalked in this way. Finn also found that 15% had received e-mails or instant messages that were insulting, harassing or threatening.

Cyberstalking has the advantage of anonymity and so increases opportunities for antisocial behaviour. It is also attractive to stalkers because there is no face-to-face contact with the target, therefore more risks can be taken with less fear of reprisal (Eytan and Borras).

The impact of stalking…

In a postal survey in Germany (Dressing *et al.*), researchers discovered that 11.5% of respondents had been the victims of a stalker. Most of the victims were women and most of the stalkers were men.

The effects on psychological health appeared significant. Most victims reported that they had changed their lifestyles after being stalked, and described various physical and mental responses to having being stalked. These included agitation (56% of those who reported having been stalked), anxiety symptoms (44%) and depression (28%).

IDA Explaining stalking in terms of insecure attachment…

Tomin measured stalkers' retrospective childhood attachment styles and their current adult attachment. To see if stalkers detained under the Mental Health Act were less securely attached than non-stalkers, she compared them to two other groups: 24 people detained in the same way but with no history of stalking, and a non-clinical community sample of 33. It was found that the stalkers had significantly more evidence of insecure adult attachment styles than the control group.

Tolerance to cyberstalking…

Sheridan and Grant argue that cyberstalking may provide less reinforcement than traditional forms of stalking because in the latter, stalkers are better able to observe the impact of their activities on the victim.

Cyberstalkers may also develop a tolerance to Internet- and phone-based harassment with the result that they need more and more extreme activities to experience the same thrill.

Perceptions of cyberstalking…

Evidence suggests that cyberstalking may not be taken as seriously as other forms of stalking. For example, Alexy *et al.* gave students a brief description of a real-life case of cyberstalking. Although this was a serious case that resulted in prosecution, only 30% of the students judged the behaviours involved to be 'stalking'.

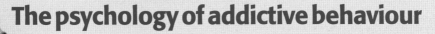

The psychology of addictive behaviour

Division A Models of addictive behaviour
Biological models of addiction
Cognitive models of addiction
Learning models of addiction
Explanations for specific addictions

Division B Factors affecting addictive behaviour
Vulnerability to addiction
The role of media in addictive behaviour

Division C Reducing addictive behaviour
Models of prevention
Types of intervention

Specification

The psychology of addictive behaviour	
Models of addictive behaviour	• Biological, cognitive and learning models of addiction, including explanations for initiation, maintenance and relapse. • Explanations for specific addictions, including smoking and gambling.
Factors affecting addictive behaviour	• Vulnerability to addiction including self-esteem, attributions for addiction and social context of addiction. • The role of media in addictive behaviour.
Reducing addictive behaviour	• Models of prevention, including theory of reasoned action and theory of planned behaviour. • Types of intervention, including biological, psychological, public health interventions and legislation, and their effectiveness.

Chapter 14

Models of addictive behaviour >
Factors affecting addictive behaviour
Reducing addictive behaviour

Biological models of addiction
Cognitive models of addiction
Learning models of addiction
Explanations for specific addictions

The psychology of addictive behaviour >

Biological models of addiction

The genetics of addiction

Family studies

Alcohol dependence has been linked to genetic inheritance, with heritability estimates of 50–60% (McGue).

Illicit drug abuse has also been shown to have high heritability estimates of 45–79% (Agrawal and Lynskey).

Twin studies

Kendler *et al.* analysed data from the *Virginia Twin Registry* in the USA and found that a common genetic factor linked to a general predisposition towards behavioural disorders, which may lead to alcohol dependence or illicit drug dependence, but alternatively may lead to *antisocial behaviour disorders*.

What is inherited?

Research has found a link between the gene for the D_2 dopamine receptor (DRD$_2$) and alcoholism. The A1 variant of this gene is more commonly found in alcoholics (Noble *et al.*) and among children born to alcoholics (Blum *et al.*).

The A1 variant is also more common among smokers (about 50% compared to 26% of non-smokers) (Comings *et al.*).

Noble *et al.* proposed that the DRD$_2$ gene is the *'reward gene'*. Individuals with the A1 variant appear to have fewer dopamine receptors in the brain's pleasure centres. Drugs increase dopamine levels by stimulating what few dopamine receptors exist. Addiction is maintained because it is only with the drug that such individuals feel good.

Genetic explanations can account for individual differences...

Some people are more vulnerable to develop an addiction because of their genetic predisposition (i.e. the diathesis-stress model).

This may also explain why some people are more resistant to treatment for their addictive behaviours, and more likely to relapse.

There is research support for the role of dopamine...

Mice, like humans, develop a craving for the drug cocaine, but those that are bred to lack another dopamine receptor (the D_1 dopamine receptor) do not self-administer cocaine when given the chance to do so. This reinforces the claim that dopamine plays a key role in addiction (Caine *et al.*).

Dopamine has also been implicated in non-drug addictions, e.g. Bostwick and Bucci reported the successful treatment of sex addiction using *nalextrone*, a drug that blocks the release of dopamine. Blocking the reward extinguished the addictive power of that behaviour.

The findings for the role of the DRD$_2$ gene are inconsistent...

Several subsequent studies (e.g. Edenberg *et al.*) have failed to find any relationship between alcoholism and the DRD$_2$ gene, or have found only a very weak relationship.

DRD$_2$ may not be the reward gene...

Comings *et al.* found that the A1 gene variant occurred in people with several disorders, including autism and Tourette's syndrome, at least as often as it appeared in alcoholics.

This finding creates a problem for the idea of DRD$_2$ being a 'reward' gene, since people with autism and Tourette's syndrome are not thought to be especially pleasure-seeking.

IDA *Biological explanations are reductionist...*

They reduce a complex phenomenon such as addiction down to a relatively simple level of explanation, i.e. an imbalance of brain chemicals or the influence of specific genes.

Whilst there are potential advantages to this approach (e.g. effective drug treatments) it ignores all other potential influences (e.g. irrational thought processes, social context etc.), as we shall see on the next few pages.

The disease model: The role of dopamine in addiction

Initiation

Addictive drugs stimulate the brain's reward circuit, e.g. crack cocaine activates dopamine receptors in the mesolimbic pathway. Lasting memories are created that link the drug to a pleasurable reward.

Incentive sensitisation theory (Robinson and Berridge) suggests that repeated exposure to drugs of abuse increases the sensitivity to their desirability.

Maintenance

Chronic exposure to drugs eventually results in a reduction in the activity of these positive reward circuits (*downregulation*) and the drug levels that are needed to trigger the brain reward system increase (Koob and Kreek).

Relapse

The brain continues to receive difficult-to-resist signals of imminent reward, even if the addict knows that a reward is not really coming. This is because the frontal cortex has become less effective at making decisions and judging the consequences of actions.

There is research support...

Volkow *et al.* gave *Ritalin* (lifts dopamine levels) to adult volunteers. Using brain scanning, they found that those who enjoyed the sensation had fewer D_2 receptors than those who hated it. This would explain why some people, after experimenting with drugs, might go on and develop an addiction, and others, despite the same initial experience, would not.

A link between dopamine and poverty...

An experiment with monkeys (Grant *et al.*) showed that animals that lost social status also lost D_2 receptors. This has implications for human beings whose lives are characterised by poverty and stress, whereas the dopamine systems of those who have more stimulating lives are less likely to need an artificial boost from alcohol or drugs.

IDA *The issue of animal research...*

Hackam and Redelmeier argue that even high-quality animal studies of drug addiction rarely replicate in human research. There have, however, been some successes.

For example, Czoty *et al.* used monkeys to establish the feasibility of treating cocaine addiction by substituting a less addictive 'replacement' drug that mimics the action of cocaine, but has less potential for abuse.

Implications for treatment...

Neurochemical explanations create the possibility that addiction may be treated by various pharmacological methods. Such an approach is certainly more progressive than those that treat drug addicts as delinquents who must be punished.

Cognitive models of addiction

The self-medication model

Initiation

Gelkopf et al. proposed that choice of drug or activity depends on the specific effect an individual desires, e.g. a person suffering anxiety selects alcohol. The drug/activity may not actually make things better but is believed to have that effect.

Maintenance and relapse – a paradox

Many smokers smoke to relieve stress yet report higher levels of stress than non-smokers, and their levels of stress *decrease* when they stop smoking (Cohen and Lichtenstein).

It may be that each cigarette temporarily relieves stress because it relieves the withdrawal symptoms that arise when a smoker can't smoke (Parrott).

There is a similar effect with alcohol, as the 'rush' of intoxication may help people forget their troubles in the short-term, but in the long-term only exacerbates them.

There is research support...

The model predicts that an addict fails to control the impulse to self-medicate, a failure of ego control. A meta-analysis found, as predicted, that participants with substance abuse disorders showed significant failures in ego control compared with a control group (Gottdiener et al.).

The model also predicts that some form of psychological distress must precede drug use. Sanjuan et al. found that sexually abused women were more likely to turn to alcohol and other drugs to remove sexual inhibitions than were non-abused women.

However...
There are many cases of addiction where there are no psychological problems to be overcome.

IDA The issue of whether addiction is a myth...

Davies argues that addiction is a myth. 'Addicts' use the language of addiction (e.g. 'I can't control myself') when talking to health workers or the police, but when talking to their peers their language suggests they are exercising preferences that are rational and understandable, given the circumstances in which they live.

On the other hand...

West suggests this is not supported by observations of addictive behaviour in real life. West argues that the phenomena of addiction (e.g. cravings and compulsions) are very real.

Expectancy theories

Initiation

Expectancy theories (e.g. Brandon) propose that addiction develops because of expectations an individual has, where the benefits outweigh the costs.

For example, heavier drinkers have been shown to have more positive expectancies about the effects of alcohol compared to light drinkers (Southwick et al.).

Maintenance and relapse

Brandon suggests long-term addiction is influenced by unconscious expectancies involving automatic processing. This would explain the loss of control typical of addiction.

Such expectancies can also be manipulated to prevent relapse, e.g. Tate et al. told smokers that they should expect no negative experiences when abstaining. This led to fewer reported somatic effects (e.g. the 'shakes') and psychological effects (e.g. mood disturbance) than a control group who were not so primed.

Subjective evaluation of expected outcomes...

Leigh found that the more favourably people evaluated the effects of drinking, the greater was their overall alcohol use. This suggests that the subjective evaluation of expected effects might be an important determinant of drinking behaviour, supporting expectancy theory.

Addiction or consumption?...

Expectancy theory is concerned more with consumption (e.g. of alcohol) than addiction per se and only rarely does it consider loss of control (which is typical of addiction). It is not clear what role expectancies play in the development of this loss of control.

Expectancy theories and publication bias...

The selective publication of positive results gives an unrepresentative view of this research area, particularly when the number of studies published is relatively small, replications are few, and contradictory findings are frequent (Saunders).

IDA Gender bias in alcohol expectancies...

Men, compared to women, have been found to have stronger positive expectancies about the effects of alcohol (e.g. Sher et al.).

However, other studies (e.g. Carey) found no gender differences in expectancy, suggesting that such conclusions may be gender biased.

Rational choice theory

Initiation

Becker and Murphy proposed that addicts make a rational choice concerning the current and future 'utility' of their drug taking, drinking or gambling. 'Utility' refers to the relative satisfaction received from an item and is a concept taken from economics. Individuals must weigh up the costs incurred against the benefits they are likely to receive.

Maintenance and relapse

Addicts are rational consumers who look ahead and behave in a way that is likely to maximise the preferences they hold.

Can explain how some addicts stop...

If any activity is measured in terms of its utility for the individual, they may reach a point where the negatives outweigh the positives (e.g. harmful effects outweigh the pleasure) and they decide to quit. In contrast, the 'out of control' view can't explain how people come to quit.

IDA Real-world application...

Drugs can be treated in the same way as other consumer behaviours, i.e. by changing their utility for the individual (e.g. making them more expensive, harder to get or illegal).

Not all addicts are rational...

Griffiths found that fruit machine addicts thought irrationally e.g. they thought they were more skilful than they actually were, and were more likely to make irrational verbalisations during play than non-addicts.

Chapter 14

Models of addictive behaviour >

Biological models of addiction
Cognitive models of addiction
Factors affecting addictive behaviour
Learning models of addiction

The psychology of addictive behaviour >

Reducing addictive behaviour
Explanations for specific addictions

Learning models of addiction

Operant conditioning

Initiation, positive reinforcement

Positive reinforcement results in an increase of dopamine in an area of the brain called the mesolimbic system.

This effect can be produced by natural reinforcers (e.g food) or by addictive drugs (e.g. cocaine, nicotine) (White) or by anything pleasurable (e.g. gambling).

Griffiths, in discussing slot machine addiction, points to physiological rewards (e.g. getting a buzz from winning), psychological rewards (e.g. the near miss), social rewards (e.g. peer praise) as well as financial rewards from winning.

Maintenance and relapse, negative reinforcement

After repeated exposure to certain drugs, withdrawal symptoms appear if the drug is discontinued. Because withdrawal effects are unpleasant, any reduction in these effects (from continuing to take the drug) acts as negative reinforcement.

Strengths of an operant conditioning explanation…

Operant conditioning requires no conscious awareness, which explains why addicts can still experience a conscious desire to stop but nevertheless continue (West).

Operant conditioning also explains why addicts show reduced eating drives. Addiction creates acquired drives that are hard to satisfy, and have priority over other drive states (e.g. food).

Problems for an operant conditioning explanation…

Operant conditioning explains addiction in terms of consequences. However, Robinson and Berridge point out that many people take addictive drugs, yet relatively few become addicts. This suggests that other psychological factors are involved in the transition from consumption to addiction.

IDA Evolutionary value of occasional reinforcement…

In real life the positive consequences are likely to be occasional rather than consistent, because taking a drug (or getting drunk) will not always lead to a sense of relief. There is an evolutionary advantage to learning from occasional reinforcement – the world is an unpredictable place, so organisms need to learn adaptive behaviours that on average work to their advantage.

Classical conditioning

Initiation, secondary reinforcers

Stimuli that precede or occur at the same time as a learned stimulus (such as a drug) may become secondary reinforcers by association.

For example, alcohol-related stimuli (e,g, pub sounds) elicit the same physiological responses as alcohol (Glautier et al.).

Maintenance and relapse

UCS (drug) leads to disequilibrium (UCR) as the drug challenges the body's internal regulation.

Stimulus accompanying drug dose becomes a CS, leading to a compensatory response from body in anticipation of the effects of the drug.

If this occurs in the absence of the anticipated drug the body is in a state of disequilibrium. The individual experiences this as withdrawal, and is motivated to take drug to alleviate symptoms.

There is research support…

Classical conditioning suggests that the cues associated with drug taking are an important factor in the maintenance of an addiction.

Evidence shows that in the absence of conditioned stimuli (cues) people cease to be addicted, e.g. soldiers who became addicted to heroin while serving in Vietnam had fewer problems with relapse after returning home (no cues), compared to heroin addicts generally who tend to return to the same environment in which they had developed their addiction (Robins et al.).

IDA Real-world application…

Drummond et al. proposed cue exposure as a form of treatment, where the cues associated with drug taking are presented without the opportunity to engage in the drug-taking behaviour. This leads to a phenomenon known as stimulus discrimination, as without the reinforcement provided by the actual drug, the association between the cue and the drug-taking is extinguished.

Social learning theory (SLT)

Initiation

SLT explains addiction in terms of outcome expectancies. The consequences of drug use may be direct or vicarious, positive or negative. This leads individuals to recognise that different drugs have different types of effect, and therefore have different outcome expectancies.

Maintenance and relapse

The fact that drugs have positive and negative effects means users are motivated to both approach (to gain the positive effects) and avoid (to avoid its negative effects) the drug. This creates an approach–avoidance conflict (West).

Addicts have also learned (through classical conditioning) to associate cues with the drug. Marlatt and George propose that the presence of multiple cues arouses 'positive outcome expectancies' which then triggers a motivation to use the drug once more.

There is research support…

Peer group influences are the primary influence for adolescents e.g. adolescents who smoke are likely to 'hang out' with other adolescents who smoke (DiBlasio and Benda).

IDA Real-world application…

This tendency to conform to the norms of a reference group has led to treatment programmes, such as resistance training, where adolescents are taught the skills to resist such influence (Botvin).

SLT and Internet addiction…

Lin et al. studied Internet addiction in students. Positive outcome expectancy predicted the level of Internet addiction; however, this was mediated by the second factor, belief in one's ability to resist, which was negatively related to the level of Internet addiction.

Implications of self-efficacy for relapse…

Among adults, those who smoke more frequently have less confidence in their ability to abstain, and among adolescents, self-efficacy predicts the onset of smoking and progression from experimental to regular use (Lawrance).

Chapter 14

Models of addictive behaviour >

Biological models of addiction
Cognitive models of addiction
Factors affecting addictive behaviour
Learning models of addiction

The psychology of addictive behaviour >

Reducing addictive behaviour

Explanations for specific addictions

Explanations for specific addictions

Smoking addiction

Initiation

Smoking may be seen as a sign of adulthood or rebelliousness, and one that promotes peer popularity.

Jarvis argues that this image is sufficient for the novice smoker to tolerate the unpleasantness of the first few cigarettes, after which the physical effects of nicotine take over.

Research supports the link between smoking and popularity…

Mayeux *et al.* found that boys who smoked at age 16 were more popular among their peers two years later. For alcohol abuse, the relationship was the other way around, i.e. popularity at age 16 predicted the onset of alcohol use.

These results highlight that popularity appears to be a risk factor for various types of hazardous behaviour during the school years.

Effects of nicotine

Nicotine affects *nicotinic acetylcholine receptors* (nAChRs) in the brain, leading to the release of dopamine in the nucleus accumbens. This creates a short-term sense of pleasure, followed within hours by lowered mood and concentration as nicotine levels drop in the blood.

There is research support for the long-term effects…

A recent Canadian study (Khaled *et al.*) lends further support to the possibility that long-term smoking may have an adverse effect on mood (depression) because it alters neurochemistry. They found that the incidence of depression was highest in current smokers and lowest in those who had never smoked. The reasons for this are not clear, but it is possible that nicotine causes changes to neurotransmitter activity in the brain, leading to an increased risk of depression (Fergusson).

Socioeconomic status (SES)

Fidler *et al.* found that smoking in the UK was associated with social and economic disadvantage, with poorer smokers tending to have higher levels of nicotine intake. Greater nicotine intake in more deprived smokers could explain why they find it harder to stop smoking.

There is research support for the link with poverty…

In a French study (Peretti-Watel *et al.*) found that specific types of neighbourhood and poor housing conditions (correlated with SES) were found to be significantly correlated with smoking and nicotine addiction.

IDA *Real-world application…*

They concluded that interventions which do not specifically target smoking but which instead contribute to improving poor smokers' living conditions, are necessary to lower the incidence of smoking.

Smoking in pregnancy

Buka *et al.* found that a mother's smoking during pregnancy did not increase the likelihood that her child will later become a regular smoker; however, the risk of their child becoming addicted to tobacco if they did begin smoking was doubled.

IDA *Gender bias in smoking addiction research…*

Nerín and Jané argue that there is an inherent gender bias in much of the research relating to smoking addiction.

The onset of smoking and development of smoking addiction follows a different pattern in men and women according to López *et al.* They found that women start smoking later than men, and that there are gender-related differences in relation to both stages and context.

Gambling addiction

Genetic factors

A twin study by Shah *et al.* found evidence of genetic transmission of gambling in men.

Black *et al.* found that the first-degree relatives of pathological gamblers were more likely to suffer from pathological gambling than were more distant relatives, demonstrating a strong genetic link.

Disentangling genetics and environment…

Familial similarity may be due to environmental rather than genetic factors. However, Slutske *et al.* found that 64% of the variation in risk for pathological gambling could be accounted for by genetic factors alone.

What is inherited?…

Genetic predisposition for gambling may work indirectly through the trait of *impulsivity*. A number of studies (e.g. Alessi and Petry) have found that impulsivity is a significant predictor of the development of pathological gambling, as well as other risky behaviours.

Sensation-seeking

Zuckerman identified individual differences in the need for optimal amounts of stimulation. Sensation seekers look for varied or novel experiences, have a lower appreciation of risk and anticipate arousal as more positive than do low-sensation seekers.

Zuckerman suggested a relationship between sensation seeking and gambling in which 'individuals entertain the risk of monetary loss for the positive reinforcement produced by states of high arousal during periods of uncertainty, as well as the positive arousal produced by winning'. The pathological gambler is seen as a person who needs this intense stimulation and excitement.

There is research support…

Blaszczynski *et al.* found that pathological gamblers had higher boredom proneness scores than a control group of non-gamblers.

However… Generally there is little support, e.g. Coventry and Brown found that those who bet on horse racing in an off-course betting shop were actually lower on sensation-seeking than non-gamblers.

Individual differences…

Coventry and Brown found inconsistencies, racetrack betters were lower in terms of sensation-seeking than non-gamblers (above) but casino gamblers were higher than non-gamblers. This suggests that gambling cannot be seen as a homogeneous activity.

This is supported by Bonnaire *et al.* who studied two groups of pathological gamblers: café games players and racetrack betters. The latter had higher scores on sensation-seeking, leading to the identification of subtypes – one (the racetrack gamblers) who play 'active' games and gamble for the associated arousal. The second subtype (the café gamers) play passive games and gamble to avoid unpleasant emotional states (e.g. boredom).

Chapter 14

Models of addictive behaviour | Vulnerability to addiction
Factors affecting addictive behaviour >
The psychology of addictive behaviour > | Reducing addictive behaviour | The role of media in addictive behaviour

Vulnerability to addiction

Self-esteem

Link with health

Abood et al. found a relationship between self-esteem and general health behaviour, with self-esteem accounting for a significant percent of the variance in health behaviours among adolescents.

There is research support...

Taylor et al. analysed data from a sample of 872 boys. Those who had very low self-esteem at age 11 were at higher risk for addiction (particularly drug dependency) at age 20.

Baumeister claimed that low self-esteem may cause people to behave in ways that are self-defeating in order to escape self-awareness.

Mobile phone usage

Bianchi and Phillips used the *Mobile Phone Problem Usage Scale* (MPPUS) with 195 males and females (mean age 36 years). Low self-esteem did not predict mobile phone usage, but did predict problem use.

Problems of determining causality...

Determining causality is a problem in studies such as Bianchi and Phillips. It is not clear in this study whether (a) heavier mobile phone use leads to poor self-esteem by generating problems associated with inappropriate use (e.g. high phone bills), or (b) whether poor self-esteem leads to higher usage and greater likelihood of inappropriate use of mobile phones. Causality can be dealt with by using longitudinal studies.

Internet usage

Armstrong et al. have found that pathological Internet usage (an indication of Internet addiction) was also more common in people with lower levels of self-esteem.

There is research support...

Niemz et al. found that 18% of their sample (371 UK students) were pathological Internet users and they had lower levels of self-esteem.

Cause or effect?... Low self-esteem may drive people to use the Internet more, but it is also possible that Internet addiction leads people to become socially isolated, leading to lower levels of self-esteem.

Attributions for addiction

Conflicting cognitions

Addiction leads to conflicting cognitions about behaviour (e.g. smoking despite health risks). Addicts may resolve this contradiction by attributing their behaviour to forces outside their control (i.e. addiction to nicotine) (Eiser).

Are attributions accurate or functional?...

Hammersley et al. found that drug users in prison often used drug use as an explanation for their crimes of theft. However, analysis suggested that the thieving preceded drug use i.e. the attributions were functional.

The detrimental nature of attributions for addiction...

Eiser and van der Plight proposed that if smokers saw themselves as addicted, this would be a major obstacle to behaviour change. By endorsing users' adoption of the 'addicted' label, agencies may well create a self-fulfilling prophecy whereby 'addicted' smokers perceive that they are not in control of their behaviour or their failure to change.

Attributions vary for different drugs

Research has shown that attributions for the behaviour of others differ according to substance type, e.g. Hatgis et al. found that attributions of personal responsibility for marijuana problems (compared to alcohol, crack cocaine and heroin) were driven by their perception that marijuana was less addictive than other substances.

IDA *Gender bias in attributions for addiction...*

Hatgis et al. found that both men and women attributed personal responsibility for drug and alcohol-related problems to men i.e. male drug and alcohol users are held more personally responsible for their problems than females.

The social context of addiction

Smoking

Smoking is linked to peers' approval together with the message that smoking promotes popularity (McAlister et al.)

- Social learning theory (SLT) (Bandura). Young people are most likely to imitate those with whom they have the most social contact. Subsequent experiences (i.e. pleasant or unpleasant) determine whether the new behaviour persists.
- Social identity theory (SIT) (Abrams and Hogg). Group members adopt as their own those norms and behaviours that are central to the social identity of the group to which they belong (e.g. being a smoker or non-smoker) .

Age differences in influence...

The influence of peers on smoking and drug use appears to wane in later adolescence, and romantic partners become increasingly important as an influence on attitudes and behaviours, particularly those that are health related (Brown et al.).

There is research support for SLT...

Research supports the claim that exposure to peer models increases the likelihood that teenagers will begin smoking (Duncan et al.).

Research supports the claim that perceived rewards such as social status and popularity are instrumental in why adolescents begin smoking and why they continue to smoke (Eiser et al.).

There is research support for SIT...

Mitchell found that adolescents are motivated to begin smoking because of the stereotypes they hold of specific social crowds but little is known about the extent to which these groups influence their members to smoke nor what happens if group attitudes conflict with an individual's own concerns to maintain a healthy lifestyle.

Heroin use

Draus and Carlson found that desire to take heroin came from belonging to a social group that uses the drug, and fears of injection were overcome by the presence of friends.

IDA *Ethical issues in addiction research...*

Lee suggests that research in sensitive areas (e.g. drug-taking) creates particular ethical issues for the researcher. When designing a study, researchers must weigh up the potential benefits (e.g. possibilities for intervention) against the potential risks (e.g. further discrimination).

Chapter 14

Models of addictive behaviour | Vulnerability to addiction
Factors affecting addictive behaviour > | The role of media in addictive behaviour
The psychology of addictive behaviour > | Reducing addictive behaviour

The role of media in addictive behaviour

Research into film representations of addiction

Sulkunen

Method: 61 scenes from 47 films were analysed regarding addictions to alcohol, drugs, tobacco, gambling and sex.

Results: The enjoyment of drugs was frequently contrasted with the dullness of ordinary life. The competent use of drugs was represented as a way of alleviating a particular problem, e.g. in *Human Traffic*, the use of ecstasy was portrayed as a way of resolving relationship problems for two of the main characters.

Gunasekera

Method: 87 of the most popular films of the last 20 years were looked at for their portrayal of sex and drug usage.

Results: Films with cannabis (8%) and other non-injected illicit drugs (7%) were less common than those portraying alcohol intoxication (32%) and tobacco use (68%), but tended to portray the use of such drugs positively and without showing negative consequences. There were no references to the consequences of unsafe sex, such as HIV transmission. The study found that only one in four films was free from negative health behaviours such as unprotected sex with new partners, cannabis use, smoking and alcohol intoxication.

Do film portrayals affect behaviour?...

Sargent and Hanewinkel surveyed a total of 4,384 adolescents who were re-surveyed a year later. They found that of those individuals who had not smoked when first surveyed, exposure to movies with smoking over the intervening year was a significant and strong predictor of whether they had begun to smoke when re-surveyed one year later.

The importance of film representations of addiction...

Byrne argues that films such as *Trainspotting* are important because they educate both addicts and the general public about addiction by creating stereotypes.

He draws a parallel with the fact that the dominant image of ECT comes not from the public information literature of the Royal College of Psychiatrists, but from the 1975 film *One Flew Over the Cuckoo's Nest*.

An alternative perspective...

Boyd argues that films actually often represent negative, rather than positive, consequences of addiction. For example, illegal drug use and addiction, claims Boyd, are depicted by physical deterioration (e.g. unkempt bodies), sexual degradation (e.g. prostitution), violence and crime (e.g. murder) and moral decline (e.g. stealing from loved ones).

IDA Ethical guidelines...

In the US, the Office for Substance Abuse Protection (OSAP) has developed guidelines about drugs for film and television writers. These recommend that writers should communicate all illegal drug use as unhealthy and harmful, that addiction should be presented as a disease and abstinence as a viable choice. There should be no references to 'recreational use of drugs', since no drug use is 'recreational'.

The role of media in changing addictive behaviour

A suitable role for the media

Television and the Internet have been identified as media that could be used to provide support for addicts and education about addiction. They are increasingly being used to promote healthy lifestyles and behaviour change such as smoking cessation and physical exercise.

Problem drinking TV programmes

Bennett *et al.* assessed the effect of the BBC programme *Psst... the Really Useful Guide to Alcohol*. Viewers showed improved alcohol-related knowledge, but did not show any change in attitude or in actual alcohol consumption.

Kramer *et al.* assessed the effectiveness of *Drinking Less? Do it Yourself!*, a five-week television self-help intervention designed to reduce problem drinking. They found that the intervention group were more successful than a control group in achieving low-risk (rather than high-risk) problem drinking, a difference maintained at a three-month follow-up.

Antidrug campaigns

In 2008, a television and Internet advertising campaign was launched in the UK to warn teenagers of the dangers of cocaine use. The adverts feature a fictional dog called Pablo, who is used by drug dealers to carry cocaine. The dog seeks out cocaine users to find out what happens to them after taking the drug.

Competitive media drives people to use drugs...

Brian Wilson, the creative genius behind the Beach Boys, used drugs such as cannabis and LSD as a creative influence. However, his use of cocaine, to which he became addicted, no longer contributed to the creative process, but was a form of self-medication as he struggled with the pressures of writing and touring. This shows how the competitive media drives some people to experiment with drugs as a creative influence, but they become victims of the drugs' addictive power (Belli).

Methodological problems...

The Kramer *et al.* study involved an intervention group, who watched the *Drinking Less?* series, and a control group who watched the series later.

- The intervention group received weekly visits from the researchers; the extra attention may explain the positive outcome for this group.
- The waiting list group were aware they would receive treatment soon, so may have postponed their behavioural change, thereby artificially inflating the magnitude of the difference between the two groups.

Correlation isn't the same as causality...

Most of the evidence about media effects on addictive behaviour is correlational, i.e. exposure to depictions of drug and alcohol use in films and on television is related to addictive behaviour. However, this does not indicate a causal relationship between exposure and addiction.

Do antidrug campaigns work?...

Hornik *et al.* concluded that the $1 billlion US *National Youth Anti-Drug Media Campaign* not only failed but also had negative effects. Why?

- The messages in the campaign were not particularly novel.
- Antidrug advertising has an implicit message that drug use is commonplace. Johnston *et al.* found that youths who saw the ads took from them the message that their peers were using marijuana, and were then more likely to imitate marijuana use themselves.

Chapter 14

Models of addictive behaviour
Factors affecting addictive behaviour
Models of prevention
The psychology of addictive behaviour > **Reducing addictive behaviour** > Types of intervention

Models of prevention

The Theory of Reasoned Action (TRA)

Main assumptions

Fishbein and Ajzen proposed a cognitive theory about the decision to engage in, e.g. taking drugs or stopping smoking. This decision can be predicted by *intentions* which are:

1. *Personal* – The individual's behavioural attitudes i.e. how desirable it seems to be.
   - Beliefs about the consequences.
   - An appraisal of the value of these consequences (i.e. good or bad).
2. *Social* – Subjective norms:
   - *Injunctive norms* – The right thing to do.
   - *Descriptive norms* – Perceptions of what other people are doing.

Application: Safe sex

Terry *et al.* studied how people responded to the threat of HIV. The possible responses included being monogamous, having non-penetrative sex and using condoms.

They found that the link between intention and behaviour was problematic for some people because they could not control the behaviour or wishes of the other partner.

Application: Gambling

Moore and Ohtsuka found that the TRA predicted gambling frequency and problem gambling. Subjective norms and attitudes predicted intentions to gamble (or not), and intentions to gamble predicted actual behaviour.

Problems of determining intention…

Intentions are often assessed by questionnaires and represent an ideal rather than the intentions that exist in the behavioural situation, and thus are poor predictors of actual behaviour (Albarracin *et al.*).

For example, a smoker may intend to give up smoking because of the threat to health. However, their actual intentions change when in a group of heavy smokers.

Intention and expectation…

Warshaw and Davis suggest a distinction should be made between behavioural intention (plans about future behaviour) and behavioural expectation (perceived likelihood of performing a particular behaviour). Only the former may have a causal effect on behaviour.

For example, a smoker may anticipate giving up smoking in five years (expectation) without having a definite plan to give up (intention).

The influence of alcohol and drugs…

Intentions tend to be measured when sober, but risky behaviours such as gambling or unprotected sex may be performed when under the influence of alcohol or drugs. In such a state, people have a reduced cognitive capacity so that only the most obvious characteristics of a situation are attended to (*alcohol myopia*) (Steele and Josephs).

MacDonald *et al.* did find that alcohol intoxication increased measured intention to engage in unprotected sex and other risky behaviours.

IDA Cultural bias and the TRA…

Bagozzi suggests that because the TRA was developed in the USA it has an individualist orientation (focuses on an individual's attitudes) and thus applies less to non-Western cultures.

Bagozzi found evidence to support this claim in that the effects of attitudes and subjective norms were greater in determining intention to eat fast food among US than among Japanese or Chinese students.

The Theory of Planned Behaviour (TPB)

Main assumptions

Ajzen extended the TRA to include *perceived behavioural control*, i.e. the extent to which the individual believes they will be able to perform the behaviour. Perceived behavioural control acts on:

1. *Intention* – The more control people believe they have over a behaviour, the stronger will be their intention to actually perform that behaviour.
2. *Behaviour* – An individual with higher perceived behavioural control is likely to try harder and to persevere for longer.

Application: Intention to change

The TRB has been successfully applied in the prediction of a wide range of social behaviours, including drug use (Umeh and Patel), stopping smoking (Rise *et al.*) and healthy eating (Conner *et al.*).

Application: Perceived control

Perceived behavioural control takes on a more important role when issues of control are associated with the performance of a task. Thus control has been found to contribute very little to the prediction of intentions to consume convenience food, but is an important predictor of the intention to lose weight (Netemeyer *et al.*).

There is research support…

A meta-analysis by Armitage and Conner found that perceived behavioural control added an extra 6% of the variance in intention compared to the assessment of attitude and subjective norm alone. This represents an improvement on the TRA.

Predicts intention rather than behaviour change…

Armitage and Conner also found that the TRB was successful in predicting intention rather than behavioural change, particularly where difficult behavioural change is concerned (e.g. addiction).

In the context of difficult behavioural change, therefore, we can make a distinction between a motivational phase which results in the formation of a behavioural intention, and a post-decisional phase which involves behavioural initiation and maintenance (Abraham *et al.*).

Both the TRA and TPB are too rational…

When filling out a questionnaire about attitudes and intentions, people may not anticipate the emotions that compel their behaviour in real life.

The presence of strong emotions may explain why people sometimes act irrationally and fail to carry out an intention (e.g. stop drinking) even when it is in their best interest to do so (Albarracin *et al.*).

IDA Real-world application…

White *et al.* examined the sun protection intentions and behaviours of young people in a high-risk sun cancer area of Australia. Results showed that the TPB components of attitude, subjective norm and perceived behavioural control were significant predictors of intentions to engage in sun protection, and these intentions were significant predictors of actual sun protection behaviour.

Chapter 14

Models of addictive behaviour
Factors affecting addictive behaviour
Models of prevention

The psychology of addictive behaviour > Reducing addictive behaviour > Types of intervention

Types of intervention into addictive behaviour

Biological interventions

Heroin addiction and methadone

Methadone mimics the effects of heroin but is less addictive. A drug abuser is given slowly increasing amounts of methadone to improve tolerance. Then the dose is decreased until the addict no longer needs methadone or heroin.

Problems with methadone treatment…

Some drug addicts can become as reliant on methadone as they were on heroin, thereby substituting one addiction for another.

The use of methadone remains controversial. Statistics show more than 300 methadone-related deaths in the UK in 2007. Because methadone consumption is often unsupervised, this has created a black market in methadone, with addicts selling their doses for only £2.

Drug treatments for gambling addiction

In the UK drug treatments have not been approved for gambling but there is evidence that they may be effective.

SSRIs increase serotonin levels. Hollander *et al.* found that gamblers treated with SSRIs showed improvements compared to a control group.

Naltrexone (a dopamine receptor antagonist) reduces the rewarding and reinforcing properties of gambling, thus reducing the urge to gamble.

Drug treatments for gambling addiction…

The Hollander study involved only ten people. A larger and longer study (Blanco *et al.*), involving 32 gamblers over six months, failed to demonstrate any superiority for the drug treatment over a placebo.

Use of naltrexone led to decreases in gambling thoughts and behaviours after six weeks of treatment (Kim and Grant).

IDA *Intervention bias…*

Cohen and Cohen describe a phenomenon called the *'clinician's illusion'* – clinicians believe that addictions are difficult to treat because they only tend to come across addicts when their condition is well advanced, too severe to effectively respond to treatment.

Psychological interventions

Operant conditioning

One way to reduce addiction is to reward people for not engaging in the behaviour.

Sindelar *et al.* tested people on methadone treatment programmes (also received counselling). One group was rewarded each time they tested negative for drugs. At the end of the programme the reward group had 60% more negative urine samples than the control group.

Reinforcement does not address underlying problems…

Although research such as the Sindelar *et al.* study have shown the effectiveness of reinforcement therapies for reducing addictive behaviour, such interventions do nothing to address the problem that led to the addiction in the first place.

This means that although a specific addictive behaviour might have been reduced, it is possible that the person may engage in a different addictive behaviour instead. A drug addict may, for example, turn to alcohol, but in most cases new addictions tend to be subtle including compulsive spending or even developing dependent relationships.

Cognitive-behavioural therapy (CBT)

The main goal of CBT is to help people change the way they think about their addiction, and learn new ways of coping more effectively.

For example, in gambling addiction cognitive errors (e.g. believing one can control and predict outcomes) play a part in maintaining gambling. Such errors are corrected by CBT.

Research support for CBT…

Ladouceur *et al.* randomly allocated 66 pathological gamblers to a cognitive therapy or to a waiting list control group. Afterwards 86% of the treatment group were no longer classed as pathological gamblers and had increased self-efficacy.

Sylvain *et al.* evaluated treatments that target cognition as well as behaviour. Pathological gamblers were given cognitive therapy, social skills training and relapse prevention resulting in improvements after treatment, with these gains maintained at one-year follow-up.

Public health interventions and legislation

Telephone smoking 'Quitlines'

Stead *et al.* found that smokers (sample =18,000) who received repeated Quitline calls increased their odds of stopping smoking by 50% compared to smokers who only received self-help materials and/or brief counselling.

IDA *Real-world application of Quitlines…*

Military personnel deployed abroad (e.g. Iraq) often increase smoking or take it up for the first time (Boos and Croft). Beckham *et al.* found that a combination of Quitline counselling and nicotine replacement therapy was highly effective in treating US military veterans.

Anti-smoking legislation

In July 2007, it became illegal to smoke in public buildings in the UK. The primary objective was to protect non-smokers from the harmful effects of secondhand smoke. It was also hoped that it would discourage smokers from smoking.

The effectiveness of smoke-free legislation…

West shows that although there was a decline in the percentage of people in the UK who smoked prior to the ban, this was followed by a rebound effect. Attempts to stop smoking were actually greater in the nine months before the ban than in the 17 months after.

The NIDA study

Government-sponsored intervention projects such as the US National Institute on Drug Abuse (NIDA) *Collaborative Cocaine Treatment Study* are designed to intervene in the cycle of personal and social problems associated with drugs.

Public health interventions…

The NIDA intervention led to reduced cocaine use, with an associated reduction in other behaviours (e.g. unprotected sex in addicts leading to a reduction in HIV) (Crits-Christoph *et al.*).

Conclusions…

Research has not tended to show that any one type of psychological treatment is superior to any other. Psychological therapies appear more effective when combined with a pharmacological treatment.

Chapter 15

Anomalistic psychology

Division A Theoretical and methodological issues in the study of anomalous experience
Issues of pseudoscience and scientific fraud
Controversies: ESP and psychokinesis

Division B Factors underlying anomalous experience
Cognitive, personality and biological factors
Functions of paranormal and related beliefs
Deception and self-deception, superstition, and coincidence

Division C Belief in exceptional experience
Psychic healing and psychic mediumship
Out-of-body and near-death experience

Specification

Anomalistic psychology	
Theoretical and methodological issues in the study of anomalous experience	• Issues of pseudoscience and scientific fraud. • Controversies relating to Ganzfeld studies of ESP and studies of psychokinesis.
Factors underlying anomalous experience	• Cognitive, personality and biological factors underlying anomalous experience. • Functions of paranormal and related beliefs, including their cultural significance. • The psychology of deception and self-deception, superstition, and coincidence.
Belief in exceptional experience	• Research into: psychic healing, out-of-body and near-death experience, psychic mediumship.

Chapter 15

Theoretical and methodological issues >

Factors underlying anomalous experience

Anomalistic psychology > | Belief in exceptional experience

Issues of pseudoscience and scientific fraud

Controversies: ESP and psychokinesis

Issues of pseudoscience and scientific fraud

Pseudoscience in studies of anomalous experience

A pseudoscience is a field of study that masquerades as a science but lacks certain important characteristics, such as:

- *Irrefutable hypothesis* – Pseudoscientific studies often have hypotheses that are non-falsifiable, e.g. a researcher may find no evidence of ESP but then claim that the lack of supporting evidence occurs because the presence of skeptics causes the phenomena to disappear.
- *Carefully controlled, replicable research* – Replication is the means by which findings can be confirmed as valid.
- *Theory to explain the effects* – The aim of scientific research is to construct explanations for observations made about the world. Many paranormal phenomena have not, as yet, been given explanations that are likely.
- *Burden of proof* is with the sceptic rather than the believer (as in true science). Such disproof is often difficult because e.g. the hypothesis lacks falsifiability or it is difficult to prove that a photo is fake.
- *Ability to change* – In science explanations are adapted as a result of hypothesis testing, whereas anomalous experiences have continued to be explained in the same way for centuries, despite a lack of evidence.

IDA *Paranormal research is not the only example of pseudoscience...*

Freud's theory has been criticised because many of his hypotheses are unfalsifiable, e.g. his view that all men have repressed homosexual tendencies cannot be disproved. If you do find men who have no repressed homosexual tendencies, then it could be argued that they have them, it's just they are so repressed they are not apparent.

There are also many examples of scientific research where believers persist despite clear disproof, e.g. the discovery of cold fusion in 1989 (a method to produce nuclear fusion at room temperature). Subsequent research has shown that any positive results were due to poor methodology; nevertheless, there continue to be researchers investigating this topic.

Parapsychology is recognised as a science...

The American Association for the Advancement of Science (AAAS), the largest general scientific society in the world, allowed the Parapsychological Association (PA) to become an affiliated member in 1969, thus appearing to confirm its scientific status.

IDA *Ethical issues... Where's the harm?...*

There are three reasons to be concerned about paranormal research.

- Some people make a lot of money out of unfounded claims.
- As a society we should be encouraged to ask for evidence rather than respond to trends and superstitions which, in the past, have resulted in dangerous practices, e.g. the persecution of witches or the punishment of mental patients.
- Thorough research may lead to valuable discoveries, e.g. acupuncture is now accepted as a valuable therapy due to research that has demonstrated repeatable results.

Scientific fraud in studies of anomalous experience

The British mathematician S.G. Soal worked with Basil Shackleton in the 1940s, demonstrating his impressive paranormal abilities to prominent observers who vouched that there was no trickery. However, in 1960 one of his agents, Mrs Gretl Albert, reported that Soal had faked the results by changing the answer sheet to match the correct answers.

The Soal affair remains unconfirmed...

Soal never admitted the fraud and he is now dead and so cannot defend himself.

However, an analysis of the data suggests that the frequency of 4s and 5s in the answers are greater than would be expected by chance, which supports the accusation that he changed the 1s to 4s and 5s and therefore his data was fraudulent (Hansel).

J.B. Rhine founded a paranormal research lab in the US in 1930. He reported that at least 12 of the researchers in his lab had behaved dishonestly in order to get significant results.

J.B. Rhine didn't go far enough...

Rhine did report his assistants for cheating but he did not reveal who they were. This means we are unable to identify the work they were involved in and this work is likely to have been published and accepted as fact (Gardner).

Carl Sargent conducted research on ESP using the Ganzfeld technique (see page 122). A colleague reported several errors and failures to follow the protocol in the research. Sargent defended himself but left the research field thereafter, which has been taken as a confirmation of his dishonesty.

Sargent's findings continue to be used...

Despite suspicions about the fraudulent basis of the work, Sargent's findings have continued to be included in various reviews, such as Bem and Honorton's review, where nine of the 18 studies were from Sargent's lab and therefore may be fraudulent.

Uri Geller became famous in the 1970s for bending spoons and for other psychic powers. James Randi, a highly successful magician, accused Geller of being a fraud and using standard magic tricks to accomplish his allegedly paranormal feats. Geller's former manager, Yasha Katz, confessed on Italian TV to helping Geller cheat (Harris).

IDA *Fraud is found throughout scientific research...*

Sir Cyril Burt was accused of inventing data on twins to support his argument that intelligence is innate.

Many noted scientists have resorted to data-fudging (reporting data erroneously) or outright invention, including Galileo, Mendel and even Newton (Playfair).

Nevertheless, Hines argues that, historically, fraud has been more common in parapsychology than other areas of scientific investigation, possibly because the lack of positive results pushes researchers to invent them.

Controversies

Extrasensory perception (ESP)

The Ganzfeld technique

Honorton developed this to study ESP. It is argued that 'psi' (the process by which ESP occurs) is such a weak force that it is normally drowned out by other senses. This can be overcome by isolating them from sensory information (ping pong balls over eyes, earphones playing white noise). The receiver describes an image being sent and an independent judge has to match the received image to images that were sent.

Honorton published an analysis of 28 Ganzfeld studies, reporting a success rate of 38%; 25% would be performance at the chance level.

Conclusions challenged

Hyman claimed that Honorton's studies were flawed in terms of lack of security and erroneous statistical analyses.

Hyman reanalysed the data and concluded there was no evidence of psi.

Honorton further reanalysed the data (using different techniques) and found that the data continued to provide supporting evidence.

Joint communiqué

In order to resolve their differences Hyman and Honorton jointly developed a better controlled technique, *autoganzfeld*. Honorton *et al.* reported the results of 11 autoganzfeld studies producing a hit rate of 34%, a significant effect.

Controversy continues

Milton and Wiseman reviewed 30 further, well-controlled Ganzfeld studies and concluded that these studies showed no significant effects.

Procedural criticisms...

The receiver's descriptions often involve a number of images (e.g. 'I see the Lincoln Memorial ... it's the 4th of July ... fireworks'). This means there is scope for subjective interpretation about what counts as a match (Carroll).

Wooffitt analysed Ganzfeld interviews and found that sceptical researchers didn't encourage the 'receivers' to elaborate their images, whereas interviewers who believed in psi often did, which led to more positive results (a kind of researcher bias).

The file–drawer effect...

Researchers have been accused of leaving certain studies out of meta-analyses (filing them away) which, by doing so creates a different set of conclusions.

The sheep–goat effect...

The file–drawer effect is particularly directed at researchers who are 'sheep' (people who believe in psi as opposed to non-believers who are called 'goats').

The sheep–goat effect applies to participants as well. Schmeidler and McConnell collected evidence from more than 1,000 participants, finding that sheep tended to score above chance whereas goats show results at the level of chance or even negative results (called 'psi missing').

The psi assumption

Carroll argues that psi can only be regarded as an explanation for observed effects if all other possibilities can be excluded (e.g. selective reporting, poor experimental design, deliberate fraud etc).

Furthermore, the question should be asked, if psi exists, why are participants not correct 100% of the time and also able to actually describe the picture in the Ganzfeld task exactly.

Criticisms of the Milton/Wiseman review...

This review was subsequently criticised because it included studies that had not followed the Ganzfeld protocol. When these anomalous studies were removed, and some more recent studies added, a significant result was again obtained (Bem *et al.*).

Psychokinesis (PK)

Macro-PK (visible to the eye) e.g. moving furniture and bending metal spoons.

Heath claimed that most people possess such powers but don't display them because their conscious mind 'interferes'.

Batcheldor 'trained' people by starting with a fake levitation event and then gradually building up belief during repeat sittings, leading to the ability to levitate objects.

Micro-PK (small effects on probabilistic systems)

Random event generator (REG), an electronic coin flipper. Volunteers are asked to produce more heads than tails, or vice versa. When the scores across all trials from 12 years of research were combined, the effect size was very large (greater than a probability of 1 in 10^{13}) (Jahn *et al.*).

Split-beam laser – Participants were invited to try to influence the activity of a split-beam laser on the web. Their laser output was more active than participants who did not try to influence activity (Stevens).

Challenge to the validity of such demonstrations...

Randi arranged a hoax (Project Alpha) where two amateur magicians volunteered for testing at The McDonnell Laboratory for Psychical Research. They were able to fool the scientists for four years through more than 160 hours of experiments.

The importance of belief...

Participants were shown a video of a fake psychic placing a bent key on a table. Those who heard the psychic say the key was continuing to bend later were more likely to report further bending than participants in a no-expectation condition (Wiseman and Greening).

IDA Making comparisons with the scientific approach...

The results from PK studies, if accepted, violate well-established laws of physics. In addition, most scientists require a higher standard of proof than the weak effects that have been observed (Sagan), excessively large data sets almost inevitably produce significant effects.

The effect size should be increasing not decreasing...

Bierman analysed a large number of paranormal studies conducted since the time of J.B. Rhine, including micro-PK studies. He concluded that there has been a steady decline in the effect size.

Usually, if there is a real effect, the size of the effect becomes greater over time, because scientists are progressively better able to identify and control extraneous variables. In contrast, increasing control has had the opposite effect in paranormal research – which suggests that the phenomena are not real.

Factors underlying anomalous experience

Cognitive factors

General cognitive ability or intelligence.

Lower intelligence might mean being less accurate at judging whether a psychic event in fact has a normal explanation.

Research (e.g. Gray) has found that believers have lower levels of academic performance than sceptics.

Some research has found the opposite...

A survey of *New Scientist* readers (more than half hold a science degree) found that 67% regarded ESP either as an 'established fact' or 'a likely possibility' (Evans).

In general research has not found a difference in terms of cognitive ability (except for syllogistic reasoning) (Wiseman and Watt).

Finding links between distantly related materials (e.g. seeing a spherical object in the sky and believing it to be a UFO).

Brugger *et al.* showed that believers are more likely to see faces or words where none exist.

This is not a negative tendency...

Researchers have found a link between creativity and paranormal beliefs (e.g. Thalbourne). People who believe are more creative, whereas non-believers are not and may even lose out because they fail to detect meaningful connections.

Probability misjudgment

Believers tend to underestimate statistical likelihood on *probability judgment tasks* (e.g. generating random numbers, Brugger *et al.*). This would lead them to reject coincidence as an explanation for paranormal events.

It might be low cognitive ability...

Musch and Ehrenberg controlled for differences in general cognitive ability and found this reduced the difference between believers and non-believers on probability judgment tasks to zero. So it may be that poor probability judgments are due to low cognitive ability and not a component in paranormal belief.

Fantasy proneness is the tendency to become so deeply absorbed in a fantasy that it feels as if it actually happened.

Evidence suggests that believers are more fantasy prone, e.g. Dixon *et al.* demonstrated a link between belief and mental imagination.

Validity of research studies...

Belief in the paranormal is measured using a set of statements about paranormal phenomena e.g. the *Paranormal Belief Scale*, which covers phenomena such as UFOs and the Loch Ness monster. This may not be a valid measurement because it covers such a wide range of different beliefs.

Personality factors

Neuroticism

Research has found a link between paranormal beliefs and neuroticism (tendency to experience negative emotional states) (e.g. Williams *et al.*).

IDA *A psychodynamic approach*

Paranormal beliefs may create a distance from reality as a defence mechanism to reduce the negative emotional states (e.g. anger) associated with neuroticism.

Schizotypy

Irwin and Green found a link between paranormal belief and schizotypy in the cognitive-perceptual domain (e.g. tendency to have hallucinations and disordered thinking).

IDA *A pathological approach...*

This research implies that belief in the paranormal is in some sense pathological. A link with narcissism has also been found – a personality disorder where an individual is full of self-importance (Tobacyk and Milford).

Extraversion

Honorton *et al.* conducted a meta-analysis of 60 published studies relating extraversion to ESP and found an overall positive correlation.

However... Links have not been found with other mental disorders, e.g. bipolar disorder (Andrews and Lester).

Some research has found a positive correlation between paranormal belief and mental health, e.g. self-actualisation (Clarke).

Locus of control

Research has shown a correlation between external locus of control (events are explained in terms of some external determinant) and paranormal belief (e.g. Allen and Lester).

The relationship is not consistent...

Some forms of psi phenomena (e.g. superstition) correlate positively with an external locus of control (Wolfradt).

The unreliability of results may be, in part, due to the way paranormal belief is measured (see above).

Biological factors

Right hemisphere over-activation

Research has found it in believers as compared to non-believers (e.g. Pizzagalli *et al.*).

Link between cognitive and biological factors...

Research has also found that the right hemisphere activity is associated with processing links between distantly related material (Wiseman and Watt).

High levels of dopamine

Brugger *et al.* found that people with high dopamine levels were more likely to interpret coincidental events as having meaning. Giving *L-dopa* (a drug that increases dopamine levels) to sceptics had the same effect.

However... It is quite a leap from identifying right hemisphere and dopamine activity to assuming that this explains pattern detection (i.e. associating distantly related materials). In addition, subsequent research by Brugger's team has not replicated the dopamine effect (Palmer *et al.*).

Genes

Koenig *et al.* found that MZ twins were more likely than DZ twins to have the same religious views, and Bouchard *et al.* found that religious belief is related to belief in the paranormal.

IDA *An evolutionary approach...*

It might be argued that a belief in paranormal phenomenon is not adaptive because erroneous connections are made, however there are times when learning such links would be adaptive (see the psychology of superstition and coincidence on page 125).

Chapter 15

Cognitive, personality and biological factors

Theoretical and methodological issues

Functions of paranormal and related beliefs

Factors underlying anomalous experience >

Deception and self-deception, superstition and coincidence

Anomalistic psychology >

Belief in exceptional experience

Functions of paranormal and related beliefs

Functions of paranormal beliefs

Evolutionary approach

Belief in anomalous experience extends across all cultures, suggesting it is innate and has evolved for an adaptive purpose.

It may enable individuals to stop worrying and then they can be more productive, increasing their reproductive success.

Psychodynamic explanations

The functions of paranormal beliefs can be related to psychological needs:

- *Defence mechanism* used by anxious people to overcome uncertainty.
- *Sense of control* – Childhood experiences, such as parental divorce or frequently moving home, may create a need for a greater sense of control that is provided by paranormal beliefs.
- *Abuse and fantasy proneness* – Abuse in childhood might lead to fantasy proneness (i.e. tendency to create fantasies instead of dealing with reality).

IDA *Is it the belief or the actual ability that is adaptive?*…

Paranormal abilities (e.g. ESP and PK) may actually exist and have evolved because they confer an advantage on individuals who possess them. However, if this were true we would expect to see an increase in such abilities over the course of human history.

Therefore we must conclude that it is the belief rather than the actual ability that is adaptive.

There is research support for sense of control…

Watt *et al.* found that people with predicted childhood experiences (e.g. frequent moving home) were more likely to hold paranormal beliefs. A second line of evidence comes from the Gulf War (1991). In the areas (e.g. Israel) attacked by Iraqi missiles (low sense of control), there was a rise in superstitious belief (Henderson).

There is research support for fantasy proneness…

French and Kerman recruited participants with a history of childhood abuse and found a correlation between childhood trauma, fantasy proneness and paranormal belief.

Criticism of the psychodynamic approach…

Wiseman and Watt suggest it is mistaken to see paranormal beliefs as pathological (e.g. implied by the psychodynamic approach). Some beliefs create positive self-fulfilling expectations.

Functions of related beliefs – religion

Psychodynamic explanation

Freud believed that rituals allow us to feel a sense of control over unconscious conflicts and that religion protects us from our fears, e.g. the finality of death.

Credulity

Hood suggests the willingness to believe is adaptive at a young age (accepting what you are told). This becomes part of religious beliefs, trusting people with special powers.

Pre-scientific societies

People required answers to questions about the world, e.g. why do people die? Even today there are some questions that only religion provides the answers for.

Spiritual healing

Any treatment has some effectiveness due to the placebo effect. Therefore belief in any treatment is adaptive because it increases the likelihood of survival.

Some research does not show a correlation…

While many studies have found a correlation between paranormal beliefs and religiosity, this is not true of all studies (e.g. Beck and Miller). This may be because scales measuring paranormal beliefs include beliefs that don't form any part of religion, e.g. UFOs.

Science might be seen as a form of religion…

Science is often portrayed as the antithesis of religion – the former is rational and evidence-based, while the latter is irrational and organised around faith. However, some (e.g. Stenmark) argue that science is like a religion in that it is something people believe in, though Dawkins argues that science is a matter of belief (which then leads to a search for evidence), whereas religion is a matter of faith (not questioning).

IDA *Is religion adaptive?*…

Research shows that people who are religious have greater self-control (McCullough and Willoughby) and better physical and mental health (Schumaker).

In contrast… Dennett argues that religion is not directly adaptive but, instead, is a by-product of other mental faculties that have been selected for different reasons, such as Theory of Mind, which allows people to deceive others.

Cultural significance

The form of belief varies across cultures, showing that such beliefs are related to social factors. The possible adaptive significance of such social factors might include:

- *Imagination* – Evolved to think about things that don't physically exist, leading to the uniquely human 'transcendental social', which unites cultural groups and the dead with the living (Bloch).
- *Social bonding* – Religious behaviour evolved because it links human beings into coherent and successful groups, which then have a competitive edge over other groups (Wilson).
- *Morality* – Religion maintains moral behaviour.

Individual versus group selection…

Natural selection functions at the level of an individual's genes, which suggests that behaviours that are good for the group would not be selected. However, any behaviour that enhances the success of a group also benefits the individuals within the group and therefore individuals in the group are more likely to be naturally selected.

IDA *A sociological approach*…

Marx suggested that organised religion is a social institution created to maintain a culture. The adaptive nature of religion is therefore nothing to do with religious experience but mainly to do with its cultural value.

Gender differences are an example of subcultural differences…

Women have a greater global belief in the paranormal, whereas men express more belief in UFOs and extraterrestrials (Rice), possibly because men are expected to take a greater interest in science and this might lead them to focus on more science-oriented phenomena.

Deception and self-deception, superstition and coincidence

The psychology of deception

The evolution of deception

Deception evolved because being able to deceive others (Machiavellian intelligence) gives an individual power. This means they may become leaders (e.g. priests, shamen) and ultimately may have greater reproductive success.

Practising deception

Magicians and psychics mask deception by e.g. diverting attention, appearing to have no motivation to deceive and emphasising their honesty.

Detecting deception

People are not good at detecting deception and may be least effective when they are face-to-face (Wiseman).

Anomalous experiences don't always involve deception...

The psychology of deception only relates to some anomalous experiences, e.g. not out-of-body experience or UFOs.

Is the use of deception harmless?...

In cases where deception is involved, such as during a séance, it could be argued that such events are relatively harmless. However, Wiseman points out that there are stories of people handing large sums of money over to psychics or, in one case, a young man committing suicide after being told by a psychic that he would die young.

IDA Links across the specification...

In order to deceive someone else, the deceiver has to know what is in the other person's mind. Psychologists call this Theory of Mind (ToM). ToM is the understanding that each of us constructs about what is in someone else's mind. This ability first develops around the age of three or four (see pages 75 and 76).

The psychology of self-deception

Psychodynamic explanation

Freud suggested that a person consciously believes one thing while unconsciously believing another, and thus is capable of self-deception.

Evolutionary explanation

Trivers suggests that deceivers who mask their deception have a selective advantage. Successful deception involves self-deception – being able to believe your own 'lie'.

The implication of this is...

Believers in paranormal phenomena are more likely to have psychological problems because they have repressed certain thoughts According to Freud, this is likely to lead to mental disorder. There is some evidence for this (see page 123).

Using the psychodynamic approach to explain fraudulent researchers...

Fraudulent researchers (see page 121) have such a strong desire to find evidence for paranormal phenomenon that this may push the knowledge of what they are doing into their unconscious mind.

The psychology of superstition

Behaviourist explanation

Skinner proposed that superstitions develop through operant conditioning where an accidental stimulus-response link is learned, and he demonstrated this with pigeons learning 'ritual behaviours'.

Evolutionary explanation

Causal thinking is adaptive, e.g. learning to link poisonous mushrooms with illness.

However, such thinking leads to Type 1 errors (you believe in a casual relationship when there isn't one). Type 1 errors are 'tolerated' in order to avoid disastrous Type 2 errors (being ignorant of causal relationships) (Beck and Forstmeier).

This explanation has been challenged...

Various studies (e.g. Staddon and Simmelhag) have shown that ritual (superstitious) behaviours in pigeons are unrelated to food rewards and are produced as frequently before any reinforcement takes place. Therefore reinforcement is not an explanation for superstitious behaviour.

These explanations don't account for cultural superstitions...

The explanations on the left only account for how individuals acquire personal superstitions. There are also culturally transmitted superstitions, e.g. the number seven is lucky in the UK, whereas in Thailand the lucky number is nine.

It may be that people adopt cultural superstitions because they provide a sense of control. Whitson and Galinsky showed that people who were given a reduced sense of control were then more likely to develop superstitions.

The psychology of coincidence

Probability misjudgment

Believers in paranormal phenomena tend to underestimate statistical likelihood on *probability judgment tasks* (see page 123). This would increase their desire for causal explanations of coincidence, because they believe that such events are not likely to co-occur by chance.

Illusion of control

Explanations for coincidence give a sense of order and increase feelings of control.

Research has found that believers show a greater illusion of control (e.g. Ayeroff and Abelson).

An alternative explanation...

Kahneman and Tversky suggest that people use various heuristics (strategies to solve problems) such as representativeness.

For example, some people understand that short runs of tossing a coin will not be representative of theoretical probability of 50:50, whereas other people expect short runs to match the theoretical probability (the gambler's fallacy).

There is research support...

Whitson and Galinsky found that reduced control led participants to detect patterns where there were none.

One of the strengths of this study was that lack of control was experimentally manipulated (rather than varying naturally) and therefore we can conclude that it *caused* the observed changes.

Psychic healing and psychic mediumship

Research into psychic healing

Psychic healing refers to any method used to alleviate health problems by purely mental means, e.g. faith healing, laying on hands (therapeutic touch, TT).

Research supporting psychic healing

Wirth compared wound healing in patients treated with TT or with no treatment. The patients were not aware of the treatment they received, thus eliminating placebo effects. Wirth found that patients treated with TT healed faster.

Wirth was involved in another study that looked at the effect of prayer on infertile women. Those who were prayed for by Christian strangers were twice as likely to become pregnant as those who had no one praying for them (Cha *et al.*).

Research not supporting psychic healing

Lyvers *et al.* recruited 20 volunteers suffering from chronic back pain and randomly assigned them to a control group or treatment from a psychic healer. They found no evidence for psychic healing but did find evidence that believers were more likely to think they had received healing benefits.

Rosa *et al.* studied 21 TT practitioners. A TT practitioner sat on one side of a screen and placed their hands through two holes in the screen. On the other side, an experimenter placed one of her hands about four inches above the practitioner's right or left hand. TT practitioners should be able to detect the energy field of the hand, but in fact their performance was not even as good as chance – they were correct only 44% of the time.

Why do people believe in psychic healing?...

It may be successful either due to the placebo effect, spontaneous recovery or because recovery is only temporary and later relapses are not reported.

Criticisms of Wirth and his research...

Various issues question the scientific honesty of the research:
- The study of wound healing has not been replicated (Wirth *et al.*).
- Researchers who wished to discuss his research have failed to be able to contact him (Solfvin *et al.*).
- One of the authors of the prayer study withdrew his name, saying he had nothing to do with the study.
- Wirth has been convicted of criminal fraud.
- Cha has been accused of plagiarism in another journal.

Nevertheless, worryingly, the study continues to be cited and taken as evidence for the power of prayer (Flamm).

Criticisms of the study by Rosa et al....

TT supporters point out that the study was designed by a nine-year-old girl, though it was published in a reputable journal.

TT supporters have also claimed the study was invalid because the experimenter was not ill, which might affect their aura (Hines).

Long *et al.* repeated the study with ordinary people (not TT practitioners) and a distance of only three inches. The results were better than chance, possibly because of body heat. Glickman and Gracely controlled body heat and the results were just at the chance level.

IDA *Research on psychic ability lacks a scientific approach...*

Research should be carried out by reputable researchers at reputable institutions and be published in peer-reviewed journals. This is rarely true of 'studies' of psychic healing and mediumship.

Scientists should 'police' bad science, which is why Flamm has taken issue with Wirth's research (which was conducted at a reputable institution and published in a reputable journal).

Research into psychic mediumship

Research supporting psychic mediumship

The Scole Report (Keen *et al.*) reported on more than 500 filmed 'experiments' where objects materialised and flew about the room, and voices were heard.

Schwartz *et al.* tested five mediums with two sitters (women who had recently had several bereavements). The sitters could not be seen and were only allowed to answer yes or no. The two sitters judged the accuracy of mediums' statements as 83% and 77% (respectively). When the same statements were given to a group of undergraduates, 36% were rated as accurate, suggesting that the mediums' performance was above chance.

Research not supporting psychic mediumship

In the mock séance conducted by Wiseman *et al.* believers tended to be taken in by events even though participants knew it was fake.

In another study O'Keeffe and Wiseman arranged for five mediums to give readings for five sitters. Each sitter read all of the 25 readings that were produced and rated the personal relevance of each statement. The ratings were actually lowest for the statements written about them.

Criticisms of the study by Schwartz et al. ...

The accuracy of the mediums' statements was demonstrated by comparing the ratings given by the sitters and students – however, since the statements would have been geared towards older women who had experienced deaths in recent years, it is not surprising that the students judged the statements as less accurate.

Explaining the apparent success of mediums...

A talented medium picks up information from various clues, e.g. the sitter's tone of voice and the sitter's replies to previous statements.

A medium (aka cold reader) also relies on general statements, e.g. 'I see a recent loss of life' or 'I see the letter J' (this is similar to the Barnum effect). Sitters then often offer elaborations.

Responses can be used later in the conversation to convince listeners of their abilities (Wiseman and O'Keefe).

Roe reports that many sitters are aware of this, but nevertheless remain convinced.

IDA *Ethical issues...*

Spiritualism is big business, which means that mediums may resort to complex and convincing strategies.

For example, the medium might hire an accomplice to visit a regular sitter. During the visit, he asks to use the toilet and is able to steal a treasured possession. Later the medium asks if the person has lost something treasured and tells her where it can be found (Hines).

Out-of-body and near-death experience

Research into out-of-body experience (OBE)

Out-of-body experience is the sensation of being awake and seeing your own body from a location outside your physical body. About 15–20% of people have experienced an OBE (Blackmore).

Naturally occurring OBEs

Green studied 400 accounts of OBEs:
- 20% of cases involved another body ('parasomatic' rather than 'asomatic').
- 25% were linked to psychological stress.
- 12% occurred during sleep.

Artificially induced OBEs

Alvarado reviewed laboratory studies where OBEs were induced by e.g. relaxation, hypnosis, audio-visual stimulation. The participants were asked to identify objects that were out of sight of their physical body. One person (Miss Z) was able to read out a randomly selected five-digit number placed in another room (Tart).

Physiological studies of OBEs

Subjects are very relaxed but awake, and not having dreams (Blackmore).

Blanke *et al.* induced OBEs accidentally by electrically stimulating the *temporal-parietal junction* (TPJ) in a woman who suffered epilepsy in that region.

Subsequently, they found that stimulation of the TPJ using *transcranial magnetic stimulation* resulted in OBEs, whereas stimulation of other areas did not.

Individual differences…

OBEs are reported more often by individuals who are paranormal believers, more fantasy prone, score higher on hypnotisability and on dissociation (ability to separate different aspects of conscious activity) (Gow *et al.*, Irwin). Such characteristics go some way to explaining why such individuals have OBEs.

There is no evidence to link OBEs with mental illness, though OBEs may make people feel they are losing their mind (Gabbard and Twemlow).

Difficulties with studying OBEs…

It is difficult to study natural OBEs because they occur without predictability and, even if a researcher were present, the OBE would cease as soon as the subject reported it. Therefore, most research is conducted on artificially induced OBEs in laboratory settings that are not equivalent to natural OBEs (Holden *et al.*).

Explaining OBEs…

Paranormal explanations suggest that something beyond our current understanding is happening. However, Alvarado's review did not find evidence that the parasomatic body had physically moved out of the physical body. He did acknowledge some exceptional cases, but perhaps these can be explained in terms of suspect methodology (e.g. subject might have the opportunity to see the target prior to the test).

Psychological explanations suggest that OBEs are related to sensory disturbance. Blackmore proposes that normally we view the world as if we were behind our eyes. In situations where sensory input breaks down, the brain attempts to reconstruct the visual field using memory and imagination. Ehrsson demonstrated that an OBE can be created by scrambling a person's visual and touch sensations using video displays so a person sees their own back as if they were sitting behind themselves.

Research into near-death experience (NDE)

Near-death experience occurs when a person is close to death. It may also occur after fainting or in stressful or threatening situations. The experiences range from one of serenity (floating, seeing a light) to extreme fear.

Naturally occurring NDEs

As many as 20% of heart attack survivors report having a NDE (Fox). NDEs may be higher in children (Atwater), though children's reports may be less reliable.

Ring interviewed 100 people who had NDEs, finding that about 60% of survivors reported a sense of peace, 33% reported OBEs, 25% said they entered a tunnel and a few said they had experienced a kind of 'life review'.

Nelson *et al.* found that people with NDEs were more likely to experience 'REM intrusions' (the brain is awake but flips into an REM state that may disrupt the integration of sensory information).

Artificially induced NDEs

Research has found that the drug ketamine can produce the classic symptoms of NDEs.

IDA Reductionism…

The reductionist view is that the mind is the product of chemical processes. However, if mental experiences occur when the brain is inactive (e.g. in a NDE), this shows the mind is separate from the physical body (Parnia). This is relevant to the *mind–body problem*.

Cultural similarities and differences…

NDEs are a universal experience. They are found in many cultures and reports date back to antiquity, sharing consistent features (e.g. going through a tunnel, feelings of peace, OBEs).

However, there are differences, e.g. in India NDEs involve encounters with Hindu figures and in Japan there are no instances of any light appearing (Augustine).

Such similarities and differences suggest that both psychological and physiological factors are involved.

Explaining NDEs…

Psychological (and paranormal) explanations suggest that NDEs are solely mental experiences. Van Lommel *et al.* followed 344 cardiac survivors for eight years. They found that those who had an NDE subsequently regarded it as a life-changing, spiritual experience. Those who didn't have an NDE continued to fear death.

Physiological explanations include the suggestion that *endorphins* are released at time of pain or stress and these lead to feelings of euphoria and detachment (Carr).

An alternative physiological explanation is that NDEs are caused by *hypoxia* (lack of oxygen) created by an REM intrusion, cardiac arrest or fainting. Hypoxia creates a flood of the neurotransmitter glutamate, which causes neuronal death. The brain's response is to produce a protective blockade, which is triggered by ketamine (Jansen).

Research and scientific method

Division A The application of scientific method in psychology

Major features of science
The scientific process
Validating new knowledge

Division B Designing psychological investigations

Selection and application of appropriate research methods
Reliability, validity and sampling
Ethical considerations in research

Division C Data analysis and reporting on investigations

Inferential analysis, probability and significance
Descriptive and inferential statistics
Analysis and interpretation of qualitative data
Research methods glossary

Specification

This section builds on the knowledge and skills developed at AS level.

Psychological research and scientific method	
The application of scientific method in psychology	• The major features of science, for example replicability, objectivity. • The scientific process, including theory construction, hypothesis testing, use of empirical methods, generation of laws/principles (e.g. Popper, Kuhn). • Validating new knowledge and the role of peer review.
Designing psychological investigations	• Selection and application of appropriate research methods. • Implications of sampling strategies, for example, bias and generalising. • Issues of reliability, including types of reliability, assessment of reliability, improving reliability. • Assessing and improving validity (internal and external). • Ethical considerations in design and conduct of psychological research.
Data analysis and reporting on investigations	• Appropriate selection of graphical representations. • Probability and significance, including the interpretation of significance and Type 1/Type 2 errors. • Factors affecting choice of statistical test, including levels of measurement. • The use of inferential analysis, including Spearman's Rho, Mann–Whitney, Wilcoxon, chi-square. • Analysis and interpretation of qualitative data. • Conventions of reporting on psychological investigations.

Chapter 16

The application of scientific method in psychology	>	Major features of science
Designing psychological investigations		The scientific process
Research methods >	Data analysis and reporting on investigations	Validating new knowledge

The application of scientific method in psychology

Major features of science

- *Empiricism* – Information is gained through direct observation or experiment rather than by reasoned argument or unfounded beliefs.
- *Objectivity* – Scientists' expectations should not affect what they record.
- *Replicability* – The validity of any study is demonstrated by exact replication. If the outcome is the same this affirms the original results.
- *Control* –Scientists seek to demonstrate causal relationships using the experimental method. In order for this to be a 'fair test' all other conditions must be kept the same i.e. controlled.
- *Theory construction* – Science aims to use facts to construct theories, which will help us understand and predict the natural phenomena around us.

The scientific process

Induction (reasoning from particular to general).

Observations → produce testable hypothesis → conduct a study to test hypothesis → draw conclusions → propose a theory.

Pre-20th century science largely used the principles of induction, e.g. Newton observed the behaviour of physical objects and produced laws.

Deduction (reasoning from general to particular).

Observations → propose a theory → produce testable hypothesis → conduct a study to test hypothesis → draw conclusions.

This approach involves starting with a theory and looks for confirming instances, e.g. Darwin proposed the theory of evolution and then sought data to prove his theory.

The hypothetico-deductive model (Popper)

Theories/laws about the world come first and are used to generate expectations/hypotheses, which can be falsified.

'No amount of observations of white swans can allow the inference that all swans are white, but the observation of a single black swan is sufficient to refute that conclusion.' (Popper).

Scientific research is desirable…

Early psychologists sought to create a science of psychology to enable them to produce verifiable knowledge.

Psychology is a science…

It shares the goals of all sciences and uses the scientific method. However, simply using the scientific method may be just 'dressing up', i.e. using the words but the underlying concepts are not relevant (Miller).

However…

Kuhn claimed that psychology could not be a science because, unlike other sciences, there is no single paradigm (i.e. a shared set of assumptions). Therefore Kuhn suggested psychology was a 'pre-science'.

Psychological research lacks objectivity and control…

In psychology the object of study reacts to the researcher leading to problems that reduce validity, e.g. experimenter bias and demand characteristics.

However, the *uncertainty principle* describes the fact that, even in physics, it is not even possible to measure something without changing its 'behaviour' (Heisenberg).

Are the goals of science appropriate for psychology?…

The psychiatrist R.D. Laing, in discussing the causes of schizophrenia, claimed that science was inappropriate for psychology. Science takes a nomothetic approach, aiming to make generalisations, whereas Laing thought an idiographic approach was more appropriate to studying human behaviour.

This is supported by the fact that psychological approaches to treating mental illness that are based on scientific principles have had only modest success, suggesting that the goals of science may not be appropriate.

Qualitative research…

Some psychologists advocate more subjective, qualitative methods of conducting research. However, these methods can still be validated.

For example, data from interviews, discourse analysis, observations, etc. can be triangulated – the findings from these different methods are compared with each other as a means of verifying them and making them objective.

Validating new knowledge

Peer review refers to the assessment of scientific work by others who are experts in the same field. The intention of peer review is to ensure that research is of high quality.

The Parliamentary Office of Science and Technology suggests that peer review may be used for:

- *Allocation of research funding* – Government and charitable bodies who fund research need to decide which research is likely to be worthwhile.
- *Publication of research in scientific journals and books* – Peer review aims to prevent incorrect or faulty data entering the public domain. Prior to peer review research was simply published and the burden of proof lay with opponents.
- *Assessing the research rating of university departments* – All university science departments are expected to conduct research, which is assessed in terms of quality (*Research Assessment Exercise*, RAE). Future funding for the department depends on receiving good ratings from a peer review.

Unachievable ideal…

It isn't always possible to find an appropriate expert with the same specialist interest to review research.

Anonymity…

Anonymity allows a reviewer to feel they can be honest, but may result in dishonesty, e.g. if a person wishes to settle an old score. Some journals now favour open reviewing.

Publication bias…

Peer review tends to favour the publication of positive results, possibly because editors want research with important implications to increase their journal's standing.

Preserves the status quo…

Peer review results in a preference for research that does not challenge existing theory. Kuhn suggested that science is generally resistant to large shifts in opinion.

An alternative…

Online blogs, encyclopedias and journals invite comments as a means of peer reviewing.

Chapter 16

The application of scientific method in psychology | Selection of appropriate research methods
Designing psychological investigations > | Reliability, validity and sampling
Research methods > | Data analysis and reporting on investigations | Ethical considerations in research

Selection and application of appropriate research methods

Method/technique		Nature and use	Advantages and weaknesses
Experiments In all cases there is an IV and DV. Design: repeated measures, independent groups or matched pairs.	Laboratory experiment	IV is manipulated by an experimenter to observe its effect on the DV. Laboratory experiments are highly controlled.	+ Can draw causal conclusion. + Extraneous variables minimised. + Can be easily replicated. − Contrived, tends to lack mundane realism. − Investigator bias and participant effects.
	Field experiment	More natural surroundings, IV is directly manipulated by the experimenter. Field experiments are less controlled.	+ Can draw causal conclusion. + Usually higher ecological validity. + Avoids some participant effects. − Less control. − May have demand characteristics.
	Natural experiment	IV is not directly manipulated, participants not randomly allocated.	+ Allows research where the IV can't be manipulated for ethical/practical reasons. + Enables psychologists to study 'real' problems. − Cannot demonstrate causal relationships. − Inevitably there are many extraneous variables. − Investigator and participant effects.
Studies using a correlational analysis		Co-variables examined for positive, negative or zero correlation.	+ Can be used when it is not possible to manipulate variables. + Can rule out a causal relationship. − People often misinterpret correlations. − There may be other, unknown variables.
Observational techniques Design: the use of behavioural categories, and time or event sampling.	Naturalistic observation	Everything left as normal, all variables free to vary.	+ Can study behaviour where it isn't possible to manipulate variables. + High ecological validity. − Poor control of extraneous variables. − Observer bias, low inter-observer reliability.
	Controlled observation	Some variables (e.g. the environment) controlled by the researcher.	+ Can manipulate variables to observe effects. − Less natural, reduced ecological validity. − Investigator and participant effects. − Observer bias, low inter-observer reliability.
	Content analysis (quantitative or qualitative)	Indirect observation of behaviour based on written or verbal material such as interviews or TV.	+ High ecological validity because it is based on what people do. + Can be replicated easily because sources are publicly available. − Observer bias.
Self-report techniques Design: may involve open or closed questions.	Questionnaires	Set of written questions.	+ Can be easily repeated, so lots of people can be questioned. + Respondents may be more willing to reveal personal information. + Does not require specialist administrators. − Leading questions, social desirability bias. − Biased samples.
	Interviews (structured or unstructured)	In unstructured interviews, the questions are in reply to the respondent's answers, conducted in real time.	+ More detailed information collected. + Can access unexpected information. − Social desirability bias, interviewer bias, inter-interviewer reliability, leading questions. − Requires well-trained personnel.
Case studies		Detailed study of a single individual, institution or event. Involves many different techniques e.g. interviews, psychological tests.	+ Rich, in-depth data collected. + Used to investigate unusual instances of behaviour. + Complex interactions studied. − Lacks generalisability. − May involve unreliable, retrospective recall. − Researcher may lack objectivity.
Other methods		Cross-cultural studies, meta-analysis	

Chapter 16

| The application of scientific method in psychology | Selection of appropriate research methods |
| Designing psychological investigations > | Reliability, validity and sampling |

Research methods > | Data analysis and reporting on investigations | Ethical considerations in research |

Reliability, validity and sampling

Reliability

Internal reliability is a measure of the extent to which something is consistent within itself (e.g. all questions on an IQ test should be measuring the same thing).

External reliability is a measure of consistency over several different occasions.

Experimental research

Reliability refers to the ability to repeat a study and obtain the same result i.e. replication.

Replications are conducted to test the reliability/validity of the original result – if the same result is obtained a second time this shows that the result is more likely to be legitimate (i.e. valid).

It is essential that all conditions are the same when conducting a replication, otherwise, if the results are now different, this may be due to the changed conditions rather than a lack of validity.

Observational techniques

Observations should be consistent which means that ideally two observers should produce the same record.

Assessing reliability: inter-rater (or inter-observer) reliability is a measure of the extent to which two (or more) observers agree, calculated by dividing total agreements by total number of observations. Should be at least +.80.

Reliability can be improved through training observers in the use of, e.g. coding systems.

Self-report techniques

Internal reliability can be assessed using the split-half method – compare a person's performance on two halves of a questionnaire or test, there should be a close correlation in the scores from both halves of the test.

External reliability can be assessed using the test–retest method – a person is given a questionnaire/interview/test on one occasion and then this is repeated again after a reasonable interval (e.g. a week). If the measure is reliable the outcome should be the same.

Validity

Internal validity concerns what goes on inside a study – whether the researcher did test what they intended to test.

External (ecological) validity concerns things outside a study – the extent to which the results of the study can be generalised to other situations and people.

Experimental research

Internal validity is affected by extraneous variables (EVs) that act as an alternative IV. If changes in the DV are due to EVs rather than the IV, then conclusions about the effect of the IV on the DV are erroneous.

External validity can be affected by the contrived and artificial nature of laboratory experiments but this is not always true, e.g. in a memory task. It is often more important to consider issues such as whether participants were aware they were being studied (reduces the realism of their behaviour) and whether the task itself was artificial and thus was low in mundane realism (reduces the generalisability of the results).

Observational techniques

Observations will not be valid (nor reliable) if the coding system/behaviour checklist is flawed, e.g. some observations may belong in more than one category, or some behaviours may not be codeable (reduces the internal validity of the data collected).

The internal validity of observations is affected by observer bias – what someone observes is influenced by their expectations. This reduces the objectivity of observations.

Observational studies are likely to have high ecological validity because they involve more natural behaviours.

Self-report techniques

Face validity: Does the test look like it is measuring what the researcher intended to measure? For example, are the questions obviously related to the topic?

Concurrent validity: This can be established by comparing performance on a new questionnaire or test with a previously established test on the same topic.

External validity of self-report techniques is likely to be affected by biased sampling strategies.

Sampling

Sampling techniques aim to select a representative sample from a target population in order to be able to generalise from the sample to the target population. A sample that is not representative is described as biased i.e. leaning in one direction. A biased sample means that any generalisations lack external validity.

- *Opportunity sample* – Using those people who are most easily available. It is the easiest method to use but inevitably biased because the sample is drawn from a small part of the target population.
- *Volunteer sample* – Participants are selected by asking for volunteers, this can enable access to a variety of participants (e.g. advertisement in a newspaper), making the sample more representative. However, such samples are biased because participants are, e.g. likely to be highly motivated (= volunteer bias).
- *Random sample* – Participants are selected from a target population using a random number technique (e.g. the lottery method, names from a hat or using a random number generator). This method is potentially unbiased because all members of the target population have an equal chance of selection, but may be biased if some people refuse to take part.

- *Stratified and quota samples* – Subgroups (strata) within a population are identified (e.g. different age groups). Then a predetermined number of participants are taken from each subgroup in proportion to their numbers in the target population. In stratified sampling, this is done using random techniques, in quota sampling it is done using opportunity sampling. This method is more representative than other methods because there is proportional representation of subgroups. However, opportunity sampling may lead to bias.
- *Snowball sampling* – Start with a one or two people with, e.g. eating disorders and ask them to direct you to some other people with eating disorders and so on. This is useful when conducting research with participants who are not easy to identify but is prone to bias because only a limited section of the population is contacted.

Chapter 16

The application of scientific method in psychology	Selection of appropriate research methods
Designing psychological investigations >	Reliability, validity and sampling
Research methods >	Data analysis and reporting on investigations	Ethical considerations in research

Ethical considerations in research

Ethical issues with human participants

Ethical issues

- *Informed consent* – Participants must be given comprehensive information concerning the nature and purpose of a study and their role in it, in order that they can make an informed decision about whether to participate. However, such information might reveal the study's aims and affect participants' behaviour.
- *Deception* occurs when a participant is not told the true aims of a study (e.g. what participation will involve). Thus the participants cannot give truly informed consent. However, it might be argued that some deception is relatively harmless and/or can be compensated for by adequate debriefing.
- *Right to withdraw* – Participants should have the right to withdraw from a study if they are uncomfortable in any way. However, the loss of participants may bias the study's findings.
- *Protection from harm* – Participants should not experience negative physical effects (e.g. physical injury) or negative psychological effects (e.g. lowered self-esteem). However, it may not be possible to estimate harm before conducting a study.
- *Confidentiality* – A participant's right to have personal information protected.
- *Privacy* – A person's right to control the flow of information about themselves.

Dealing with ethical issues…
Debriefing…
A post-research interview to inform participants about the true nature of a study, and restore them to the state they were in at the start of the study.
Ethical committee…
A group of people within a research institution that must approve a study before it begins. May consist of both professional and lay people.
Ethical guidelines…
Concrete, quasi-legal documents that establish principles for standard practice and competence. The current British Psychological Society (BPS) code of ethics and conduct:

- *Respect* for the dignity and worth of all persons, including standards of privacy and confidentiality and informed consent. Observations of behaviour in public are only acceptable in situations where people would reasonably expect to be observed by strangers. Intentional deception (lack of informed consent) is only acceptable when it is necessary to protect the integrity of research and when the nature of the deception is disclosed to participants at the earliest opportunity.
- *Competence* – Psychologists should maintain high standards in their professional work.
- *Responsibility* – Psychologists have responsibility to clients, the general public and the science of psychology. This includes protecting participants from physical and psychological harm, and debriefing participants to inform them of the nature and conclusions of the research, to identify and deal with any unforeseen harm.
- *Integrity* – Psychologists should be honest and accurate. This includes reporting research findings accurately and bringing instances of misconduct by other psychologists to the attention of the BPS.

Punishment…
A professional organisation, such as the BPS, punishes psychologists who contravene the code with disbarment from the society.

Socially sensitive research
'Studies in which there are potential social consequences or implications, either directly for the participants in research or the class of individuals represented by the research' (Sieber and Stanley), e.g. research on inter-racial differences in IQ.

Dealing with such issues…
Psychologists may prefer to avoid socially sensitive research, but this means that such groups may miss out on any of the potential benefits from the research (e.g. increased funding or wider public understanding). Ignoring these important areas of research would amount to an abdication of the 'social responsibilities' of the psychological researcher (i.e. their duty to society to study important areas of human behaviour).

Ethical issues with non-human animals

Reasons for conducting research using non-human animals
- Animals may be studied because they are interesting in their own right and such research may benefit animals.
- Animals offer the opportunity for greater control and objectivity in research procedures.
- Animals may be used when we can't use humans, e.g. research on the effects of emotional deprivation or on effects of drugs to treat mental illness.
- Human beings and non-human animals have sufficient of their physiology and evolutionary past in common to justify conclusions drawn from the one being applied to the other. However, it can be argued that animals tested under stressful conditions may provide very little useful information.

Is 'science at any cost' ever justifiable?…
Sentient beings…
Animals do respond to pain, but there is little evidence that animals other than primates have self-awareness. However, equally, some humans lack sentience (e.g. some brain-damaged individuals).
Speciesism…
Discrimination on the basis of species is no different to racism or sexism (Singer). However, Gray argues that we have a special duty of care to humans so speciesism is not equivalent to, for example, racism.
Animal rights…
Singer's view is a utilitarian one, i.e. if animal research can alleviate pain and suffering it is justifiable. Regan argues that there are no circumstances under which animal research is acceptable.

Existing constraints…
- The BPS publishes guidelines for research with animals.
- The UK *Animals (Scientific Procedures) Act* (1986) requires that animal research only takes place at licensed laboratories with licensed researchers on licensed projects.
- The 3 Rs (reduction, replacement, refinement) is a means of protecting animals, as the need for animal research continues, e.g. British law requires that new drugs are tested on at least two species of live mammal.

Chapter 16 | Inferential analysis, probability and significance

The application of scientific method in psychology | Descriptive and inferential statistics
Designing psychological investigations | Analysis and interpretation of qualitative data
Research methods > | Data analysis and reporting on investigations > | Research methods glossary

Inferential analysis, probability and significance

Probability and significance

Significance

A statistical term indicating that a set of research findings is sufficiently strong for us to accept the research hypothesis under test.

Example: In an experiment Group A perform a task while there is loud music playing, whereas Group B perform the same task with no music.

Null hypothesis: There is no difference between Group A and Group B in their performance on this task.

Alternative hypothesis: There is a difference between Group A and Group B in their performance on this task.

The results show that there is a difference between the mean score for Group A and the mean score for Group B:

• This pattern could have arisen by chance, and then it would not be correct to conclude that there is a real difference between the groups. We should accept the null hypothesis.

• This pattern did not arise by chance and is therefore described as significant. We conclude that there is a real difference between the groups. We reject the null hypothesis and accept the alternative hypothesis.

Probability

A numerical measure of the likelihood or chance that certain events will occur.

We cannot be certain that an observed effect was due to chance or not but we can state how certain we are. In general, psychologists use a probability of $p \leq 0.05$, which means that there is a 5% possibility that the results did occur by chance. In other words, there is a 5% probability that the results occurred even though there was no real difference/association between the populations from which the samples were drawn. (NB that ultimately we are interested in making a statement about the population(s) from which the samples are drawn.)

Significance level

The level of probability (p) at which it has been agreed to reject the null hypothesis.

In some studies psychologists want to be more certain – such as when they are conducting a replication of a previous study or considering the effects of a new drug on health. Then, researchers use a more stringent probability, such as $p \leq 0.01$ or even $p \leq 0.001$. In other studies a more lenient level of $p \leq 0.10$ might be used, such as when conducting research into a new topic.

Type 1 and 2 errors

A researcher may erroneously accept a hypothesis that is false.

Type 1 error – Rejecting a null hypothesis that is true. This is more likely to happen if significance level is too high (lenient, e.g. 10%).

Type 2 error – Accepting a null hypothesis that is in fact not true. This is more likely to happen if the significance level is too low (stringent, e.g. 1%).

Inferential analysis

Inferential tests

Procedures for drawing logical conclusions (inferences) about the population from which samples are drawn.

In order to work out whether a difference is or is not significant we use inferential tests. Such tests permit us to work out, at a given probability, whether a pattern in the data from a study could have arisen by chance or whether the effect occurred because there is a real difference/correlation in the populations from which the samples were drawn.

Different inferential tests are used for different research designs, e.g.:

• Spearman's rho: correlation, data is ordinal or better.
• Chi-square: difference or association, nominal data only.
• Mann–Whitney U: difference, independent groups, data is ordinal or better.
• Wilcoxon T: difference, repeated measures, data is ordinal or better.

Observed and critical values

Two values used to determine whether the results of a study occurred by chance or are significant.

The value that is calculated for any set of data is called the *observed value* (so called because it is based on the observations made). It is also sometimes called the *calculated value* – because it is calculated.

To decide if this observed (calculated) value is significant this figure is compared to another number, found in a table of critical values. This is called the *critical value*, which is the value that the observed value must reach in order for the null hypothesis to be rejected.

There are different tables of critical values for each different inferential test. To find the appropriate critical value in a table we need to know:

• *Degrees of freedom* (df) – In most cases we get this value by looking at the number of participants in the study (N). In studies using an independent groups design there are two values for N (one for each group of participants), which are called $N1$ and $N2$. In the case of the chi-squared test we calculate df on the basis of how many 'cells' there are.

• *One-* or *two-tailed test* – If the hypothesis was a directional hypothesis, then we use a one-tailed test, if it was non-directional we use a two-tailed test.

• *Significance level* – The researcher decides on a suitable probability, usually $p \leq 0.05$. This means that the null hypothesis will be accepted or rejected if there is a chance of 5% that this is erroneous. Higher or lower significance levels may be used in some kinds of research, e.g. 10% may be used for a new area of research, allowing a greater margin of error. 1% may be used when researching the effects of drugs when we want to be more certain of our conclusions.

Descriptive statistics

Measures of central tendency inform us about central (middle or average) values for a set of data.

- *Mean* – Calculated by adding up all the scores and dividing by the number of scores. It makes use of the *values* of all the data but can be unrepresentative of the data as a whole if there are extreme values. It is not appropriate for nominal data.
- *Median* – The middle value in an ordered list. It is unaffected by extreme scores because not all values are reflected in the median. It is not appropriate for nominal data.
- *Mode* – The value that is most common in a data set. It is the only method appropriate when the data are in categories i.e. nominal data, but can be used for all kinds of data. It is not a useful way of describing data when there are several modes.

Measures of dispersion inform us about the spread of data.

- *Range* – Calculated by finding the difference between the highest and lowest score in a data set. This is easy to calculate but may be affected by extreme values.
- *Standard deviation* – Expresses the spread of the data around the mean. This is a more precise measure because all of the values of the data are taken into account. However, some characteristics of the data are not expressed, such as the influence of extreme values.

Graphs provide a means of 'eyeballing' the data and seeing the results at a glance.

- *Bar chart* – The height of the bar represents frequency. Suitable for words and numbers, i.e. all levels of measurement.
- *Scattergram* – Suitable for correlational data, a dot or cross is shown for each pair of values. If the dots form a pattern going from bottom left to top right this indicates a positive correlation, whereas top left to bottom right suggests a negative correlation. If there is no detectable pattern there is a zero correlation.

Levels of measurement

When deciding which test to use you may need to identify the level of measurement that was used.

- *Nominal* –The data are in separate categories, e.g. grouping your class into people who are tall, medium or short.
- *Ordinal* – Data are ordered in some way, e.g. lining your classmates up in order of height. The 'difference' between each item is not the same.
- *Interval* – Data are measured using units of equal intervals, e.g. when counting correct answers or measuring your classmates' height.
- *Ratio* – There is a true zero point as in most measures of physical quantities.

Inferential statistics

Deciding what test to use

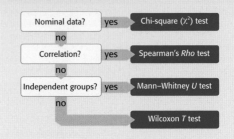

Justifying our choice

Below are a variety of possible justifications that could be used in an exam question. In each case, full reference to the data has been made, as well mentioning other important criteria for deciding which test to use. In an exam question we must shape our justification to fit the particular scenario presented.

Spearman's rho

A test of correlation is needed as the hypothesis predicted a correlation. The data involved ratings made by participants that are ordinal data. This means we should use Spearman's rho (test of correlation, ordinal data).

Chi-squared

As the data have been put into categories, they are classified as nominal data. The results are independent in each cell, and the expected frequencies in each cell are greater than 4. The appropriate inferential test to use is therefore a chi-square test (test of association, independent groups, nominal data).

Mann–Whitney

A test of difference is required because the hypothesis predicts that there will be a difference between the two groups. The design is independent groups as participants were allocated to one of two treatment groups, and the data were scores on a test (ordinal data). Therefore the Mann–Whitney test is suitable (test of difference, independent groups, ordinal data).

Wilcoxon

A test of difference is required because the hypothesis predicts that there will be a difference between the two conditions. The design is repeated measures as all the participants were tested twice. The data were scores on a memory test, which are interval data. Therefore a Wilcoxon test was chosen (test of difference, related groups, interval data).

Analysis and interpretation of qualitative data

Coding

Coding is the process of identifying categories, themes, phrases or keywords that may be found in any set of data.

For example, when analysing observational data the researcher identifies a number of categories and then allocates each individual observation to one of the categories, or when analysing the transcript of an interview the researcher identifies a variety of themes (such are feeling upset, thinking about the future) and then works through the entire text annotating each sentence of the interview.

Coding is not a superficial categorisation but a thoughtful process trying to understand the meaning of the data. The categories or themes are decided upon in one of two ways:

- Top-down approach (e.g. *thematic analysis*) – codes represent ideas and concepts from an existing theory/explanation. For example the clinical characteristics of schizophrenia may be used as categories to code self-descriptions from patients diagnosed with schizophrenia.
- Bottom-up approach (*grounded theory*) where the codes/categories emerge from the data. Thus codes remain grounded in the observations rather than generated beforehand by existing views. This is popular in an area that has not been well researched or in order to develop new insights.

The analysis of qualitative data requires repeated reviewing of the data in order to consider further categories, to re-assess meaning and re-assign codes.

Summarising the data

Later the behavioural categories can be used to summarise the data.

For example, the categories or themes may be listed or examples of behaviour within the category may be represented using quotes from participants or descriptions of typical behaviours in that category.

It is also possible to count frequency of occurrences in each category, thus qualitative data is turned into quantitative data. Finally a researcher may draw conclusions.

Validity and reflexivity

The traditional approach in psychology claims there is one real world and *quantitative* research seeks to discover that reality or 'truth' – validity is a measure of the extent to which that has been achieved.

The *qualitative* approach denies the existence of any one 'real' world. Nevertheless qualitative researchers acknowledge the need for reflexivity, the recognition that a researcher's attitudes, biases etc. have an unavoidable influence on the research they are conducting. The impact of reflexivity cannot be avoided but it can be monitored and reported.

The validity of qualitative research findings may be demonstrated using *triangulation*, comparing the results from a variety of different studies of the same thing or person. The studies are likely to have used different methodologies. If the results agree this supports their validity. If the results differ then this can lead to further research to enhance our understanding.

Reliability is a component of validity and can be checked, for example, by looking at inter-rater reliability when more than one person has coded the data.

Comparing quantitative and qualitative data

	Advantages	Weaknesses
Quantitative data	Easier to analyse because data in numbers. Produces neat conclusions.	Oversimplifies reality and human experience (statistically significant but humanly insignificant).
Qualitative data	Represents the true complexities of human behaviour. Gains access to thoughts and feelings, which may not be assessed using quantitative methods with closed questions. Provides rich detail.	More difficult to detect patterns and draw conclusions. Subjective analysis can be affected by personal expectations and beliefs (although quantitative methods may only appear to be objective but are equally affected by bias).

Chapter 16

The application of scientific method in psychology | Inferential analysis, probability and significance
Designing psychological investigations | Descriptive and inferential statistics
Analysis and interpretation of qualitative data

Research methods > Data analysis and reporting on investigations > Research methods glossary

Cohort effects occur because group of participants that has unique characteristics because of time-specific experiences during their development, such as growing up during the Second World War. This can affect both *cross-sectional studies* (because one group is not comparable with another) and *longitudinal studies* (because the group studied is not typical).

Control condition/group The condition (in a repeated measures design) or group (in an independent groups design) that provides a baseline measure of behaviour without the experimental treatment (IV), so that the effect of the experimental treatment may be assessed.

Correlation coefficient A number between −1 and +1 that tells us how closely the co-variables in a correlational analysis are related.

Counterbalancing An experimental technique used to overcome order effects. Counterbalancing ensures that each condition is tested first or second in equal amounts.

Covert observations Observing people without their knowledge, e.g. using one-way mirrors. Knowing that your behaviour is being observed is likely to alter your behaviour.

Critical value The value that a test statistic must reach in order for the null hypothesis to be rejected.

Cross-sectional study One group of participants of a young age is compared with another, older group of participants, with a view to investigating the effect of age on the behaviour in question.

Dependent variable (DV) A measurable outcome of the action of the *independent variable* in an experiment.

Experimental realism The extent to which participants become involved in an experiment and are less influenced by cues about how to behave.

Experimenter effects *See investigator effect.*

Hawthorne effect The tendency for participants to alter their behaviour merely as a result of knowing that they are being observed.

Independent variable (IV) An event that is directly manipulated by an experimenter in order to test its effect on another variable – the *dependent variable* (DV).

Investigator effect Anything that the investigator does which has an effect on a participant's performance in a study, other than what was expected. This includes investigator/experimenter bias.

Longitudinal study Observation of behaviour over a long period of time, possibly looking at the effects of age on a particular behaviour (such as moral development) by repeatedly testing/interviewing a group of participants at regular intervals.

Operationalised Providing variables in a form that can be easily tested.

Order effect In a repeated measures design, an extraneous variable arising from the order in which conditions are presented, e.g. a *practice effect* or *fatigue effect*.

Participant variables Characteristics of individual participants (such as age, intelligence, etc.) that might influence the outcome of a study.

Peer review The practice by academic journals and research assessments of using scientific experts to assess other scientific experts.

Pilot study A small-scale trial of a study run to test any aspects of the design, with a view to making improvements.

Presumptive consent A method of dealing with lack of informed consent or deception, by asking a group of people who are similar to the participants whether they would agree to take part in a study. If this group of people consents to the procedures in the proposed study, it is presumed the real participants would have agreed.

Quasi-experiments Studies that are 'almost' experiments (e.g. natural experiment) but lack one or more features of a true experiment, such as full experimenter control over the IV or *random allocation* of participants to conditions. Quasi-experiments cannot therefore claim to demonstrate causal relationships.

Role play A controlled observation in which participants are asked to imagine how they would behave in certain situations and act out the part. This method has the advantage of permitting the study of certain behaviours that might be unethical to study or difficult to find in the real world.

Single blind A type of research design in which the participant is not aware of the research aims or of which condition of the experiment they are receiving. *See double blind*

Situational variables Factors in the environment that could affect the DV, such as noise, time of day or the behaviour of an investigator.

Structured interview Any interview in which the questions are decided in advance.

Structured (systematic) observations An observer uses various 'systems' to organise observations, such as behavioural categories and sampling procedures. Unstructured observations are when an observer records all relevant behaviour but has no system. This technique may be chosen because the behaviour to be studied is largely unpredictable.

Systematic sample A method of obtaining a representative sample by selecting every fifth or tenth person. This can be a random sample if the first person is selected using a random method and then every fifth or tenth person is selected.

Zero correlation In a correlation co-variables are not linked at all.

Glossary

Page numbers are provided for most terms, except those that are common throughout the book

ACC (anterior cingulate cortex) A region of the brain involved in various autonomic functions as well as rational cognitive functions, such as reward anticipation, decision-making, empathy and emotion. Page 105

Acculturation effect Adopting the characteristics and behaviours of the surrounding culture (particularly among non-natives). Page 41

ACTH (adrenocorticotropic hormone) A hormone released by the pituitary gland, which stimulates the adrenal glands. Page 8

Adaptive Any physical or psychological characteristic that enhances an individual's survival and reproduction, and is thus likely to be naturally selected. Page 9, 13, 18, 22, 29, 38, 39, 43, 44, 46, 51, 63, 76, 80, 86, 92, 98, 109, 114, 123, 124, 125

Adrenaline A hormone associated with arousal of the autonomic nervous system, and also a neurotransmitter. Pages 92, 94

Agonistic buffering Refers to situations where a male (e.g. a baboon) carries an infant as a signal to inhibit aggression from dominant animals, thus allowing them to approach individuals to which they normally have no access. Page 64

Agonist A drug that binds to and alters the activity of a receptor, as distinct from an antagonist drug. Page 80

Agoraphobia A fear of being in places or situations from which escape might be difficult (or embarrassing). Pages 91, 92, 93, 95

Alternative hypothesis A testable statement about the relationship between two variables. Page 133

Amphetamines A group of drugs that increase focus and wakefulness by increasing levels of adrenaline, serotonin and dopamine in the brain. Pages 36, 80

Amygdala A group of nuclei in the brain forming part of the limbic system and involved in emotional processing and memory. Pages 22, 43, 92, 105

Androgyny The combination of masculine and feminine characteristics. Page 54

Anomalous experience An umbrella term for experiences that do not currently have a scientific explanation.

ANS (autonomic nervous system) Governs the body's involuntary activities (e.g. stress, digestion, heart beat) and is self-regulating (autonomous). Page 92

Antagonist A drug that binds to a receptor but which does not alter the activity of the receptor, as distinct from an agonist. Page 80, 119

Antipsychotic drugs Medication used with schizophrenia and other psychotic conditions. Pages 36, 80, 81, 82, 83

Anxious-ambivalent (resistant) attachment A form of insecure attachment where an infant feels uneasy about strangers and about exploring their environment, even with their attachment figure present. The infant will be ambivalent when the mother returns (seeking closeness but also rejecting when approached). Page 109

Appearance-reality distinction The ability (or inability) to understand that what something looks like (its appearance) does not represent how things really are (reality). Pages 53, 69

Attachment disorder A disorder characterised by an inability to interact or relate to others, associated with a lack of early attachments. Page 30

Attachment style The characteristic way an individual responds in relationships, such as being trusting and close (secure attachment) or wary and sometimes rejecting (insecure attachment). Pages 30, 109, 110

Attribution theory or **attributional style** An account of how, or the manner by which, we explain the causes of our own and other people's behaviour to ourselves. Page 14, 87, 116

Attrition The loss of participants from a study over time, which is likely to leave a biased sample or a sample that is too small. Page 89

Autism A mental disorder that usually appears in early childhood and typically involves avoidance of social contact, abnormal language, and so-called 'stereotypic' or bizarre behaviours. Pages 51, 60, 75, 76, 77, 98, 106, 112

Barnum effect Tendency for people to accept general statements (Barnum statements) as an accurate description of themselves. Page 126

Basal ganglia 'Basal' refers to the fact this region is found in the 'basement' of the brain. Pages 46, 98

Behavioural categories Dividing a target behaviour (such as attachment or sociability) into a subset of behaviours. Pages 130, 135, 136

Behaviourist An approach to explaining behaviour which holds the view that all behaviour can be explained in terms of learning (i.e. nurture or environment), referring only to the behaviours themselves rather than any internal mechanisms – thus 'behaviourism'. Pages 74, 77, 93, 101, 107, 125

Beta-blockers (BBs) Decrease anxiety by reducing the activity of adrenaline and noradrenaline, which are part of the sympathomedullary response to stress. Pages 92, 94

Biological preparedness The ability of some organisms to associate significant (i.e. in terms of survival) combinations of stimuli, responses and reinforcers. Pages 44, 61, 92, 93

Bipolar disorder A mental illness that includes both manic and depressive episodes. Mania is characterised by an elevated and expansive mood, delusions, overactivity and impulsive behaviour. Pages 79, 123

Bottom-up Processing which starts from the base elements of the system (the physical stimulus or data itself), as distinct from top-down processing. Pages 17, 18, 19, 20, 21, 135

Broca's area An area in the frontal lobe of the forebrain, usually in the left hemisphere, related to speech production. Page 77

CAT scan Computerised axial tomography, a method of detecting activity in the living brain to determine the function of different regions. Page 80

Caudate nucleus A region of the brain located in the basal gangia and an important part of the brain's learning and memory system. Pages 98, 100

CBT see cognitive-behavioural therapy.

Circadian rhythm A pattern of behaviour that occurs or recurs approximately every 24 hours, such as the sleep–wake cycle. Pages 7, 8, 9, 10, 11

Circular reactions A feature of the sensorimotor stage in Piaget's theory, to describe the repetitive actions which enable an infant to learn new schema linking sensory and motor experiences. Page 69

Classical conditioning Learning that occurs through association. A neutral stimulus is paired with an unconditioned stimulus, resulting in a new stimulus-response (S-R) link. Pages 25, 61, 63, 93, 99, 114

Clinical Refers to medical practice, thus a non-clinical population refers to a group of people with no incidence of the target illness, a sub-clinical population refers to a group of people who have some of the symptoms of the target illness but not enough to be diagnosed with the disorder. Pages 36, 41, 88, 91, 92, 97, 99, 106, 110, 131

Clinician A health professional, such as a doctor, psychiatrist, psychologist or nurse, who deals with the diagnosis and treatment of mental disorder. Pages 79, 85, 91, 119

Closed questions Questions that have a range of answers from which respondents select one; produces quantitative data. Page 130, 135

Cognitive style An individual's characteristic way of thinking. Pages 51, 60, 93

Cognitive therapy (CT) A form of psychotherapy which attempts to change a client's thoughts and beliefs as a way of treating maladaptive behaviour. It differs from cognitive-behavioural therapy because the latter involves some element of behavioural techniques. Pages 83, 87, 101, 119

Cognitive-behavioural therapy (CBT) An approach to the treatment of mental disorders combining both cognitive and behavioural approaches. Pages 47, 83, 89, 93, 95, 100, 119

Collectivist A culture characterised by the extent to which things are shared – groups live and work together sharing tasks, belongings and valuing interdependence. Japan and Israel are examples of collectivist societies. Pages 31, 72, 74, 75

Comorbidity The presence of two or more coexisting morbid conditions or diseases. Pages 79, 86, 91, 97, 98

Compound conditioning Where an unconditioned stimulus is associated with two or more neutral stimuli so that either will produce the conditioned response. Page 63

Concordance rate A measure of similarity (usually expressed as a percentage) between two individuals or sets of individuals on a given trait. Pages 15, 66, 80, 86, 92, 98

Concurrent validity A means of establishing validity by comparing an existing a test/questionnaire with the one you are interested in. Pages 91, 131

Conditioned A response that has been created through classical or operant conditioning. Pages 19, 92, 101

Conditioned response (CR) In classical conditioning, the response elicited by the conditioned stimulus i.e. a new association has been learned so that the neutral stimulus (NS) now produces the unconditioned response (UCR), now called the CR. Pages 61, 93

Conditioned stimulus (CS) In classical conditioning, the neutral stimulus (NS) after it has been paired with the unconditioned stimulus. The NS now elicits the unconditioned response UCR, now called a conditioned response (CR). Pages 61, 63, 93, 114

Confederate An individual in a study who is not a real participant and has been instructed how to behave by the investigator/experimenter. May act as the independent variable. Pages 54, 107

Configural process Using the relationship between separate features (i.e. the configuration) to help in recognising an object or a face. Page 23

Conservation The ability to distinguish between reality and appearance, for example to understand that quantity is not changed even when a display is transformed. Pages 53, 69

Construct validity A means of assessing the validity or trueness of a psychological test by demonstrating the extent to which performance on the test measures an identified underlying construct. Page 91

Cortisol A hormone produced by the adrenal gland that is associated with stress. Pages 7, 10, 36, 51, 86

Counterconditioning Being taught a new association that runs counter to the original association, thus removing the original association. Page 95

Covert desensitisation Using the principles of systematic desensitisation but only imagining the hierarchy of situations from least to most fearful. Page 95

CR See conditioned response.

Critical period A limited window in biological development during which certain characteristics develop. Pages 21, 46

Cross-cultural research A kind of natural experiment in which the IV is different cultural practices and the DV is a behaviour such as attachment. Pages 19, 20, 21, 31, 48, 56, 75, 97, 130

CS See conditioned stimulus.

Cuckoldry The reproductive cost inflicted on a man as a result of his partner's infidelity. The consequence of cuckoldry is that the man might unwittingly invest his resources in offspring that are not his own. Pages 29, 38

D_2 dopamine receptor One of at least five different dopamine receptor subtypes. A receptor is located at the receiving end of a synapse to receive neurotransmitters being transmitted across the synapse. Pages 80, 82, 112

Decentration The ability to focus on more than one aspect of a problem, overcoming the problem of centration (thinking focused on one aspect of a problem, e.g. height, and ignoring other features, e.g. width). Page 69

Defence mechanism In psychoanalytic theory, the strategies used by the ego to defend itself against anxiety, such as repression, denial and projection. Pages 99, 123, 124

Degrees of freedom (df) The number of values which are free to vary given that the overall total values are known. Page 133

Delayed sleep phase syndrome A disorder where a person's major sleep episode is delayed by two or more hours of the desired bedtime. Pages 9, 11, 14

Demand characteristic A cue that makes participants unconsciously aware of the aims of a study or how the researchers expect the participants to behave. This may act as a confounding variable. Pages 33, 69, 129, 130

Depressive attributional style An individual's preferred method of explaining what has caused their own or another person's behaviour. Page 87

Descriptive statistics Methods of summarising a data set such as measures of central tendency and dispersion, and the use of graphs. Page 134

Determinist The view that an individual's behaviour is shaped or controlled by internal or external forces rather than an individual's will to do something. Pages 7, 8, 30, 46, 48, 50, 51, 52, 56, 98

Diathesis-stress model The view that individuals inherit a susceptibility for a disorder (diathesis) which develops only if the individual is exposed to certain environmental conditions (stress). Pages 14, 15, 45, 46, 86, 87, 92, 93, 112

Differentiation theory The idea that perceptual (and cognitive) development occurs by learning to distinguish between different classes of objects. Page 19, 21

Directional hypothesis States the direction of the predicted difference between two conditions or two groups of participants. Page 133

Discovery learning Learning through personal enquiry and constructing your own knowledge, rather than being told the answers to questions and presented with pre-constructed categories. Page 72

Dopamine A neurotransmitter produced in the brain, involved in sexual desire and the sensation of pleasure. Unusually high levels of dopamine can be associated with schizophrenia. Pages 36, 46, 48, 80, 81, 82, 92, 94, 98, 112, 114, 115, 119, 123

Double blind Neither the participant nor the experimenter is aware of the research aims and other important details, and thus have no expectations. Page 88

DRD_2 gene The gene which encodes the D_2 subtype of the dopamine receptor. Page 112

DSM (The Diagnostic and Statistical Manual of Mental Disorders) This is a classification system of mental disorders published by the American Psychiatric Association. It contains typical symptoms of each disorder and guidelines for clinicians to make a diagnosis. The most recent version is DSM-IV-TR. Pages 14, 79, 85, 91, 97

Dysthymia A chronic condition characterised by depressive symptoms that occur for most of the day, more days than not, for at least two years. Page 85

DZ (dizygotic) Non-identical twins formed from two fertilised eggs (or zygotes). Pages 15, 37, 66, 80, 86, 92, 98, 123

Ecological approach Explanations based on observations of animals in their natural environment. Pages 18, 56, 65

Ecological validity A form of external validity, concerning the ability to generalise a research effect beyond the particular setting in which it is demonstrated, to other settings. Ecological validity is established by representativeness (mundane realism) and generalisability (to other settings). Pages 74, 130, 131

ECT *See electroconvulsive therapy.*

EEA (environment of evolutionary adaptation) The environment to which a species is adapted and the set of selection pressures that operated at this time. For humans, this is thought to be the African savannah approximately two million years ago. Pages 44, 51, 109

EEG (electroencephalograph) A method of detecting activity in the living brain, electrodes are attached to a person's scalp to record general levels of electrical activity. Pages 8, 11, 15

Effect size A measure of the strength of the relationship between two variables. Pages 105, 122

Ego Part of Freud's conception of the structure of the personality, the ego is driven by the reality principle, which makes the child accommodate to the demands of the environment. Pages 81, 93, 113

Egocentric Seeing things from your own viewpoint and being unaware of other possible viewpoints. Pages 69, 70, 74, 76

Eidolic An image that represents objects in three dimensions, as if it were the real thing. The opposite is an epitomic image. Page 20

Electro-convulsive therapy (ECT) The administration of a controlled electrical current through electrodes placed on the scalp. The electrodes induce a convulsive seizure which can be effective in relieving an episode of major depression. Pages 82, 88, 117

EMG (electromyography) A technique for recording the electrical activity produced by skeletal muscles. Page 29

Empathy Being aware of and identifying with another person's feelings. Pages 74, 75, 76, 77, 103, 105

Empirical A method of gaining knowledge which relies on direct observation or testing. Pages 60, 95

Enactive skills Learning or thinking in terms of body actions, i.e. in action. Pages 55, 71

Endogenous Internal. Page 9

Endorphins Neurotransmitters released in response to pain that act as the body's natural painkiller. Page 127

Enrichment theory The view that perceptual (and cognitive) development occurs as a result of experience; the development of schemas enriches the impoverished sensory input. Page 21

Entrain The process of bringing bodily rhythms into synchronisation with an external influence. Pages 7, 8, 9, 10, 14

Epitomic An image which extracts the basic elements i.e. the 'epitome', or perfect example, of the object. Epitomic images are easier to draw than eidolic ones. Page 20

ESP (extrasensory perception) The ability to acquire information without the direct use of the five known physical senses. Pages 121, 122, 123, 124

Event sampling An observational technique in which a count is kept of the number of times a certain behaviour (event) occurs. Page 130

Exogenous External. Page 8, 9

Experimenter bias *See investigator bias.*

Extraneous variables In an experiment, any variable other than the independent variable that might potentially affect the dependent variable and thereby confound the results. Pages 31, 122, 130, 131

Extraversion Exhibited by an individual who is outgoing and impulsive, and seeks greater excitement and more dangerous pastimes. This is possibly because they have a lower level of cortical arousal and therefore need more stimulation to experience the same sense of excitement as introverts. Pages 70, 109, 119

Face validity A means of establishing validity by considering the extent to which a test/questionnaire looks as if it is measuring what it intends to measure. Page 131

Factor analysis A statistical technique used to identify the variables that explain correlations between scores on tests of different abilities. Page 58

False belief A mistaken opinion arising from incorrect reasoning. Pages 75, 76

Falsify The attempt to prove something wrong. Pages 58, 121, 129

Felt-responsibility hypothesis The view that people behave in a prosocial, altruistic manner because empathy leads you to feel responsibility for another person's distress. Page 74

First-degree relatives Closest genetic relatives – parent, sibling, or offspring. Pages 15, 86, 98, 115

First-rank symptoms The symptoms that distinguish schizophrenia from other psychotic disorders. Page 79

Flooding Treating phobias by exposing the patient to the feared stimulus without any gradual build-up as in systematic desensitisation. Page 95

fMRI (functional magnetic resonance imaging) A method used to scan brain activity while a person is performing a task. It enables researchers to detect which regions of the brain are rich in oxygen and thus are active. Pages 77, 105

Frontal cortex The front (auterior) region of the cerebral cortex, containing the motor cortex and prefrontal cortex. Involved in fine motor movement and thinking. Pages 43, 77, 98, 100, 112

Frontal lobe A region in each hemisphere of the frontal cortex. It is located in front of (anterior to) the central sulcus and above the lateral fissure. It contains the prefrontal cortex. Pages 58, 77

GABA (Gamma-amino-butyric-acid) A neurotransmitter that regulates excitement in the nervous system, thus acting as a natural form of anxiety reducer. Pages 94, 100

Gambler's fallacy The mistaken belief that the probability of an event occurring increases or decreases depending on recent events. Page 125

Gender dysphoria Having negative or conflicting feelings about one's sex or gender role. Page 54

Gender identity disorder (GID) The psychiatric classification for people experiencing gender dysphoria. Page 54

Gender schematic Individuals who consider gender an important factor in a person's behaviour, and tend to classify people as male or female and respond to them accordingly. Page 54

Gender The psychological characteristics associated with being male or female, as distinct from 'sex' which is a biological fact.

Gene A unit of inheritance which forms part of a chromosome.

Generalised anxiety disorder An anxiety disorder that involves excessive worry about anything and everything. Pages 86, 91

Genetic engineering The deliberate manipulation of the genes of an unborn child, with the intent of making them 'better' in some way, e.g. less aggressive. Page 37

Ghrelin A hormone produced by the stomach cells, and thought to increase feelings of hunger. Pages 43, 48

Glutamate The most common excitatory neurotransmitter in the brain which is thought to be involved in learning and memory. Excessive amounts, caused by brain injury or illness, cause neuronal damage and cell death. Page 127

Growth hormone A hormone that stimulates growth and cell reproduction. Pages 7, 8, 11, 12

GSR (galvanic skin response) A measure of ANS activity indicating emotional arousal (increased sweatiness of the skin increases electrical conductivity). Pages 23, 92

Habituation method A method of testing infants' perceptual abilities by exposing them to a certain stimulus until they get used to it (i.e. habituate) and show less interest when later shown the same stimulus because it is no longer novel. Page 19

Heritability The ratio between (a) genetic variability of the particular trait and (b) total variability in the whole population. Pages 66, 92, 112

Holistic process Perceiving the whole display rather than the individual features and/or the relations between them. Page 23

Horizon-ratio relation The proportion of an object that is above the horizon divided by the proportion below. Two objects of the same size on a flat surface will have the same horizon ratio. Page 18

Hormone Hormones are chemical substances that circulate in the blood and only affect target organs. They are produced in large quantities but disappear very quickly. Their effects are slow in comparison to the nervous system, but very powerful. Pages 7, 8, 11, 12, 29, 42, 43, 48, 50, 51, 52, 53, 54

Hypocretin A neurotransmitter that regulates sleep, appetite and energy conservation. Page 15

Hypothalamus A part of the brain that functions to regulate bodily temperature, metabolic processes such as eating, and other autonomic (ANS) activities including emotional responses. Pages 9, 43, 54

Hypothetico-deductive reasoning An approach to problem-solving where a person starts with many possible hypotheses and eliminates erroneous ones through testing, thus arriving at the correct solution. Page 69, 129

ICD (International Classification of Disease and Related Health Problems) The classification scheme produced by the World Health Organisation for both physical and mental disorders. Pages 79, 85

Iconic skills Learning or thinking through visual images. Page 71

Idealistic thinking Thinking in terms of abstract principles such as love, liberty and justice. Page 69

Idiographic An approach to research that focuses more on the individual case as a means of understanding behaviour rather than a way of formulating general laws of behaviour (the nomothetic approach). Pages 91, 129

Immature See mature.

Imposed etic A technique or theory developed in one culture and then used to study the behaviour of people in a different culture with different norms, values, experiences etc. Pages 20, 21, 31, 56, 67

Insecure attachment A form of attachment between infant and caregiver that develops as a result of the caregiver's lack of sensitive responding to the infant's needs. There are two main subtypes: insecure-avoidant (children who tend to avoid social interaction and intimacy with others) and insecure-resistant (ambivalent) (children who both seek and reject intimacy and social interaction).Insecure attachment is associated with poor subsequent cognitive and emotional development. Pages 47, 109, 110

In vivo desensitisation Using principles of systematic desensitisation where a patient has direct experience of the hierarchy of situations from least to most fearful (as distinct from covert desensitisation). Page 95

Independent groups design An experimental design where participants are allocated to two (or more) groups representing different experimental conditions. Allocation is usually done using random techniques. Pages 130, 133, 134

Individualist A culture that values independence rather than reliance on others, in contrast to many non-Western cultures that could be described as collectivist. Page 26, 31, 70, 72, 75, 118

Inferential statistics Procedures for making inferences about the population from which samples are drawn. Pages 133, 134

Information-processing theory An approach to explaining behaviour based on a computer analogy, i.e. the concept that mental processes are similar to computer processes. Pages 59, 71

Infradian rhythm A pattern of behaviour that occurs less often than once a day, such as the human female menstrual cycle. Page 8

Ingroup Those individuals who, for whatever reason, are part of or accepted by the group of people with whom we usually identify. Page 53, 109

Innate Behaviours that are a product of genetic factors. These may be apparent at birth or appear later through the process of maturation.

Insomnia Problems with falling asleep or staying asleep despite the opportunity to do so. Pages 10, 11, 14, 94, 100

Inter-interviewer reliability The extent to which two interviewers produce the same outcome from an interview. Page 130

Inter-observer/rater reliability The extent to which there is agreement between two or more observers or raters involved in observations of a behaviour. Pages 79, 85, 91, 97, 130, 131, 135

Internal working model A mental model of the world that enables individuals to predict and control their environment. Page 30

Intersex A person who has a mismatch between internal genitalia, external genitalia and/or gender identity. Pages 50, 54

Intervening variable A variable that comes between two other variables that can explain the relationship between those two variables. Page 11

Interviewer bias The effect of an interviewer's expectations, communicated unconsciously, on a respondent's behaviour. Pages 91, 97, 130

Investigator/experimenter bias The effect that an investigator/experimenter's

expectations has on the participants, and thus on the results of a research study. Pages 19, 21, 129, 130, 136

IQ test A test of intelligence, IQ is the score derived from such tests, the letters stand for 'intelligence quotient' because the score used to be calculated by dividing test score by age. More recent tests use norms to work out a person's IQ based on their score and age. Pages 7, 58, 59, 60, 65, 66, 67, 75, 100, 131, 132

Jealousy A state of fear or suspicion caused by a real or imagined threat to one's current status. Page 29, 38, 75

Jet lag A physiological condition caused by desychronisation of the body clock as a consequence of travelling across time zones. Pages 8, 9, 10

Ketamine A drug used medically as an anaesthetic and also used as a recreational, hallucinogenic drug. Page 127

Kibbutz A kind of collectivist farming community found in Israel where everything is shared including the childcare arrangements. Page 74

Klüver-Bucy syndrome A syndrome caused by injury to the temporal lobes of the brain and characterised by memory defects, hypersexuality and diminished fear reactions. Page 43

Lateral hypothalamus Part of the hypothalamus, stimulation of which is thought to lead to the onset of eating behaviour. Damage to the lateral hypothalamus leads to reduced food intake. Page 43

Learned helplessness Occurs when an animal finds that its responses are ineffective, and thus it learns that there is no point in responding and behaves passively in future. Page 87

Leptin A hormone produced by fat cells and involved in the regulation of appetite. Page 48

Life event Commonplace experiences that involve change from a steady state. Pages 81, 86, 87, 89

Limbic system A system of structures lying beneath the cortex (subcortical), including the amygdala, hippocampus and hypothalamus. The region is associated with emotional behaviour. Pages 94, 100

Linear perspective Parallel lines that recede into the distance appear to get closer together, providing information about depth. Page 20

Locus of control An aspect of our personality; people differ in their beliefs about whether the outcomes of their actions are contingent on what they do (internal control) or on events outside their personal control (external control). Page 123

Machiavellian intelligence The ability to intentionally deceive another individual. It requires a Theory of Mind in order to comprehend what the other knows or doesn't know. Pages 64, 65, 76, 125

Major depressive disorder (MDD) Also known as 'major depression', 'clinical depression', or 'unipolar disorder', MDD is a condition characterised by a long-lasting depressed mood or marked loss of interest or pleasure in all or nearly all activities. Pages 85, 86

MAOI (Monoamine oxidase inhibitor) Creates higher levels of neurotransmitters of the monamine group such as serotonin, noradrenaline and dopamine. Pages 12, 94

Mark test See mirror test.

Matched pairs design An experimental design where pairs of participants are matched in terms of key variables such as age and IQ. One member of each pair is placed in the experimental group and the other member in the control group. Page 130

Mature/maturation The process of ripening. In psychological terms it means a change that is due to innate factors rather than learning. Page 8, 11, 12, 15, 19, 29, 46, 53, 65, 69, 71, 73, 74, 75, 76, 115

Melatonin A hormone mainly produced in the pineal gland which induces sleep. Page 7, 8, 9, 10, 11

Mental module The assumption within evolutionary psychology that the human mind comprises a number of innate 'structures' that have evolved because they had adaptive functions for our ancestors. Pages 23, 76, 98

Mesolimbic pathway Begins in the ventral tegmental area of the midbrain and connects to the limbic system. It is involved in experiences of reward and reinforcement. Pages 112, 114

Meta-analysis A researcher looks at the findings from a number of different studies in order to reach a general conclusion about a particular hypothesis.

Metabolic processes The chemical processes that occur within any living organism to produce energy. Pages 8, 13

Microsleep Small periods of sleep during the day which possibly enable some physiological recovery to take place. The individual may not be aware they have been asleep. Page 12

Mirror neuron (MN) A neuron that responds to actions performed by oneself as well as when the same actions are performed by others. Page 77

Mirror test An investigative technique used to assess self-awareness by, for example, putting red colour on an individual's nose and showing them their image in a mirror. The individual demonstrates self-awareness if they touch their nose. Pages 64, 75

Modelling The process of imitating another's behaviour, which involves cognitive representations of the modelled activities as well as abstractions of the underlying rules of the modelled behaviours. Pages 30, 33, 41, 55, 93, 95, 104

Mood disorder A mental disorder in which disturbance of mood is the central feature. Pages 79, 85

Motion parallax As we move, objects that are closer to us move farther across our field of vision than more distant objects, providing information about depth. Page 19

MRI (magnetic resonance imaging) Produces a three-dimensional image of the static brain which is very precise. A magnetic field causes the atoms of the brain to change their alignment when the magnet is on and emit various radio signals when the magnet is turned off. A detector reads the signals and uses them to map the structure of the brain. Page 65

Müller-Lyer illusion Illusion created by fins at the end of a line such that one line looks longer (fins pointing out) than the other (fins pointing in). Pages 17, 18, 20

Mundane realism Refers to how a study mirrors the real word. The experimental environment is realistic to the degree to which experiences encountered in the environment will occur in the real world. Pages 25, 130, 131

MZ (monozygotic) Identical twins formed from one fertilised egg (or zygotes). Pages 15, 37, 66, 80, 86, 92, 98, 123

Nativist The view that development is determined by innate factors, that most abilities simply need fine tuning but do not depend on experience for their development. Page 69

Natural selection The major process that explains evolution whereby inherited traits that enhance an animal's reproductive success are passed on to the next generation and thus 'selected', whereas animals without such traits are less successful at reproduction and their traits are not selected. Pages 39, 46, 52, 65, 76, 80, 124

Nature Those aspects of behaviour that are innate and inherited. Nature does not simply refer to abilities present at birth but to any ability determined by genes, including those that appear through maturation. Pages 14, 15, 18, 19, 21, 50, 51, 74, 75, 76, 77

Need for cognition (NC) A personality variable describing people who enjoy tasks that involve high cognitive effort, such as analysing arguments and brain teasers. Page 106

Negative correlation Describes a correlation where, as one co-variable increases, the other decreases. Pages 13, 39, 107, 130, 134

Negative reinforcement Increases the probability that a behaviour will be repeated because it leads to escape from an unpleasant situation. Pages 41, 62, 93, 99, 101, 114

Neocortex or 'new' cortex is the six-layered covering of the brain. About 95% of the cerebral cortex is neocortex so that

gradually the terms have come to mean the same. The 'old' cortex or 'archicortex' is mainly the limbic system and basal ganglia. Pages 64, 65

Neuropeptide Y (NPY) A neurotransmitter believed to be important in the control of appetite and eating behaviour, especially in response to leptin. Page 43

Neuroticism The tendency to experience negative emotional states such as anxiety, anger, guilt and depressed mood. Individuals cope poorly with stress and are often self-conscious and shy. Pages 109, 123

Neurotransmitters Chemical substances, such as serotonin or dopamine, which play an important part in the workings of the nervous system by transmitting nerve impulses across a synapse. Pages 12, 88, 94

Neutral stimulus (NS) In classical conditioning, the stimulus that initially does not produce the target response i.e. it is neutral. Through association with the unconditioned stimulus (UCS), the NS acquires the properties of the UCS and becomes a conditioned stimulus (CS) producing a conditioned response (CR). Pages 61, 63, 93, 99

Night terrors A parasomnia related to sleep walking, where nightmares occur during slow wave sleep. It may not be possible to wake a person suffering from night terrors. Page 11

Nomothetic An approach to research that focuses more on general laws of behaviour than on the individual, possibly unique, case (the idiographic approach). Pages 91, 129

Non-clinical See clinical.

Non-directional hypothesis Predicts that there will be a difference between two conditions or two groups of participants, without stating the direction of the difference. Page 133

Noradrenaline A neurotransmitter found mainly in areas of the brain that are involved in governing autonomic nervous system activity, e.g. blood pressure and heart rate. Pages 48, 86, 88, 100

NREM sleep Non-rapid eye movement sleep, which includes slow wave sleep. Pages 11, 13, 15

NS See neutral stimulus.

Nucleus accumbens A group of neurons in the frontal cortex, thought to be involved in reward, pleasure and fear. Page 115

Null hypothesis An assumption that there is no relationship (difference or association) in the population from which a sample is taken with respect to the variables being studied. Pages 133, 136

Nurture Those aspects of behaviour that are acquired through experience i.e. learned from interactions with the physical and social environment. Pages 14, 15, 18, 19, 21, 50, 51, 74, 75, 76, 77

Object permanence A child's understanding that objects that are no longer visible nevertheless continue to exist. Page 69

Observer bias The tendency for observations to be influenced by expectations or prejudices. Pages 130, 131

Occam's razor The principle that simpler explanations are preferable, if everything else is equal. Page 52

Occlusion Objects that are closer block out (or occlude) objects that are more distant, providing information about depth. Pages 19, 20

Oestrogen The primary female hormone, though also present in males in small amounts. Regulates the menstrual cycle and female development in puberty. Pages 8, 42, 54

One-tailed test Form of test used with a directional hypothesis. Page 133

Open questions Questions that invite respondents to provide their own answers rather than to select an answer that has been provided. Tend to produce qualitative data. Page 130

Operant conditioning Learning that occurs when we are reinforced for doing something, which increases the probability that the behaviour in question will be repeated in the future. Conversely, if we are punished for behaving in a certain way, there is a decrease in the probability that the behaviour will recur. Pages 25, 33, 62, 63, 93, 99, 114, 119, 125

Orbitofrontal cortex (OFC) A region of the frontal cortex, lying just above the eyes, involved in cognitive processes such as decision-making. Pages 98, 100

Outgroup Those individuals who, for whatever reason, are not part of or accepted by the group of people with whom we usually identify. Pages 53, 55

Oxytocin A hormone that also acts as a neurotransmitter. Its effect is to promote feelings of pleasure and its release is associated with bonding, trust and also orgasm. Page 51

Panic disorder Unexpected and repeated episodes of intense fear accompanied by physical symptoms. Page 94

Paranormal A general term to describe experiences that lack a scientific explanation. The term 'anomalous experience' is preferred because it has fewer negative connotations.

Parasocial relationship A one-sided relationship with someone you haven't met, such as a celebrity, which creates the illusion of a friendship. Pages 108, 109, 110

Parasomnias Sleep disorders that revolve around sleep, such as sleep walking and night terrors, as distinct from disorders of sleep, such as insomnia. Page 11, 14

Paraventricular nucleus (PVN) An area in the anterior (towards the front) part of the hypothalamus, damage to which is more recently thought to cause hyperphagia. The PVN also detects the specific foods our body needs, and seems to be responsible for many food 'cravings'. Page 43

Parental investment (PI) Any investment by a parent in an offspring that increases the chance that the offspring will survive at the expense of that parent's ability to invest in any other offspring (alive or yet to be born). Pages 28, 29

Participant effects A general term used to acknowledge the fact that participants react to cues in an experimental situation, and that this may affect the validity of any conclusions drawn from the investigation. Page 130

PET scan (positron emission tomography) A brain scanning method used to study activity in the brain. Radioactive glucose is ingested and can be detected in the active areas of the brain. Pages 58, 80, 98

Pheromones Chemical substances that are transmitted from one animal to another of the same species, affecting the other animal's behaviour. Page 8

Phototherapy The use of very bright lights to treat disruptions to biological rhythms, such as SAD and jet lag. The aim is to entrain biological rhythms and reduce levels of melatonin. Page 8, 14

Phylogenetic signal This refers to the behavioural similarities between species that are genetically similar, i.e. close on the phylogenetic scale. Page 13

Pineal gland Small gland in the brain that is stimulated by darkness or by the SCN to release melatonin, inducing sleep. Page 9

Pituitary gland Known as the 'master gland', the pituitary releases a variety of hormones that act on other glands throughout the body. Page 8

Placebo A substance or treatment which 'pretends' to be the real thing so we can observe the psychological effects of the treatment. Pages 8, 48, 82, 86, 88, 89, 94, 100, 101, 119, 124, 126

Pleasure centres A collection of structures in the brain, such as the nucleus accumbens, that produce great pleasure when activated. Page 112

Population In psychological research, all the people about whom we wish to make a statement, also called the 'target population'. Pages 80, 99, 104, 131, 133

Positive correlation Refers to when, in a correlation, co-variables both increase together. Pages 13, 36, 37, 38, 41, 48, 58, 64, 65, 71, 98, 108, 123, 134

Pre-operational A stage in Piaget's theory of cognitive development where a child (aged between two and seven years) is able to use symbols to represent experience (e.g. language) but lacks the ability to operate on concepts with internally consistent, adult logic. Pages 53, 69, 72, 76

Predictive validity A means of assessing the validity or trueness of a psychological test by correlating the results of the test with some later behaviour; the ability to predict something it should theoretically be able to predict. Page 79

Prefrontal cortex Section of the cerebral cortex at the front of the brain associated with working memory and planning. Pages 67, 81

Premotor cortex A region of the motor cortex responsible for the sensory guidance of movement. Page 77

Proband The first person who seeks treatment for a genetic disorder; other relatives are then contacted to see if they also have the disorder in order to investigate genetic factors. Pages 86, 92

Progesterone A female hormone that increases after ovulation and is important in pregnancy. Page 8

Psychosurgery Surgery that involves severing fibres or removing brain tissue with the intention of treating disturbed behaviour for which no physical cause can be demonstrated. Modern psychosurgery techniques, such as deep brain stimulation, do not involve permanent damage. Pages 94, 100

Psychotic A loss of contact with reality, consistent with serious mental illness, which typically includes delusions, hallucinations and disordered thinking. Pages 12, 79, 80, 91, 97

Qualitative data Data that expresses the 'quality' of things including descriptions, words, meanings, pictures, texts and so on. Qualitative data cannot be counted or quantified but they can be turned into quantitative data by placing them in categories. Pages 45, 130, 135

Quantitative data Data that represent how much or how long, or how many, etc. there are of something; i.e. a behaviour is measured in numbers or quantities. Pages 130, 135

Reductionist An approach which breaks complex phenomenon into more simple components, implying that this is desirable because complex phenomena are best understood in terms of a simpler level of explanation. Pages 80, 99, 112, 127

Regression A form of defence mechanism where an individual deals with anxiety by returning to an earlier ego state rather than coping with unacceptable impulses in an adult way. Page 81

Reliability A measure of consistency both within a set of scores or items (internal reliability) and also over time so that it is possible to obtain the same results on subsequent occasions when the measure is used (external reliability). Pages 42, 79, 85, 91, 97, 130, 131, 135

Religiosity Refers to various aspects of religious activity and belief, as well as how religious a person is. Page 124

REM sleep Rapid eye movement sleep, during which the body is paralysed except for the eyes. REM sleep is often equated with dreaming, though dreams also occur in NREM sleep. Pages 8, 11, 12, 13, 15, 127

Repeated measures design An experimental design where each participant takes part in every condition under test. Pages 130, 133, 134

Replication If a finding from a research study is true (valid) then it should be possible to obtain the same finding if the study is repeated. This confirms the validity of the finding. Pages 112, 113, 121, 123, 126, 129, 130, 131, 133

Representative sample A sample selected so that it accurately stands for or represents the population being studied. Pages 66, 104, 131, 136

Repressed A form of defence mechanism whereby anxiety-provoking material is kept out of conscious awareness as a means of coping. Pages 93, 99, 121, 125

Reproductive fitness A measure of the success of an individual in passing on their genes to the next generation and beyond. Pages 38, 65

Retinal disparity The difference in the images received by the retina in the right and left eye. Page 19

Retinal image The image formed on the retina, a region of the eye containing photosensitive cells (rods and cones) which record light energy. Pages 17, 19

Retinal size The true size of an object as recorded on the retina, as opposed to the perceived size when factors such as distance are taken into account. Page 19

Sally Anne test A method used to assess an individual's understanding of false beliefs and Theory of Mind. Sally puts a ball in her basket and leaves the room, Anne moves the ball to her box. When Sally returns, where does she think her ball is? The answer is 'in the basket' but some children, after observing Anne's actions, would say Anne's box because they don't comprehend that someone else may be thinking something different to themselves. Pages 75, 76

Sampling The process of taking a sample intended to be a representative selection of a target population. Pages 30, 37, 130, 131, 136

Scaffolding An approach to instruction that aims to support a learner only when absolutely necessary i.e. to provide a support framework (scaffold) to assist the learning process. Pages 71, 72

Schema A cluster of related facts based on previous experiences, and used to generate future expectations. Pages 21, 53, 54, 55, 69, 87

Selective pressure In evolutionary theory, demands made by the environment resulting in one set of genes being favoured over another. This is the mechanism of natural selection. Pages 13, 51, 52, 65

Self-actualisation A person's motivation to maximise their achievements and fulfill their potential. Page 123

Self-efficacy The belief that we can perform competently in a given situation. Pages 33, 55, 114, 119

Self-esteem The feelings that a person has about their self-concept. Pages 45, 47, 54, 75, 95, 110, 116, 132

Self-fulfilling prophecy A prediction that comes true simply because of the expectations generated by the prediction that was made. Our beliefs generate expectations which affect our own perceptions and other people's behaviour. Page 14, 81, 116, 124

Self-monitoring The extent to which an individual is able to observe their own behaviour to check that their behaviour is appropriate and/or desirable. Page 108

Semi-structured interview An interview that combines both structured and unstructured interviews. The interviewer has some pre-established questions but also develops questions in response to the answers given. Pages 91, 97

Sensorimotor The co-ordination of sensory and motor experiences, such as hand–eye coordination. Pages 19, 69

Serotonin A neurotransmitter found in the central nervous system and implicated in many different behaviours and physiological processes, including aggression, eating behaviour, sleep and depression. Pages 8, 36, 37, 46, 48, 86, 88, 92, 94, 98, 100, 119

Sex A biological fact, as opposed to gender.

Sexual selection A key part of Darwin's theory explaining how evolution is driven by competition for mates, and the development of characteristics that ensure reproductive success. Pages 28, 48, 65, 109

Shift lag A physiological condition caused by dyschronisation of the body clock as a consequence of working shifts at different times of day and night. Pages 9, 10

Sleep walking A parasomnia that occurs during slow wave sleep and entails a range of activities normally associated with wakefulness (e.g. eating, getting dressed, walking about); the person has no conscious knowledge of what they are doing. Pages 11, 14, 15

SLT See social learning

SNS (sympathetic nervous system) The part of the autonomic nervous system that is associated with physiological arousal and 'fight or flight' responses. Pages 92, 94

Social cognition The study of how cognition (i.e. thinking, beliefs, perception) influences social behaviour. Pages 75, 76, 77

Social constructionist An approach to studying and explaining human behaviour in terms of its social context rather than any objective reality. Social constructionists believe that, if behaviour is separated from social context, then its true meaning is lost. Pages 52, 54, 71

Social desirability bias A tendency for respondents to answer questions in a way that they think will present them in a better light. Pages 36, 130

Social identity theory An important part of our personal identity is determined by the various social groups to which we belong. Page 116

Social learning (social learning theory, SLT) Learning through observing the behaviour of others, mentally rehearsing the behaviours they display, then later imitating them in similar situations. Pages 29, 33, 37, 41, 53, 55, 65, 93, 114, 116

Social phobia A phobia of situations involving other people, such as speaking in public or being part of a social group. Pages 91, 92, 94, 95

Socioeconomic status (SES) A measure of an individual's or family's social and economic position, based on income, education, and occupation. Pages 66, 67, 92, 103, 115

Specific phobia A phobia of specific activities or objects, such as bathing or spiders. Page 91

Split-half method A method of assessing internal reliability by comparing two halves of, for example, a psychological test to see if they produce the same score. Page 131

SSRIs (selective serotonin re-uptake inhibitors) Commonly prescribed drugs for treating depression. They work by selectively preventing the re-uptake of serotonin from the synaptic gap, thus leaving more serotonin available at the synapse to excite surrounding neurons. Pages 46, 48, 86, 88, 94, 98, 100, 119

Sub-clinical *See clinical.*

SWS (slow wave sleep) Stages 3 and 4 of NREM sleep when brain waves have low frequency and high amplitude. This stage of deep sleep is associated with bodily growth and repair, such as the production of growth hormones. Pages 8, 11, 12, 13, 15

Symbolic Learning or thinking using abstract symbols. Pages 69, 71

Synapse A small gap separating neurons. It consists of the presynaptic membrane (which discharges neurotransmitters), the postsynaptic membrane (containing receptor sites for neurotransmitters) and a synaptic gap between the two. Pages 80, 88, 100

Systematic desensitisation A process by which a patient is gradually exposed to (or imagines) a threatening situation under relaxed conditions until the anxiety reaction is extinguished. Pages 93, 95, 101

Target population In a research study, the group of people that the researcher is interested in. The group of people from whom a sample is drawn. The group of people about whom generalisations can be made. Page 131

Test–retest method A method used to check external reliability. The same test or interview is given to the same participants on two occasions to see if the same results are obtained. Pages 85, 97, 131

Testosterone Hormone produced mainly by the testes in males, but also occurring in females. It is associated with the development of secondary sexual characteristics in males (e.g. body hair), but has also been implicated in aggression and dominance behaviours. Pages 36, 50, 52

Texture gradient Objects that are closer to the viewer appear more widely spaced, providing a cue to depth or distance. Page 18, 20

Thalamus A structure lying under the cortex (subcortical) that has been described as the great relay station of the brain because most sensory information first goes to the thalamus, where it is processed and sent on to the cerebral cortex. Page 98

Theory of Mind (ToM) An individual's understanding that other people have separate mental states and that they see the world from a different point of view from their own. Pages 51, 75, 124, 125

'Theory' theory (TT) A theory of human development that proposes a middle ground between pure innateness, on the one hand, and the role of experience, on the other. Pages 21, 77

Three mountains task Designed by Piaget to investigate perceptual perspective-taking ability in children. A child is asked to identify the hypothetical view of three mountains seen by a doll placed in different positions. Pages 69, 76

Time sampling An observational technique in which the observer records behaviours in a given time frame, e.g. noting what a target individual is doing every 30 seconds. Page 130

Tolerance The progressive reduction of the effect of a drug (or other addiction) due to its continued use. Pages 110, 119

Top-down Processing that starts from an overview of a system, as opposed to bottom-up processing, such as using previous experience and context to enrich sensory input. Pages 17, 18, 19, 20, 21, 135

Tourette's syndrome A neurological disorder characterised by tics (sudden involuntary movements or vocalisations (such as swear words) which are repeated excessively. Pages 98, 99, 112

Trait hostility Describes people with a hostile personality i.e. they are hostile across situations. Page 105

Tryptophan An essential amino acid found in the diet, particularly in milk, cheese, fish, nuts and chocolate. Tryptophan is a precursor of the neurotransmitter serotonin, and melatonin, a hormone related to sleep. Pages 48, 86

Two-tailed test Form of test used with a non-directional hypothesis. Page 133

Type 1 error Rejecting a null hypothesis that is true. This is more likely to happen if significance level is too high (lenient, e.g. 10%). Pages 125, 133

Type 2 error Accepting a null hypothesis that is in fact not true. This is more likely to happen if the significance level is too low (stringent, e.g. 1%). Pages 125, 133

UCR See unconditioned response.

UCS See unconditioned stimulus.

Ultradian rhythm A pattern of behaviour that occurs more often than once a day, such as the cycle of sleep stages that occurs every 90 minutes during sleep Page 8

Unconditioned response (UCR) In classical conditioning, the innate reflex response to a stimulus, the innate reflex when presented with food. Page 93

Unconditioned stimulus (UCS) In classical conditioning, the stimulus that inevitably produces an innate reflex response, such as food producing a salivation response. Pages 61, 93

Unstructured interview An interview that starts out with some general aims and possibly some questions, and lets the interviewee's answers guide subsequent questions. Pages 130, 136

Validity Refers to the legitimacy of a study, the extent to which the findings

can be applied beyond the research setting as a consequence of the study's internal and/or external validity. Pages 7, 33, 37, 53, 60, 79, 81, 83, 85, 91, 97, 122, 123, 129, 130, 131, 135

Ventromedial hypothalamus Part of the hypothalamus, stimulation of which is thought to lead to the termination of eating behaviour. Damage to the ventromedial hypothalamus leads to excessive food intake. Page 43

Vicarious reinforcement Learning not through direct reinforcement of behaviour, but through observing someone else being reinforced for that behaviour. Pages 33, 55

Visual agnosia The brain's inability to recognise objects, including words (alexia) and faces (prosopagnosia). Page 23

Visual cliff A laboratory apparatus to investigate depth perception in babies and other young animals. It consists of a large glass sheet with patterned material directly below the glass on one side, and a foot below on the other. This apparatus creates the visual illusion of a cliff, while protecting the subject from injury. Pages 18, 19

Visual constancy We continue to see the shape, size, colour etc. of familiar objects as being the same despite changing retinal images due to perspective and/or lighting conditions. Page 19

Volunteer bias A form of sampling bias caused by the fact that volunteer participants are usually more highly motivated than randomly selected participants. Page 131

Working memory An area of memory that deals with information that is being worked on, equivalent to short-term memory. It is divided into separate stores representing different modalities. Pages 59, 81

Xenophobia A fear and distrust of strangers, although this is now popularly recognised as a fear and distrust of foreigners. Page 39